# TALLEYRAND

MACMILLAN AND CO., Limited
LONDON · BOMBAY · CALCUTTA · MADRAS
MELBOURNE

THE MACMILLAN COMPANY
NEW YORK · BOSTON · CHICAGO
DALLAS · ATLANTA · SAN FRANCISCO

THE MACMILLAN COMPANY
OF CANADA, LIMITED
TORONTO

TALLEYRAND IN HIS DECLINING YEARS
After the portrait by Ary Scheffer

# TALLEYRAND

BY

## COMTE DE SAINT-AULAIRE

Translated from the French
by

### GEORGE FREDERIC LEES

and

### FREDERICK J. STEPHENS

With an Introduction by
the former

NEW YORK
THE MACMILLAN COMPANY
1937

COPYRIGHT

PRINTED IN GREAT BRITAIN
BY R. & R. CLARK, LIMITED, EDINBURGH

# CONTENTS

TALLEYRAND

## CHAPTER IX

## CHAPTER X

## CHAPTER XI

## CHAPTER XII

## FRONTISPIECE

TALLEYRAND IN HIS DECLINING YEARS. After the portrait by Ary Scheffer.

# INTRODUCTION

ON the reading of the riddle of that sphinx-like statesman and diplomatist, Charles Maurice de Talleyrand, every fresh contribution to his life and times has thrown some new light, and thus, gradually but surely, the complete portrait of one of the most remarkable men of five distinct periods in French history—the days of Louis XVI and the Revolution, those of Napoleon and the Empire, the reign of Louis XVIII and his successors, Charles X and Louis Philippe—has been revealed. During his own lifetime, when historians were too near to him to understand his motives thoroughly, the features of that portrait were still indistinct and his contemporaries knew not whether to call him sphinx or comedian—or both.

"We did not know what to make of him", says Macaulay in the course of his review of Hallam's *Constitutional History*, and while referring in general terms to those troubled times in history when "a laxity of principle, without which no public man can be eminent or even safe, becomes too common to be scandalous". But Macaulay himself, thanks to his profound reading of history and his equally deep knowledge of mankind, had already begun to read the Talleyrand riddle when he continued to remark that "his manifold treasons by no means seemed to destroy his influence, or even to fix any particular stain of infamy on his character. . . . His countrymen did not seem to be shocked: for there was scarcely one Frenchman distinguished in the State or in the army, who had not, according to his talents and opportunities, emulated the example. The rapidity and violence with which change followed change in the affairs of France towards the end of the last century had taken away the reproach of inconstancy, unfixed the principles of men, and produced in many minds a general scepticism and indifference about principles of government." And our great historian and critic added that "our own Shaftesbury was surely a far less respectable man than Talleyrand".

The literature which has grown up around the romantic and most diversified life of Talleyrand is enormous, and in the still more gigantic library of books on his great collaborator, Napoleon, he is also to be seen playing one of the leading parts on the stage of history. Pamphlets on his work and opinions were innumerable during the period of the Revolution, and many of them—rare documents to-day—have come down to us. About 1853, when Michaud published an account of his political and private life, and above all in 1870, when Amédée Pichot's *Souvenirs intimes* appeared, we were beginning to understand the importance of the great diplomatist's rôle in history, past and present. Talleyrand's own view of himself—those *Memoirs* which the Duc de Broglie edited and annotated —did not appear until 1891–92. By that time his letters to Mme Adélaïde and his correspondence with Comte de Jaucourt, Interim Minister of Foreign Affairs during the Vienna Congress, had also been published. It was then that the character of the ex-Bishop of Autun became sufficiently clear for such historians as Ferdinand Lolliée— who wrote two standard works on Talleyrand, in 1910 and 1917—to produce much more complete studies of his life. Since then and within the last few years we have had M. Lacour-Gayet's monumental work in three volumes. And now, in the following pages, we have this fine contribution to the life of a statesman whose work, as will be seen, still lives after him.

The lives of men of genius—and especially those who have taken a part in international politics—are subject to so many points of view that, among historical writers of different nationalities, unanimity as regards motive or the credit for the achievement of this or that momentous task in world-politics is well-nigh impossible. We do not expect, nor perhaps do we hope, to find uniformity of views in those two notable books on the same theme as this work —one in German by Herr Hans Blei, and the other in English by Mr. Duff Cooper. Diversity of opinion is indeed welcome to the impartial student of history, and the differences in their points of view which we note in those writers on Talleyrand who are not Frenchmen are surely an additional proof of the many-sided and fascinating character of that superman of the diplomatic world.

Nothing is more interesting than comparison between the two biographical studies just mentioned and that which the Comte de Saint-Aulaire has written; comparison, not with the object of giving one or the other the palm, but with that of knowing all we can of a man who was many men rolled into one—Nobleman and Priest, Statesman and Diplomatist, Opportunist, Financier, and Hedonist; the most vital and prolific human spark of his day; a man who, when he came face to face with "that new phenomenon in politics", as Macaulay calls the Revolution, which aimed at the reform of great abuses and at which honest men rejoiced, made up his mind to await events and act accordingly. For Talleyrand was neither the "divinely inspired prophet" nor the "obstinate fool" to whom Macaulay refers in his admirable summing-up, in some dozen lines, of "that great blessing to mankind", the French Revolution. If not a good man in the puritanical sense of the word, he was certainly a wise one, and gifted with the most astounding gift of prevision.

That was Macaulay's estimate of Talleyrand, whom he depicts at Holland House relating his "conversations with Barras at the Luxembourg, or his ride with Lannes across the field of Austerlitz".

To his task of giving us one of the most analytical and at the same time picturesque and anecdotal studies of Talleyrand yet written, the Comte de Saint-Aulaire has brought his special knowledge as a distinguished French diplomatist; and it is interesting to note, in passing, that he himself, when French Ambassador in London between 1920 and 1924,[1] was one of this Prince of Diplomatist's successors. Moreover, as a writer on historical themes, he holds a high place as the author of *La Mythologie de la Paix* (1930) and *Cardinal de Richelieu* (1932), the latter being a close study of that Cardinal and Dictator who must be placed in the same category as Talleyrand—among those statesmen who have shown remarkable constructive ability. It is especially Talleyrand the Constructor whom he depicts for us in the following pages; Talleyrand "the good Frenchman, a lover of his country" who, though he might feather his own nest when opportunity offered, was nevertheless able to foresee the most distant events and prepare to safeguard Peace and the welfare of humanity.

In the present stage of international politics such a work as this is of intense interest, both to the professional diplomatist and that "man in the street" who can now follow

[1] The following biographical details may be added. The Comte de Saint-Aulaire was born in 1866, was educated at the École des Sciences Politiques, and was a member of the Diplomatic Corps from 1893 to 1924. He has held the following posts: Chargé d'affaires in Lima (Peru), 1896; Chargé d'affaires at Santiago (Chili), 1897; First Secretary in Vienna, 1909; Minister in Vienna (1909–1912), Morocco (1912), Bucharest (1917), Warsaw (1920); Ambassador in Madrid (1920) and in London (1920–24). He is a Grand Officer of the Legion of Honour.

with fairly sound judgment the moves on that chess-board of the nations, which is very much the same to-day as it was in the days of the Revolution and the Empire of Napoleon Bonaparte. Though the combinations of the game are certainly different, the principles underlying it are often identical, and, in reading the Comte de Saint-Aulaire's pages (apart from those in which he touches upon his hero's work for an alliance with England and the part he played in obtaining the Independence of Belgium, in which some authorities may be inclined to see rather the hand of Palmerston than that of Talleyrand) we are continually coming face to face with an exposition of some of those human and political truths which are eternal. We learn, for instance, what the inevitable fate of all forms of tyranny is; it is made clear to us once more how illusive is the idea of a Napoleon when he sets forth to dominate the world; our belief in the folly of militarism is strengthened; and, as we read of the effect of conscription and the no-less-disastrous blockade, which "deprived the Russians of those English articles to which they were accustomed and prevented them exporting the produce of their own country", we begin to ask ourselves when the world will begin to learn the lessons of history.

GEORGE FREDERIC LEES

## CHAPTER I

## YOUNG CHARLES MAURICE

The time I spent at Chalais made a deep impression
upon me.                                  TALLEYRAND

CHARLES MAURICE DE TALLEYRAND-PÉRIGORD was born
on February 2, 1754, at No. 4 Rue Garancière, not far
from the Sorbonne, quite near to St-Sulpice, in a quarter
which at one and the same time was the most intellectual
and pious in Paris. When, in the decline of life and
accompanied by his charming grand-niece Pauline de
Périgord, he took his last walks on the left bank of the
Seine, seeking rejuvenation and to enlighten his old age
through recollections of childhood—recollections which
were to be of some consequence as regards his conversion
—he was able to take in at a single glance the places where
he first saw the light of day and where some of the most
important acts in his religious, sentimental, and political
life had been accomplished.

Whereupon there was a discordant and all the more
touching chorus of impressions, the most lively of which
Pauline's "good uncle", as she used to call him, doubtless
kept from his grand-niece. "It was there", he said, when
passing in front of No. 4 Rue Garancière, "that I was
born." And a little further on, gazing on the towers of
St-Sulpice, he added: "It was there I was baptized, on
the very day of my birth. My godfather was my paternal
uncle, Comte de Périgord, who was attached to the person
of the Dauphin; my godmother was my maternal grand-

mother, the Marquise d'Antigny, a fervent Christian but tinged with Jansenism." We have no knowledge of the reflections suggested to him by the gloomy buildings of the St-Sulpice seminary, where he found—in lieu of a vocation which, however, was not of his seeking—some compensations. But he could not have specified their nature without offending the purity of his Antigona. It was, indeed, in the Rue Férou, opposite his cell, that he received the baptism of love; unless it were its confirmation, for, according to some of his biographers, he had come to man's estate before entering the seminary.

Although the scene of innumerable scandals, but which, being of a purely political order, could not scandalize even little girls, the neighbouring Palace of the Luxembourg—first the seat of the Directory, of which he had been the minister, and then that of the Imperial Senate, which he had managed as he liked at certain decisive times—was a less delicate subject of conversation than No. 6 Rue Férou.

It was there, forty years before, in 1797, that his mistress, Mme de Staël, had obtained for him, through the influence of Barras, the office of Foreign Affairs. There, in the same year, he had harangued Bonaparte, after the Italian campaign, and celebrated "the sweetness of his studious retreat". There, on the 18th of Brumaire, he had brought about the resignation of his protector Barras, in order to make a clear place for Bonaparte. And there, in 1814, he had pronounced the Emperor's dethronement.

Charles Maurice was the younger brother of Alexandre François Jacques, who died at the age of five years. Thus he became the elder, in fact but not legally, because the infirmity from which he suffered barred a military career. His parents deprived him of his prerogatives in favour of their third son, Archambeaud Joseph, and destined him

for the Church. This was both his luck and his mischance
—his worldly good luck, but his spiritual fatality. Despite
himself, he was to be directed along a path on which,
although loaded with all the good things of this world,
he was to compromise his salvation in the other. The fact
that he forfeited his right as an elder son without having merited such a fate partly explains his character and
conduct. His pride was wounded; his natural ambition
spurred on. He determined to recover supremacy in his
family by right of conquest, by adding unprecedented
splendour to his name; and he was prompted to revolt
against a social order of which he considered himself to
have been a victim.

Those who search for the secret of great events in
minor causes will place Talleyrand's club-foot in the same
category as Cleopatra's nose and the grain of sand in
Cromwell's bladder. He owed this propitious disgrace to
the woman with whom his parents put him to nurse, and
then as a boarder until he was four years of age. She let
him fall so badly that his right foot was dislocated; and,
it appears, an irreparable deviation was the result. He was
lame for the whole of his life. According to Dr. Cabanès,
who specialized in the study of the psychological peculiarities of celebrated men, Talleyrand suffered from a "varus
équin" club-foot. Dr. Puys, who studied the cerebral
lesions of those who suffer from this infirmity, claimed
to have discovered a correlation between it and atrophy
of the moral perception; and in support of his theory he
cites Talleyrand's case, although *his* infirmity was purely
accidental. The instance of Lord Byron, whose club-foot
was congenital, and whose lack of moral principles was
more complete than Talleyrand's, would have been more
convincing. If, as testified by Trelawny, who saw the poet
in his coffin, Byron had "the face and bust of Apollo, the

3

feet and legs of a faun", Talleyrand is said, on the faith of one of his lady friends, to have possessed "the face of an angel". But he had not the forked foot of a devil. The lameness of his conscience appears to have been independent of the other. He walked with the aid of a long stick-and-crutch, which, when carrying out his episcopal duties, he could replace by his crosier, also held in the left hand (lame people rely for support on the opposite side to that of their infirmity), so that his right hand remained free for the benediction.

When seated, he had a bad habit of tapping with his stick on the metal contrivance which supported his bad leg from the leather ring to which it was attached below the knee to his orthopaedic shoe, a roundish box—comparable to a horse's hoof—which fitted the shape of the foot.

Orthopaedy is not yet applicable in the case of moral deformities, and Talleyrand's education was to aggravate his rather than correct them. His stump of a conscience was less protected than that of his foot. Delivered into mercenary hands until the age of four, his soul was to fare no better than his body. Not that his parents were unnatural, as some modern parents may believe—and who themselves are much more so, since they voluntarily limit the number of their offspring. Parents under the old régime in France considered that fecundity was their primary duty. The father of the future Bishop of Autun, Daniel de Talleyrand, who at sixteen married the twenty-two-year-old Mlle de Damas d'Antigny, had five children: four sons and a daughter. Parents of numerous children cannot have for each of them the same solicitude they have for an only son, that unique idol for whom and in whose presence the authors of his precious days tremble. The educative value of that idolatry is, without doubt, inferior to that of the relative

4

detachment which was formerly the rule in aristocratic families. Parents considered that they had a double duty towards their offspring: the duty of bringing them up, which could be delegated to another; and the duty of assuring their future by maintaining and, if possible, increasing the family position—a duty which could be fulfilled only by themselves. Thus it was that Talleyrand's father, a colonel in the Grenadiers of France, was often with the armies, while his wife was retained at Versailles by her duties at Court.

Talleyrand, who sometimes spoke of his parents with bitterness—less to accuse them than to make excuses for them—did not, however, see an anomaly in the indifference for which he reproached them. On the contrary. On the subject of his education, he said: "What is above all things necessary is to act and to be like everybody". And he added: "The children were the heirs of the name and the family coat of arms".

This conception of the family was particularly authoritative in the case of the representatives of so illustrious a lineage as that of the Talleyrands. They could pride themselves on an extraction equal to that of the kings of France, since they descended from the Counts-Sovereign of Périgord, one of whom, Aldebert, when Hugues Capet asked him, "Who made thee Count?" replied, "Who made thee King?"—a rejoinder which is perhaps more famous than it is authentic. For it has been contested, as well as the filiation of the Talleyrands from Aldebert. The witticism attributed to Louis XVIII has often been repeated. "In their pretensions", he said, "the Talleyrands make a mistake only in a single letter: they are *du*—of the—and not *de* Périgord—of Périgord." However, one of the ancestors of Talleyrand, Prince de Bénévent, was recognized to be in the direct line of the former Counts of Périgord when

Louis XIII raised the castellany of Grignol to an earldom and the castellany of Excideuil to a marquisate in his favour. Whatever may be the historical interest in this controversy, it is of no psychological interest in the study of Charles Maurice de Talleyrand because it never existed either for him or for the majority of his contemporaries. He had no doubts whatsoever on the subject of that illustrious origin which, heraldically, gave him precedence over almost the whole of Europe and placed him on an equal footing with the remainder. It inspired him with unbounded pride—the fundamental trait in his character and one of the keys, perhaps the very one which unlocks the innermost recesses "of the most impenetrable and incomprehensible of men", to quote Mme de Staël, who, however, ought to have known *everything* about him, if to that end it suffices that she did not refuse him *anything*.

Talleyrand, the sceptic, the liberal, the revolutionary, the friend of progress and enlightenment, was, at bottom, a great feudal lord, one of the most ancient dynasts in Europe, dispossessed but not resigned, and who, amidst the turmoils of his period—the most convulsive in the whole range of history—saw nothing save opportunities to reconquer and develop, under forms adapted to the circumstances, his antique prerogatives. He exerted himself by exercising first of all a more modern and less exceptional prerogative, sufficiently widespread during revolutions to become common law, which consists in exalting oneself above the maxims of ordinary ethics. What was most personal in him and which came from the consciousness of his origin was his greed of power, sought after for himself alone and as a means of enjoyment; for this future bishop was the very opposite of an ascetic. It was also his inborn habit to negotiate with the great people of this world—kings, emperors, and popes—on

6

an equal footing, when he was not, amidst his bowing and scraping, treating them with a feeling of contempt, due to the consciousness of his double superiority—his nobility and his intellectuality.

But Talleyrand, the feudal lord, was not merely that. If this hereditary trait was so strongly marked as to make the hidden unity of a character and a destiny equally contrasted, to the point of apparently belonging to several very different men, this descendant of the Counts of Périgord had no lack of choice among his ancestors in order to borrow from them gifts or tendencies which varied, moderated, renewed his feudalism, and, finally, served it. The majority were formidable fighting men, as witness their name derived from "Taille-Rang" (*Anglicè*, "Rank-Slasher"), a nickname evoking mighty blows with the sword amidst the ranks of the enemy. His grandfather had been killed at the siege of Tournai in 1745, his great-grandfather at the siege of Barcelona in 1714. Through the women of his house Talleyrand had in his veins the blood of still more famous warriors: Montluc, the celebrated Gascon captain, the terror of the Protestants; the great French admiral, Jean de Vienne, who succeeded in making a landing in England, and who was killed, at the head of his troops, at the battle of Nicopolis. Talleyrand was to possess his audacity and energy; but to make another use of them. And he was to have no more scruples in politics than Montluc had had in warfare. Among his kindred there were personages less fierce, and these included two of Louis XIV's ministers, the great Colbert and Chamillart.

In Talleyrand's family there were also a number of saintly prelates, the nearest of whom was his uncle, his father's brother, Alexandre Angélique, the coadjutor in 1766 of Monseigneur de la Roche-Aymon, Archbishop of

Rheims, whose successor he became in 1777. Having been Archbishop-Duke of Rheims, he was, in 1817, to be Cardinal-Archbishop of Paris. On the women's side the majority, in default of an historical part, possessed a reputation for charm, wit, piety, and virtue. His mother especially, whose household was on a most solid foundation despite her being six years older than her husband, was most attached to her duties, as they were understood in those days. In the full-length portrait which adorns the dining-room at the Château de Valençay she has an expression—which one feels was quite natural—of seriousness, delicacy, and authority. Her son, whose errors must have sorely grieved her, traced, with a pious and delicate hand, the following portrait of her mind: "When visiting my mother I chose those hours when she was alone, in order to enjoy the graces of her mind to the full. When in conversation nobody ever appeared to me to possess a charm comparable to hers. There was not the slightest trace of affectation in her. *She spoke wholly in delicate shades of meaning; a witticism never escaped her lips; for that would have been to have said too much. Witty remarks are remembered, and all she desired was to please and retain no further hold on what she said.*" Her son inherited from her that feeling for delicate shades. But he was also to cultivate the art of wit. And, above all, he was to make a point of never losing anything. His mind appertained to the art of succeeding rather than to the art of pleasing, which is likewise a way to success. It was to be a weapon and an investment rather than a game and a gift. He was to exploit instead of displaying it, as his mother did, for the improvement of the minds of others.

If Talleyrand's conscience was ever at peace, because it capitulated without a fight, we cannot say as much of his subconscious self, the arena of his ancestors—feudal lords

8

and servants of the monarchy, crusaders and libertines, sturdy warriors and saintly prelates. Amidst that intestine struggle, amidst such a "clashing of hereditary traits", to use the expression of a psychiater, it is not easy to count the blows and award the palm of victory. In Talleyrand's case, however, the victory was not indecisive. It ever belonged to the shades, which were to be his best allies in the conquest of realities. If, to speak like his great enemy, Chateaubriand, he bivouacked under the tent of the dead, he was to choose the flag of the dead to aid him the better to live his own life.

Man, as has been said, is the sum-total of his race. That is perhaps true when all his ancestors resemble each other. But it is erroneous in the contrary case, because one cannot sum up different or opposite values. Man is then, not the addition, but the synthesis of his race, a synthesis which evades analysis, at any rate as far as the proportions and mutual reactions of its composite parts are concerned. The test-tube at the bottom of which they will some day perhaps be calculated has not yet been invented. An unstable synthesis, moreover, by virtue of unknown laws and in accordance with the play of the will which presides over the combination of its elements. With Talleyrand, the more or less conscious will-power was to favour, among so many elements in which the heart and even the soul had its part, those who were to be of a disposition to procure for him what Pascal called the grandeur of the flesh, or the grandeur of position.

There we have Talleyrand's true vocation. Far from counteracting it, the early experiences of his life were to confirm it. The feelings on which it was nourished— pride, ambition, and concupiscence—are among those which, if they do not succumb, are strengthened by the obstacles they encounter and the blows they receive. They die through satiety, but live through inanition. The latter régime was inflicted, in his childhood, owing to the craving for honours and pleasures which consumed the youth Charles Maurice. Hence, as Freud's disciples will say, that phenomenon of repression which was to determine his future—a suppressed and acute libido which was to burst forth on its first contact with the world and overthrow all principles.

Talleyrand's parents were not wealthy. His father had barely his pay as a colonel, while his mother's dowry amounted to an income of only 15,000 livres. That would have been amply sufficient to live in a noble style in the provinces. But in Paris, and under an obligation to cut a figure at Court, it was almost poverty. Pregnant with her second child, Charles Maurice, Mme Talleyrand wrote to her mother to ask for baby-linen, so as not, she said, to be "the counterpart of the Holy Virgin". The future Prince de Bénévent was not, however, born in a stable and, even in his worst days, was never to sleep on straw. Yet his parents could only satisfy the exterior requirements of their rank by curtailing their interior budget, and at the same time that of their offspring. More ease would have permitted greater supervision and averted the accident which crippled for life the future eldest child of the family—it would have averted that double drama of his childhood and adolescence: the fall and the consecutive priesthood, a double drama which was to command the comedy of his whole existence.

When Charles Maurice, awaiting an appropriate age—that is to say, six years—to be placed as a boarder at the Collège d'Harcourt, was sent to Périgord to his great-grandmother, the Princesse de Chalais, so that he might benefit by a change of air and consolidate his delicate state of health, he proceeded there accompanied, not by a tutor, whom his parents felt they could not afford, but by a trustworthy woman, Mlle Charlemagne, and not in a post-chaise but in the common Bordeaux stage-coach, which made the journey in seventeen days. Who can say whether that stage-coach was not destined to lead him rapidly, though by circuitous ways and not those of virtue, to fortune? At that tender age, when self-esteem is so keen and the recollections of which are ineffaceable, the child who later was to dazzle Europe by his pageantry must have felt, on utilizing for the first time the common conveyance of the period, the same feeling of vexation which, in our days, would be that of the conceited offspring of a great but penniless lord on stepping into a motor-bus when it was side by side with the Rolls Royce of a less well-born comrade. Meditating over that silent and all the more bitter humiliation, he must have dreamed of a brilliant revenge. That Bordeaux stage-coach, in which he once more travelled two years later, and still with Mlle Charlemagne, was perhaps the unknown predecessor of the luxurious berlins which were to convey His Most Serene Highness from Court to Court over the main roads of Europe. The relative poverty of his parents was to incite him to leave nothing undone to escape from the inequality between his fortune and his rank. There, perhaps, is one of the sources of what will be called—using too summary a word—his venality, but where it is more just to see an eagerness less delicate as regards conduct than taste.

If that journey to Périgord awakened the little patrician's self-esteem while mortifying it, his sojourn there flattered that feeling and caused it to bloom. In that province, the cradle of his family, which still held first rank there, and where the influence of the new age had not touched, however so lightly, the most distant traditions; in that Château de Chalais, rebuilt in the seventeenth century but side by side with the ancient donjon, still standing (as also the other neighbouring castle of the Talleyrands, Excideuil), his feudal fibre awakened and resuscitated in him the soul of the eleventh century, bequeathed to him by his ancestors, and which he was to preserve under various masks, while combining it with the most modern spirit. These ancient and half-crumbling ramparts of Chalais and Excideuil are long since powerless from a military standpoint; but socially and morally they are still the impregnable strongholds of the pride of the nobility. The life people led there resembled more that of the neighbouring cottages than the splendour Talleyrand was to know at Valençay; but life there was more truly noble than at Court and in the palaces which copied its magnificence. Whilst at Versailles, and in the provinces which borrowed its tone, all grandeur was eclipsed by the royal grandeur, and encountered at the foot of the throne an often victorious competition through the recent glory, beauty, fortune, or favour of the monarch; the Lords of Chalais enjoyed an absolute suzerainty, which, if no longer sanctioned by institutions, was intact as regards manners and customs. Everything—things and beings—proclaimed it: those lofty walls which testified to the ancient power of the race, and the little village girls who, according to a still existing custom, stopped, on meeting the Lady of the Manor, to curtsy to her in courtly fashion. To young Maurice that was a call to the will for power rather than a lesson in democratic equality. That object lesson was to be completed by his great-grandmother, a very great lady who had frequented the Court of Louis XIV. "She possessed", he says in his memoirs, "the genius of the Montmart family. That was her name." Under the gaze of the family portraits,

she was to initiate him into the splendour of thei
In the evenings their history was embellished
fied to legendary proportions by narratives a
retainers who formerly played a great part in the education
of young noblemen. These "domestics", in the etymological sense of the word, belonged from generation to
generation to the "House", which was regarded as not
only an abode but as a family. They were even prouder of it
than their masters and transmitted its traditions more faithfully, for the simple reason that they did not go to Court.

The Châteaux of Chalais and Excideuil, with all the
possessions attached to them, belong to-day to a home
founded by the Talleyrand family. If his shade were at
times to wander there he would surely experience a
double surprise. He would note that his name, often cursed
by his contemporaries, is now blessed there by everyone.
And at Excideuil he would meditate on the vanity of
revolutions on learning that, during the last war, the
war of "democracy and law", the Republic imprisoned
undisciplined soldiers in the oubliettes of the donjon.
For if his Périgordian Bastille, with its two donjons
without an opening—a castle blinded and walled up like
a sepulchre—has lost its battlements, it still retains its
gloomy dungeons. The soldier-citizens who were huddled
together there must, each according to his turn of mind,
have consoled themselves with the thought that they were
there by virtue of a law which theoretically gave expression
to their will, or else they regretted the Middle Ages on re-
flecting that obligatory military service did not then exist.

"The time I spent at Chalais made a deep impression
upon me", says Talleyrand in his memoirs.[1] The best

---

[1] *Mémoires du Prince de Talleyrand*, publiés avec une préface et des
notes par le Duc de Broglie. Paris, Lévy, 1891–95. 5 vols.—Translators' note.

proof of this is that it is the only period of his life of which he speaks in detail. He learnt the Périgordian dialect there. Better lessons still did he learn. "To those early years", he writes, "I owe the general tendency of my conduct. If I have displayed affectionate, even tender feelings without over familiarity, if I have retained under different circumstances a certain loftiness without being haughty, if I love and respect old people, it was at Chalais, it was by my grandmother's side that I absorbed all those good feelings with which I saw my relatives surrounded in that province, and amidst which they experienced delight." He also learnt, and above all was to remember, that his family held the leading place in the district and received almost royal honours there. "Several noblemen of ancient extraction formed for my grandmother a sort of Court, with naught of the vassalage of the thirteenth century about it, but at which deferential manners were blended with the most elevated feelings. . . . They took a pleasure in accompanying her every Sunday to the parish mass, each carrying out at her side duties which were ennobled by the great politeness with which they were performed. Next to my grandmother's prayer-stool was a little chair for myself."

He wrote those lines more than half a century after his sojourn in Périgord, and the vividness of his recollections testify to their influence on his life. Supposing that he ever encountered at Chalais one of those ancient peasant women who, in a province disposed to be more credulous than firm in religious belief, cast children's horoscopes, she must surely have predicted that the Masses which he attended on his little chair prepared him to dominate mankind rather than to serve God, and contributed to his formation —or deformation—more than the Masses he himself was to celebrate would contribute to his sanctification.

In September 1760 Mlle Charlemagne took the child who had been entrusted to her care back to Paris, again by stage-coach and in seventeen days. If faith is to be placed in his memoirs, an old servant awaited him at the coach-office and, there and then, without taking him to his parents' house, shut him up at the Collège d'Harcourt. Arriving at eleven in the morning, he was at the refectory table at noon. He was not yet seven years of age. However, he recalled those college days without bitterness. His schoolfellows of that age, which is pitiless, were not without deference for his name nor without taste for his charm. Although unable to take part in his comrades' games, he was to make lifelong friends among the "Harcourtians". If in political life Talleyrand was to distinguish himself by unfaithfulness (which, however, applied to régimes rather than to doctrines), he was to prove himself remarkably staunch in friendship. Smallpox, which attacked him at the age of eleven, was the chief event of his life when a boarder at school. He recovered and without being pock-marked, as Mirabeau, Camille Desmoulins, Robespierre, and Danton were. Nor was he to be more marked by the ideological epidemics of the Revolution. His scepticism and common sense vaccinated him against *that* sort of contagion.

When, in 1816, he recalled his college days, he summed them up as follows: "I worked tolerably well; my comrades liked me, and I accustomed myself fairly cheerfully to my position". The indolence, charm, and plasticity of his nature already made their appearance. He was not a brilliant pupil. But he gives one to understand that he would have been had he only liked. He does not tell us whether he disdained scholastic success because, in his opinion, a scholar who is strong in his exercises is not exempt from being a self-conceited pedant, or because the career imposed upon him did not appear to him to be worthy of his efforts. He was not a "plodder"; but he reflected, observed, meditated, and dreamed. That inner work was to be more fruitful than industry in class. He has described himself as retiring within himself owing to "the troubles of his early years", thus contracting "the habit of thinking all the more profoundly". His precocity was not merely intellectual, according to one of his biographers, who attributes to him, at the age of fifteen, a triple liaison with three sisters, Maria, Amy, and Sophie —likewise a symbol, he adds, of the three forms of government, Republic, Empire, and Restoration—all of whose favours he was to enjoy without marrying any one of them. Whether that adventure was symbolic or not, Talleyrand was not to be content with being the Don Juan of Constitutions.

His lost right to primogeniture left him with a resentment which impelled him to exaggerate his grievances against his parents and formulate them with a "perverseness" which, however, denotes less delicacy as regards his feelings than as regards the way he expressed them. Here is how he explained his family's apparent indifference whilst he was at school: "I understand now that my parents, being determined, in accordance with what they regarded as the family interest, to guide me to a profession for which I showed no disposition whatsoever, were distrustful of their courage in carrying out that project should they have seen me too often. That fear is a proof of a tenderness for which I am grateful to them." He even asserts that he never knew the happiness of sleeping beneath the parental roof. But that is hardly likely. He may actually have sojourned with his parents at Versailles, as is claimed under the authority of an anecdote which, if disputable—like the majority of the stories of which he is the hero—at any rate possesses a documentary value from the point of view of his reputation. His shrewd mind and charming grace having induced his parents to use him for confidential missions, they are said to have sent him, during Lent, to Paris, to call on the Archbishop and negotiate their reconciliation with Heaven, owing to an involuntary transgression during the period of fasting. M. and Mme de Talleyrand had inadvertently partaken of the contents of a barrel of pork, which they mistook for tunny. Terribly alarmed, they are said to have sent young Maurice to lay the case before His Eminence, and ask for his advice as regards the necessary reparation. One may wonder how, in their religious conscience, such scruples could accord with the determination to devote to the Church a son whose soul was in no way sacerdotal and whose ecclesiastical career was destined to be a long sacrilege. But those were the morals of the day. . . . If M. and Mme de Talleyrand still retained doubts as to Maurice's piety, the manner in which he carried out his mission must have dispelled them completely, without, however, shaking their decision. For young Talleyrand did not even set foot in the Archbishop's palace. He made no attempt whatsoever to meet His Eminence; he devoted all the money given him for his journey, and all the time at his disposal, to amusements which were all the more guilty since they were enjoyed during Lent. . . . True or not, the story is worthy of being so, for it enables us to complete his horoscope. It portends that, in the course of his diplomatic career, he would not trouble his head over any instructions, and that, as regards conduct, he would not worry himself over any rule, especially a rule of abstinence.

## CHAPTER II

## THE ABBÉ DE PÉRIGORD

I assumed the air of little Bonaparte.

Letter of October 6, 1827, to
Mme Gentil de Chavagnac

At the age of fifteen our collegian had finished his studies. The problem for his parents was to inspire him with the semblance of a religious vocation. Devoting themselves to this, they pointed out to him the worldly satisfactions with which God rewards noble lords who honour Him with their service. They said that if in His house there were many mansions, there were several doors, and the most suitable door for their son was that of ambition.

So they sent him to his paternal uncle, coadjutor to the Archbishop of Rheims. On seeing a Talleyrand in his episcopal splendour, and one soon to succeed to the see of St-Rémi, he might perchance discover that this calling was as good as any other. In order to put him in a state of grace, his journey was made more agreeable than had been the one to Chalais. They went to the expense of a post-chaise, which arrived at the college to take him— again without calling at the paternal abode—to Rheims. But, he said later, "that was because it was not becoming for my family that I should arrive at the Archbishopric by coach". And there he donned the cassock. Mme de Talleyrand wrote to her mother: "My eldest son is very comfortable in his new position", which doubtless signified that his cassock was well cut. To fit him out to measure with the soul of a priest, a less easy task, it did not suffice to attach him to the princely suite of the Archbishop Charles Antoine, Duc de Reims, Comte de la Roche-Aymon, Grand Almoner of France, an archbishop who was soon to become a cardinal. His uncle, the coadjutor, made him read the lives of churchmen who had played a great part on the world's stage: Hincmar, Archbishop of Rheims, prime minister of Charles the Bald; Cardinal Ximénès, Grand Inquisitor of Castille; Richelieu and Cardinal de Retz. The life of the last named was the only one whose lessons were destined not to be lost. During that period at Rheims he met a celebrated teacher, the Comtesse de Genlis, who gave him a good mark in these words: "He was pale and silent; but I found his face very agreeable, with an observant air which impressed me". The future diplomat already possessed one of the chief qualities of the profession: circumspection, in the etymological sense of the word, which means "taking everything into account".

At sixteen years of age he entered St-Sulpice. But he made no effort to attain a vocation refused him by God. On that score he would doubtless have considered it an impiety to oppose the design of Providence. In his diminutive breeches and little black silk cloak his mood was more sombre than his clothes. Retiring within himself, attentive to voices possessing no celestial quality, he spoke to no one, thus causing a complex of gloomy despair and glowing ambition to be mistaken for vulgar pride. But his despair was that of a man with red globules in his blood and whose senses were ablaze. Through his lameness he was deprived of all exercise, but his vitality ebbed violently in another direction; to use the jargon of psychoanalysis it suffered a "transference", destined to be full and final. His blood coursed through his veins like burning lava. The courtyard of St-Sulpice was already for him a stage on which, before a public consisting of his teachers and comrades, he wore a mask of haughty and taciturn melancholy. But behind the scenes—and even in the green-room—he took it off. Night afforded him a revenge for the day and an instalment drawn on the future. Despite his club-foot, he was over the seminary wall in a trice, using first of all the branch of a tree and then the top of a hackney-coach, stationed on the other side to facilitate the feat. He had made an appointment with the daughter of a neighbouring cook-shop keeper, a child of fourteen who, gossip had it, used to pass defiantly before the janitor, under the guise of a little pastrycook with a tray of cakes on her head, to visit Charles Maurice in his cell.

The young seminarist had at least one more adventure sufficiently unusual for him to refer to it with feeling forty-four years later, and thanks to which he said he "had escaped experiencing all the results due to melancholy brought to its highest pitch". His Superior, pleased with his assiduity in attending divine service at St-Sulpice, was in blissful ignorance of the fact that his zeal was explained by the presence of Dorothée Dorinville, who acted at the Comédie Française under the name of Suzy. He had spoken to her for the first time on a rainy day, and, like a good neighbour, had offered her the half of his umbrella to accompany her back to her home at No. 6 Rue Férou. Moreover, he entered, and cherished so pleasing a recollection of her welcome that he was to be found returning every day for the next two years. Never was he to forget Dorothée, his first love, the owner of the same name as the last object of his tenderness, the Duchesse de Dino. This first passion, followed by so many others, was the most lasting, at any rate in his memory, not only because it was the first, but also because it was the most well-assorted. Not that this great comedian had any natural affinity with a little actress. To love an actress because she was an actress was for him something far too commonplace; he loved her although she was an actress, or because she was an actress just as he was a seminarist. Said he: "Her parents had pushed her on to the stage of the Comédie Française against her will, and I, against my will, was at the seminary", which fact, by another route, forced him also to act comedy. Thus their happiness was the component of two misfortunes which found mutual consolation, and the families, without laying their heads together, had thrown the lovers into each other's arms.

When Talleyrand recalled his seminary days, the double life he led there explained his contradictions. At times he cursed, at others, blessed them. He cursed them when thinking of the restraints to which he was subjected, but especially in his memoirs where he forced the note in order to justify his apostasy before posterity. In moments of intimacy he used to confess, "When I wish to be happy, I think of St-Sulpice". Besides, in the character of Talleyrand, inconsistency was not a bar to sincerity. He was capable, without imposture, of asserting contradictory statements on the same subject. One could not ask him to be always this *or* that. Most frequently he was this *and* that. His was a case of complexity rather than duplicity.

This life of his was even triple in character: the young seminarist applied himself to work with as much zeal as pleasure, and with more fruition than from prayer. After his Périgordian training—the most effective as regards his character—and that at the Collège d'Harcourt, the most superficial of the three, the Sulpician discipline was the most effective intellectually. He spent long hours daily in the fine library of St-Sulpice devouring works of the most varied character. The object of his quest was not to find information supplementary to religious teaching, but a derivative. His preference, as he himself says, was for "books of the most revolutionary character", and books recounting the "upheavals in all countries". He knew that his miraculous draught of fishes was not to be in still waters. He echoed, in his own way and in a more practical spirit, the romantic exclamation of Chateaubriand, "Hasten, ye welcome tempests!" As he conceived it, it was not for the love of the tempest, but because the tempest alone was to bring him to the haven. The "Hell" of this library, according to the expression in use for the designation of "naughty" books, was his paradise. For him reading was an escape, a means of dispelling his phantoms and nourishing his dreams. It was also a means of preparing him to realize them by imparting to him knowledge which he was later to use under all manner of circumstances.

Thus it was that he played the part of the "little Bonaparte" of Brienne, and not merely, as he supposed, because he was equally taciturn, solitary, and out of his element. So were both under conditions and for reasons entirely different. Bonaparte was on his right path, since he possessed the military vocation, but he was neither in his element nor even in his own country, seeing that he was a Corsican recently naturalized, with a pronounced foreign accent, which made him the butt of his comrades, who nicknamed him "*La paille au nez*" ("Straw-nose"), because he pronounced his Christian name—for such it was then—"Napollione". On the other hand, at St-Sulpice, where the aristocracy of the clergy was trained, the Abbé de Périgord was not on his right road, but he was in his element. His name won for him exceptional attentions, and even privileges, if one is to judge by the toleration he enjoyed despite the liberties he took with regulations.

Nevertheless, he played his part of Bonaparte in little, otherwise and more than he supposed. Like the student Bonaparte, a feverish ambition consumed him and produced in him an insatiable thirst for reading and knowledge. Like him, he was omnivorous. With pen in hand and endowed with a marvellous memory, he was to retain everything which might be of future use. Like him, he assimilated "the contents of books which were entirely outside his profession"; and this was to enable him to excel in his profession, for one only excels in some specialism by dominating it, in other words by getting beyond its limits. If this be true of the calling of an Emperor, and if Napoleon astonished his Council of State in a juridical debate because at Brienne he had read the *Institutes* of Justinian, it is none the less true of diplomacy, which, having as its object international relations in the political, military, religious, economic, and intellectual spheres, makes use of too many specialisms to be considered one in itself. Talleyrand's reading at St-Sulpice was destined to gain for him at the Congress of Vienna an ascendancy analogous to that of Napoleon over his legal experts.

The education of these two extraordinary men, who in a few years' time were to collaborate, was similar in a profounder sense. They were two great recluses whom isolation was to bring together. At Brienne, Bonaparte was isolated not only on account of his accent but even more so by the feelings and the dreams which his origin inspired. He dreamed not of World Empire, but of the liberation of Corsica, his first fatherland. He felt he was a foreigner, and was to enter the army with the spirit of a disciplined mercenary; he experienced none of the frenzies

which were to agitate revolutionary France. He was all
the better equipped to rise above party and to reconcile
France with herself. At St-Sulpice, Talleyrand dreamed
only of his own liberation. At the bottom of his heart he
had broken with the traditions of family and class. Even
while studying theology he broke with God. But he broke
with God and his class without swearing fealty to any
other class or any other god. He was to lend himself to
all parties without giving himself to any, and he was to
yield to none of the mysticisms of the Revolution. Hence
there existed in him a sort of moral insularity which related him to that other insular man—Bonaparte. They
were, in France, and each in his own way, two outlaws,
which fact was to qualify them to dictate law in France
when the hour of reconciliation came. At that time,
because they had belonged to neither club nor faction, because the recently annexed Corsican and the feudal nobleman who had lost his way in the priesthood were in
different degrees strangers in modern France, they were to
instal themselves without effort in the position of an
arbiter, which, officially for one and later on effectively for
the other, was to be that of a sovereign, for in 1814, if
Talleyrand was not actually a sovereign, he was to play
the part of one.

There is yet another resemblance—and it follows from
the first—in that, for both, France was not to be the object
but the instrument of their ambition. Each had his centre
of gravity in himself, obedient to a movement as auto-
matic as the nature of man and society permit. This it was
which destined each to attract the other and then to
separate them when the more brilliant but more ephemeral
star of the two disappeared in the abyss. Then was Talleyrand, who never had much taste for the abyss, and who
was not content to be a mere satellite, destined to treat

Napoleon as both had treated France, as a means to an end, but not an end in itself. Then was he to rise above the Vienna horizon, where Waterloo afforded him the opportunity of his diplomatic Austerlitz.

In what manner was the future strategist of the Congress indebted to St-Sulpice for his victories? He did not owe them merely to his orgy of reading in the library, to that totality of varied knowledge which was to give him superiority over his rivals by setting a keener edge on his mind than on theirs, and furnishing it with ideas of all kinds and precedents for all situations. The doctrinal teaching of his professors was of greater use to him if, in politics, exact thinking is of greater import than vast knowledge. In March 1838, a few weeks before his death, in the striking speech he delivered at a solemn sitting of the Academy, the Prince de Bénévent paid homage to theology considered as a school for diplomacy. He made use of the occasion of the death of one of his collaborators, the mediocre Reinhard (at whom in private life he had jeered without mercy), in order to sing his own praises in his political testament, and under the guise of an eulogium of that obscure personage. Reinhard, a Protestant who, at first having studied theology, wished to become a pastor. Talleyrand seized upon this fact to demonstrate the advantage of such a discipline in diplomacy. The instances he cited were more numerous than the reasons he set forth; instances selected to illustrate by analogy his own career while implicitly recalling his own chief successes. These examples were: Cardinal Ossat, who, in spite of the intrigues of rival powers, reconciled Henri IV and the Court of Rome; Cardinal-Chancellor Duprat, who negotiated the concordat with Leo X; and Cardinal de Polignac, who, after great reverses, preserved the integrity of France by the Treaty of Utrecht. It was Talleyrand who reconciled

25

the Emperor and the Pope, notwithstanding Austria; who collaborated at the concordat of 1802; and who, after Waterloo, preserved for France her ancient limits. As for the utility of theology in preparation for diplomacy he confined himself to the observation that it had inspired Reinhard with "power and suppleness in reasoning". But could not the same be said of other disciplines, notably those of Law and Mathematics?

The ex-Bishop of Autun would have been reluctant to particularise the more specifically theological reasons for his diplomatic genius. Otherwise he might have added that these are no less moral than intellectual, and that young priests, when considering the world in the category of eternity, acquire the habit of patience, an essential condition in the case of far-reaching political designs. They also acquire the habit of secrecy, which, as Richelieu said, is the soul of business. When preparing themselves to guide the conscience of others, they explore, in the dim light of moral theology, the innermost recesses of the human heart, which, though it may be the source of all sin, is also the mainspring of all that happens. History is the record of the passions.

Talleyrand, it is true, completed that theoretical study of the passions practically. The feeling of his own weaknesses sufficed to show him the extravagance of the illusions spread by J.-J. Rousseau and Fénelon regarding the natural goodness of mankind, illusions which were to give birth to tragic realities. Personal experience confirmed in him his teachers' lessons concerning the doctrine of original sin, and strengthened it to warn him against the catastrophic optimism of those who, in home or foreign politics, multiplied the powers of evil while refusing to believe in it. The seminary also taught him the habit of meditation, even outside the realm of the spiritual life.

Those who, at least, devote no prayer to it naturally reflect on it, and their reflections, if they guide the State, are fruitful because aspiration towards the eternal and the absolute is transformed in the temporal sphere into a quest for the permanent and the essential—a law of all politics worthy of the name. Furthermore, theology is the finest school of diplomacy, since, in the widest meaning of the word, diplomacy is the art of bringing to light the most secret and necessary relations between peoples, and these relations are those of man with God. And if, in its highest sense, it is the art of attaining international harmony in the independence of nations, it approaches the conception of Christianity, which implies their unity in diversity, and it will take inspiration from scholasticism in order to apply the doctrine of universals with the subtlety of reasoning.

The grace to enlighten his politics by his theology was doubtless that which he asked of the Holy Ghost, whose image, in the form of a dove hovering in a circle of light, adorns his thesis—accepted with a dispensation at the age of twenty—entitled "Tentative" ("Temptation"), a thesis dedicated to the Holy Virgin, with an engraving representing her in a state of ecstasy, in the Annunciation, opposite the Archangel Gabriel, lily in hand.

After the period of his training, the Church was to afford him his opportunity. Outside the Church he would have had neither one nor the other. His education would have been less serious and the opportunity less favourable. It was his lameness which, while proscribing a military career, enabled him to go so far and so fast. In that calling, notwithstanding the immensity of his mind, or perhaps because of the immensity of his mind, he would have been lured to the alleys, boudoirs, and coteries more frequently than to camps and battlefields; he would have

27

been inglorious; whereas St-Sulpice was to make him a marshal in politics and one who was destined to win most brilliant victories.

While awaiting his opportunity he made preparations for it by completing his education. After leaving St-Sulpice, he had his name entered at the Sorbonne, where he passed two years, completed on March 2, 1778, by the diploma of Licentiate. Although classed as sixth, he was nevertheless placed first, in accordance with a regulation then in force, due to his rank of *nobilissimus*, for he was the highest noble on the list. This privilege, exercised apropos of an examination in theology, was not calculated to diminish his pride, upon which it conferred a kind of divine right. Without accepting the word of the historian who accuses him of amusing himself by concealing newly born infants in the beds of his Superiors, we may presume that this "bad boy" followed the example of Rabelais and even of Villon rather than that of the pious Sorbon, the confessor of Saint Louis, or the chaste Abélard. He did not pursue his theological studies beyond the Licentiate, and was never a doctor, save in licentiousness.

When frequenting the church of the Sorbonne, which contains the tomb of Richelieu, he meditated on the means to success while following an ecclesiastical career. The great cardinal—whose name by a singular omission he failed to include in his prize list of prelate-diplomats who had been crowned with laurel, cited in his discourse at the Academy in 1838—inspired the young Abbé de Périgord with none of his virtues, not even his ambition. This virtue—truly one in the etymological sense of the word, for it is a great force—Talleyrand possessed from his childhood, but it was not the virtue of Richelieu. Though in 1814 he may have safeguarded French unity as founded by Richelieu, he was not the equal of the latter in glory, and never dreamed of being so, for above aught else he looked upon power as a means of satisfying his passions, whereas in the case of the most illustrious of his predecessors, the lust of power, the only passion he had ever felt, meant above all absolute devotion to the State, which raises it to the status of a virtue in the moral as well as in the etymological sense of the word. If Talleyrand, who reaped so many advantages from the Church by entering it, and more still by leaving it, and who, if he was sincere with himself, must have recognized that he preferred himself to the State, avoided the comparison of himself even implicitly to Richelieu, as to others —to Richelieu the irreproachable priest and minister—it was perhaps out of a sense of that moral inferiority. But as he loved to lay the responsibility for his weaknesses and excesses on the errors of the age, his pride and inner consciousness did not suffer from that inferiority, in which he saw the effect of circumstances rather than of his own temperament. Had he entered public life at the beginning of the seventeenth century, the stability of institutions and customs would have afforded guarantees and imposed restraints which would have supported him on the right road, from which the anarchy and temptations of his own age were to lead him astray. It was that which induced Talleyrand, who was really great only under the monarchy, to consider himself a Richelieu deprived of a Louis XIII, even more than he was of grace.

The Abbé de Périgord had obtained a dispensation to pass in his theological thesis. He obtained another for his ordination of Sub-Deacon. He must have concluded that, when one's name is Talleyrand, dispensation is the rule— one which we shall find he punctually observed by exempting himself from all his duties. The four lesser orders (doorkeeper, reader, exorcist, acolyte) he had received only ten months before, when, on Saturday April 1, 1775, on the eve of Passion Sunday, he was ordained Sub-Deacon. On thus attaining the first of the major orders, he bound himself, according to the formula, "for ever to the service of God". On the eve of contracting this solemn obligation he passed through a violent crisis. "They wish", said he, "to make a priest of me. Very well!—you will see what a shocking individual they will produce." One of his colleagues of the cloth wrote later in his *Recollections*: "I can assert that the day he was made Sub-Deacon his temper was vile".

Was that a crisis of despair or one of conscience? Was it a matter of regret for his lost freedom, or remorse as he foresaw his apostasy? Probably both, which in his case would be merely one more contradiction. That crisis, attested by the most worthy witnesses, is a refutation of those who represented him as wholly a cynic. However, mankind being more disposed to believe in evil than in good, the dubious but unfavourable anecdotes which were afterwards retailed concerning Talleyrand were the most welcomed. Take, for instance, the anecdote which shows him, at that time, in the boudoir of Mme du Barry—a silent guest, while others are narrating their conquests, a thing which is in itself improbable, seeing that the others were Choiseul-Gouffier, Lauzan, and Narbonne, who doubtless observed the rules of the art of seduction, and were aware that in such matters discretion, even if not the first of duties, is certainly the first of interests. According to the tale, Mme du Barry, astonished by Talleyrand's reserve, asked him: "And have *you* nothing to say? Not a single conquest? Is this virtue or modesty?"—"Ah! Madame! I am deep in most melancholy reflections."—"Whatever can they be?"—"Paris is a

city", replied Talleyrand, "where it is easier to obtain
women than abbeys. . . ." After which the Marquise, then
at the height of her power, aided him to obtain his first
two benefices. Certainly Talleyrand was quite capable of
asking for them in such a way, only, when he was ordained
Sub-Deacon, Louis XV had been dead nearly a year!

He was indebted for his first benefice, St-Denis of
Rheims, to Louis XVI, who granted it on September 24,
1779, a few months after his ordination as Sub-Deacon.
So behold him, at the age of twenty-one, with an income
of 18,000 livres. The same year his name, the favour of
the Court, his reputation for intelligence, and the protection of Cardinal de la Roche-Aymon, the old Archbishop of Rheims, whom he had fascinated but not
edified, led to his appointment as deputy for the province
at the quinquennial assembly of the clergy. What was
more, notwithstanding his extreme youth he was made
promoter of the assembly. And so ably did he carry out
his duties, administrative rather than religious, that he
became the favourite for the office of Agent-General for
the clergy, in other words the representative of the clergy
for the Government in the periods between the assemblies.

Thus, while very young, he formed the habit of accepting responsibility and became initiated in the various
questions appertaining to the State, such as taxation,
finance, education, public assistance, ecclesiastical discipline, litigation, etc.; and this not only by studying them,
but by handling and controlling them. An excellent
schooling, which perfected the theoretical teaching of
St-Sulpice and the Sorbonne. In the daily grind of
difficult business, as in all those in which the spiritual and
temporal are blended, he sharpened his faculties and
adapted them to the necessities of his future career. He
acquired that which diplomats—more familiar with the

general data of international problems than with the practical means of solving them—so often lack, the sense of concrete details, for want of which the most happily conceived schemes remain in the condition of projects. At the same time, through the obligation to settle expeditiously matters which were not matters of conscience, he avoided that rock of mere theologians who have entered politics too late in life, namely, that excessive subtlety which paralyses the will. By frequently and expeditiously dealing with facts, he could correct the sterility so often found in the clash of ideas, and, notwithstanding his natural carelessness and cultivated dilettantism, he avoided that most serious fault of diplomatists who have not corrected it by the discipline of another study, the predominance of the critical spirit over that of decision, of observation over action.

It was also in 1775 that the Abbé de Périgord was a witness of a solemnity which, according to his memoirs, only left him with a recollection most unworthy of such a spectacle. He was present on June 11 at the coronation of Louis XVI in Rheims Cathedral. Next to the royal family, that of Talleyrand played the most important part. His uncle, the coadjutor of the Archbishop, officiated side by side with the Cardinal de la Roche-Aymon. His father, Comte Talleyrand, was appointed by Louis XVI to be one of the four noblemen-hostages of the Holy Phial[1]. This signal honour consisted in escorting, on horseback, the Holy Phial from the Abbey of St-Remy, where it was habitually kept, to the Cathedral, and thence back to St-Remy, after having sworn on the Gospels to sacrifice life, if need be, to its defence.

[1] *"La Sainte Ampoule"*—*"Ampulla Remensis"*—the bottle which formerly contained the sacred oil used in anointing the kings of France.—Translators' note.

The reign of Louis XVI had opened under the most favourable auspices. The young Queen, Marie Antoinette, then in the full flower of her grace and beauty, was the idol of the people. Throughout the whole kingdom reigned a delirium of joy, hope, and affection. This was shown with striking emphasis and in the most varied ways during the coronation festivals, the last of the old monarchy. It was amidst general enthusiasm that once more were solemnized the mystic espousals of the King and France.

"It was from the coronation of Louis XVI that I date my relations with several women remarkable for their diverse charms and whose friendship has never for a moment ceased to cast enchantment over my life." If he does not go so far as to enumerate those charms, he names some of the ladies. And that is all he has to say, fifty-five years afterwards, about a spectacle grandiose in itself, and to which the sequence of events lent so pathetic an aspect!

Thus, whilst under the vaulted roof where the echoes of France's history resound, the King, Queen, princes of the blood and princes of the Church knelt to implore the Divine benediction on the new reign; whilst his uncle, the coadjutor of Rheims, and his father, the hostage of the Holy Phial, joined in profoundest union in that invocation, the Abbé de Périgord—and it is he who tells us so—thought merely of ogling the pretty women.

In 1778, the Abbé de Périgord was present at a coronation of another character—the secular and even irreligious apotheosis of Voltaire, amidst the delirious admiration of Paris. The patriarch of Ferney, at the age of eighty-four, had left his retreat to be present at the first performance of *Irène*. This, for the intellectual dictator of Europe, was his coronation in the capital of the mind and the occasion of an apotheosis which imbued him with the sentiment of entering, while still alive, into immortality. Moreover, by reason of the profound emotion he experienced, it hastened his end. Among the rites of that worship there figured the presentation of some young Levites who seemed particularly qualified to sustain it. In the midst of the assembly of the faithful, the Abbé de Périgord knelt before Voltaire, who, by the laying-on of hands on the head of the initiate, bestowed his blessing upon him. If this was to be regarded as a second ordination, it conferred upon him merely the minor orders of the new religion.

False analogies have suggested the thought that "Talleyrand was a diplomatic Voltaire". Nothing is more false. The Abbé de Périgord was less faithful to the religion whose pontiff was Voltaire, than to the Catholic religion in which he was to die, without, despite certain appearances, having lived in that of the encyclopaedists. Between him and Voltaire there were formal resemblances which obscured fundamental dissimilarities. Both were remarkable for clarity, alertness, taste, irony, and an extraordinary mastery of ordinary talents. It has been said that the literary genius of Voltaire consisted in writing the language of everyone but like no one. One might say that the political genius of Talleyrand was common sense pushed to a rare degree. It is precisely in that respect that he differed from Voltaire and even opposed him. His good sense, combined with his Sulpician training and a profounder scepticism than that of the philosophers his contemporaries, sustained, as regards essential points, his mind in a tradition that his conduct flouted. If, in his manners, he belonged to the eighteenth century, in his ideas he was partly of the seventeenth; that is to say, subject to that reason which the Revolution enthroned only on its altars. Not to the syllogizing reason, parent of so many follies: understanding nothing, because it confuses everything—a fatal confusion, above all in politics, where it imposes the methods of the abstract sciences and the illusion of the absolute. Whereas in that kingdom of the concrete there is nothing absolute, according to a well-known saying, save the constancy of the relative, and, the more often, everything there depends upon reasons of which reason knows nothing. Talleyrand's realism excluded the spirit of system and that of idle fancy which, having overthrown the ideas of the seventeenth century, proceeded to overthrow its institutions, and shed rivers of blood in the name of humanity. That realism, which was based on practical reason, enlightened by experience and observation, adjusted its method to its end. It did not transfer the laws and criteria of the exact sciences into politics, "the first of the inexact sciences"—an attempt to measure cloth by the pint. That realism which was also based, perhaps unconsciously, upon religious teaching, established the knowledge of man and human societies on the doctrine of originals in, whereas the encyclopaedists based the thanklessness of man on the postulate of his natural goodness, which they raised to the rank of a dogma, with which to challenge the dogma of original sin. They set forth what they might have called the immaculate conception of the people. That denial of original sin was to be the original sin of the Revolution.

The opposition between Talleyrand and Voltaire was no less fundamental in the sphere of religion. Talleyrand was never an irreligious man. Having entered the Church without love for it, he left it without hatred. He was never to pose, like Voltaire, as Antichrist. He was never to feel, or pretend to feel, the slightest fanaticism, either in one way or the other. That would have been a lack of good taste and also of prudence, for it is never wise to

estrange any force in order to placate all contingencies.
Better not break with God, who may be a useful ally even
in this world. In face of the Catholic Church, Talleyrand
was never to be found, like Voltaire, assuming the
attitude of an enemy. That apostate was, on the whole,
merely a secularist who remained a sympathizer. But a
true sceptic he was indeed, for he doubted his own doubt.
The eighteenth-century philosophers were believers, and
even fanatics, who, with their dogmas turned inside out,
presented the appearance of devotees turned upside
down.

Talleyrand was no diplomatic Voltaire, since, in the
conduct of public affairs particularly, he adopted neither
his maxims nor his animosities. All the more was he not
so, because Voltaire would have made an execrable
diplomat, if only on account of his immense vanity, which
would have made him the plaything of all his rivals and
of all the foreign Courts. Hence his "Prussomania", which
transformed that pontiff of rationalism into an apostle of
Germanic irrationalism, and the most pellucid of our
writers into a eulogizer of the most obscure genius.
Talleyrand, who treated all sovereigns, even his own, on
a footing of equality, was far better armed for diplomatic
controversies. In the secular conflict between French
lucidity, which he represented, and German obscurity,
lucidity was destined to triumph. He was not the man to
have consented to act as Chamberlain to Frederick II. The
ex-Marquis of Brandenbourg made no impression on the
heir of the Counts-Sovereign of Périgord. Though he
became Grand Chamberlain to Napoleon I, he could show
such dignity as to look loftily down on the servility of
Voltaire at Berlin. In Voltaire, as a diplomat, there would
have been a touch of the lackey. Talleyrand, even with
sovereigns, had the air of a suzerain.

The following year the Abbé de Périgord was ordained priest. To traverse that stage he was to use cunning in his relations with the Church and appeal to the nepotism which played so great a part in his life, whether he profited by it or practised it, for, after being a privileged nephew, he was to become a most solicitous uncle. At that time the Archbishop of Paris was Christophe de Beaumont du Repaire, another Périgordian of ancient lineage. That was the sole thing he had in common with Talleyrand. His morals were as pure as those of his compatriot were dissolute, and there was nothing which could bend his inflexibility when questions of dogma, discipline, or morals were under discussion. The Abbé de Périgord preferred to place the beginning of his career under the auspices of his uncle, Alexandre Angélique de Talleyrand, promoted in 1777 to the archbishopric of Rheims. It was in that diocese that he had his name entered, after being transferred from the diocese of Paris. On the eve of his ordination and in the presence of his friend, Choiseul-Gouffier, he burst into tears. The fact that that companion of his pleasures was there proves that his despondency was less that of a soul eager for grace vainly implored than that of an egoism which resented any obstacle. His was no combat with the angel; it was the rebellion of the demons within against the violence offered them. And it was not to be long before they would take their revenge. His parents were present, profoundly impressed at his first Mass, and he administered the communion to them. What their reflections were we do not know. But everything leads us to suppose that, like blameless Christians, they trusted in Providence, hoping that grace would sanctify the newly ordained priest. They counted more on his prayers than on their own merits to assure their salvation, and in their fervent faith rejoiced that they had given a son to the Church, without being troubled by the thought that they had determined to make this child of his century—the century the least religious and the most absorbed by the present—a *sacerdos in aeternum*.

## CHAPTER III

## THE MITRED ALCIBIADES

*It is with ambition as with fire; the most common and
most precious matter feeds it equally well.*

TALLEYRAND

ACCORDING to Vitrolles, who knew Talleyrand well, the
two incentives of his existence were "love of women and
love of money". Money in order to possess women, and
women in order to obtain money. Not that he received it
from them; but that he used them in the financial and
personal negotiations which he grafted on to his diplomatic negotiations.

Thiers, who frequented Talleyrand's salon during the
Restoration, gathered there a remark which, like the
majority of his utterances, was at one and the same time
a maxim, a confession, and a sally. "Invariably", he says,
"I wished to turn the conversation to the subject of
Europe, the state of affairs—in short, politics. But he spoke
of nothing else than women. This wearied me. One day I
said to him: 'Prince, you are ever talking to me about
women; I would much rather talk politics'. He replied:
'But women *are* politics'."

One must do Talleyrand this justice: he made use of
women politically far more than he made himself useful
to them. He was in their arms, or at their feet; but never
in their hands. He does not appear to have departed from
that policy save in 1814, when his mistress, Aimée de
Coigny (Mlle Monk) converted him to the cause of the

Bourbons. But this revolutionary through ambition was a traditionalist by vocation, and his preferences accorded with the feelings of his Egeria all the more when circumstances made them conform with his ambition. Aimée de Coigny intervened merely in order to hasten a natural evolution.

Awaiting the time when he was to make use of Mme de Staël to obtain the office of Foreign Affairs, the Abbé de Périgord, when completing his political education, made gallantry the adjunct of theology. Intercourse with the wittiest women of his day refined certain of his gifts and taught him things which are perhaps essential for a diplomatist: a feeling for the most delicate shades of meaning in thought and language; the art of pleasing, of hiding his secrets while discovering those of another, of giving encouragement without compromising himself, of refusing without causing offence, of breaking off negotiations without disagreement, of shifting the faults in a quarrel, and, finally, to become friends again after having been lovers; that is to say, the art of making peace after war.

That great school of behaviour was never more in honour than during the years preceding the Revolution. After the Regency, which was a violent reaction against the austerity of the Court under Mme de Maintenon, the example set by Louis XV gave society an excuse for persevering in licentiousness. At the same time the philosophy of the eighteenth century established it as a principle and even as a dogma. Through sweeping aside the restraints of Christian morality and preaching a return to a state of nature, there was an unbridling of instinct which acquired a strength all the more irresistible when it became a fashion and a religion. To the corruption of morals was added the more formidable corruption of ideas. That new fashion and religion raged first of all among those who were to be its victims, when they spread among the people who practised, after its own fashion, the state of nature and disdain of the laws.[1] That ideological idyll ended in the Terror and war. Before the day of the sinister lawyers of the Convention, before the "headsman-scribblers of laws"—laws contrary to all divine and human laws—there came the "off-with-his-head scribblers" of books, of which those laws were merely a translation.

Those books were the favourite ones of the Court and the best society. The great novelty of the eighteenth century lay in the fact that it devoted itself to apostleship. Before then its aim had been merely to entertain the reader. Later it laid claim to his salvation through the revelation of "light". Writers became guides, magicians, prophets. And the great novelty of the Louis XVI style in conversation consisted in religion and morality, finance and politics being the principal subjects. At the suppers of the Regent—still too classical to mingle various themes —the only impropriety would have been to talk politics. But now, in drawing-rooms there was fashionable warfare against institutions—an ideological intoxication, a rage for reform. In the homes of the aristocracy a scathing attack was made on God, the King, the Queen, and principles—in short, everything which sheltered them was riddled with subversive theories and epigrams. The gayest women were not content with making a few men happy, they must also contribute to the happiness of the whole human race. Philosophers were their unspiritual

---

[1] According to Jean-Jacques Rousseau the state of nature was a state of peace, but in the opinion of the great diplomatist James Harris, Earl of Malmesbury, it was a state of war.—Translators' note.

directors. Amidst play and laughter and illusion they danced through life towards the scaffold. "Gaily we proceed", wrote the Comte de Ségur, "on a carpet of flowers which hides from us an abyss." It was not only of Louis XVI, accessible to the prevailing utopias, that one can say that he lost his head before it was severed.

The Abbé de Périgord did not lose his head and would never do so. He played his part in the prologue all the more effectively. With an impassiveness which was at one and the same time a mask and a weapon, he applied himself to seizing opportunities and avoiding the risks of the great changes which were making their appearance. The new régime, like all the régimes to follow, was to be for him not an ideal but a career, or rather a stage in his career. He prepared for it by cultivating connections in all influential circles, by putting out his feelers in all useful directions. This worldly abbé went but rarely to Court— to the official Court of Versailles; but he courted the queen of the day and above all the queen of the morrow— public opinion. Indeed, Louis XVI had, through weakness, renounced his power before it was taken away from him legally. For want of governing boldly, in accordance with Bossuet's advice to all kings, he was dominated by the forces of the Revolution. He abdicated before he was deposed. Thus took place a transfer of the sovereignty of the Crown to public opinion left to itself, that is to say to the salons, but soon to descend to the cafés, the clubs, and the street. When necessary, in the interest of his ambition, Talleyrand was to degrade himself, but all the time relying on his irony to preserve distances. He was not one of those who sought for popularity, after the fashion of one who desires a woman whilst despising her. He did not desire popularity for itself, but because it was necessary he should possess it in order to obtain something better—fortune, power, renown, without counting the women in flesh and blood who, under all régimes, figure in the casual incomes of those invested with authority.

For the time being—the Revolution still only triumphing at the summit of the society it was to destroy—Talleyrand could serve it and make use of it without leaving his own circle. He became the favourite in the most fashionable drawing-rooms. With as much science as the philosophers, but without their pedantry, with as much grace as the great lords, but more seriously, he surpassed the one and the other in the art of speaking gravely on trivial matters, lightly on grave ones, and in reaching the bottom of his subject while preserving an air of toying with it on the surface. No one knew better than he how to decant, filter, and give a sparkle to philosophy, and even to political economy.

The seduction he exercised was not merely intellectual. His contemporaries and, what is more significant, his female contemporaries depict him as an irresistible bad fellow. After having been Chérubin,[1] he rose in rank. The Duchesse d'Abrantès regarded him as a Faublas. Without being a boaster of vices he did not possess, which would have been an error in taste, he was still less a Tartuffe. He reserved his power in dissimulation for politics. In society, his face, which he later learnt to compose, was without any pretence. A follower of Lavater makes out that he can see through a being, not from the protuberances on his cranium, but thanks to the reliefs of the entire head. Look at it, he says, in profile; that profile stands out like a key, and is in fact the key to a soul, or a life. In the case of the Abbé de Périgord's there is nothing mysterious about that

[1] A character in Beaumarchais' comedy *Le Mariage de Figaro.*— Translators' note.

key. His character is clearly written on his features. His expansive forehead is that of a thinker, but his nose has the air of setting the forehead at defiance: it is the nose of a comedian, one would say, if the general effect was not that of a nobleman; a keen nose with quivering nostrils and tip-tilted as though the better to inhale all perfumes and scent out every wind. Lavater's disciple would read there sensuality, curiosity, opportunism. The fleshy lips confirm and aggravate the nose's hint. The eyes—blue according to some people, grey according to others, and therefore ambiguous like their look, which was ironical and tender—are wide open to all the scenes of life. When, in old age, they sank deep within their orbits, under heavy eyelids which sharpened his look rather than dulled it, and which, when flickering, darted forth as through two loop-holes, one might compare it to that of a cat. He had the cat's magnetic pupil; he always fell on his feet; he accepted the caresses of his familiars rather than show his affection for them; he attached himself to the houses where authority reigned rather than to its successive occupants, and his suppleness enabled him, even though he might have to flatten himself out, to pass through the narrowest doors and windows. Pamphleteers and caricaturists will also see the serpent in him. The Comtesse de Kielmansegge presented him to us in the following terms: "When M. de Talleyrand comes towards me, with heavy and tottering gait, his eyes shining forth from a head with reptilian jaw, and the smile of a hypnotist on his lips, I say to myself: 'Nature appears to have given thee the choice between tiger and serpent, and thou hast chosen the anaconda'". He did indeed possess its smooth visage, its variable shades according to its movements and the play of light. He even cast his skin with every particular season. In order to hide his infirmity as much as possible, he advanced with undulations from left to right—a sort of vertical crawl. And his look fascinated.

The list of charming prey who wrangled over him is formidable.[1] In his memoirs he set posterity an example for discretion which it has not followed. An example, however, which he set *only* in his recollections. In those days, when he tasted "the sweetness of life", he made a parade of himself—or people did it for him shamelessly. He appeared in gay company during Holy Week. He became —not then a difficult thing to do—an object of scandal. But he cared not a straw. Already he distinguished himself by his total indifference to what folk said. He considered that backbiting, calumnies, and insults obeyed the law of gravity: they descended, they did not rise. He was placed at too great a height in his own eyes not to be ever high above his enemies. In talking about him they served his purpose; it was an element of his publicity.

If he ran the risk of losing his soul, he did not lose his time. His mistresses were his allies; they used their influence to push him forward in society and even in the Church. One of them, the Comtesse de Brionne, wished to obtain for him a Cardinal's hat before the episcopate. The general agency of the clergy, of which he had been an incumbent since 1780, appeared to her to be a sufficient title, although he was barely thirty years of age. With that object in view, Talleyrand's friend concerted with the King of Sweden, Gustave III, a Lutheran prince on excellent terms with Pius VI, who, in order to be agreeable to him, promised the hat. If, despite this double patronage,

[1] See that rare book, *Les Femmes de M. de Talleyrand*, par M. le Baron de H. (Paris, Kolb, n.d.), which gives the complete history of Talleyrand's relations with the Comtesse de Flahaut, Mme de Genlis, Mme Tallien, Mme de la Châtre, Mme de Staël, Mme de Talleyrand, the Duchesse de Luynes, Mme Récamier, and others.—Translators' note.

the Abbé de Périgord did not obtain it, it was because the virtuous Louis XVI vetoed the appointment.

Whilst one of Talleyrand's mistresses strove in vain to make him a Cardinal, another, the Comtesse de Flahaut, made him the father of a son, who was himself to be the father of the Duc de Morny. This liaison was the most official of all of them, and to such a degree that it was accredited by foreign diplomatists, since the representative of the United States, General Morris, relates that, having called for news of the suffering Mme de Flahaut, he was received by Talleyrand, then Bishop of Autun, at the very time he was busy warming his lady's bed with a warming-pan.

These liaisons did not exclude more useful relations with the most important men of the day. He frequented Chanteloup, the home of the Duc de Choiseul. His name and a schoolfellow of the Collège d'Harcourt, Choiseul-Gouffier, nephew of the former minister of Louis XV, assured him the warmest welcome. He was given advice which, confirming that he gave himself, was not to be lost. The Duke pointed out the new incompatability between the ecclesiastical profession and a great political career, at a time when the whole movement of ideas was directed against the Catholic Church. "France", he said to him, "has had five Cardinal Ministers: Richelieu, Mazarin, Dubois, Fleury, and Bernis. Their time is over." Choiseul also taught him how a nobleman and minister ought to work, and especially how to make others work. "In my Ministry I always made others work more than I worked myself. You must not bury yourself under papers: you must find men to put them in order. You must manage affairs with a movement, a sign. . . ." And, together with advice, Talleyrand found at Choiseul's house the means of following him when he himself became a minister. For it was there he made the acquaintance of a professor of the Oratory, Blanc d'Hauterive, a man of the same age as himself, who was to become his principal collaborator. M. de Calonne, whose society he also frequented, recommended to him the same method—to transact business "without effort and without ceremony, in the corner of a drawing-room, or the recess of a window".

With another very different and more exceptional personage, Mirabeau, the Abbé de Périgord found more intimate but less confident relations. They possessed what was needed to attract and repel each other. They were attracted to each other through a somewhat similar singularity in their destiny. Belonging, one of them to the highest aristocracy in the kingdom, the other to the best nobility of Provence, they were, under the empire of equally unbridled ambition and sensuality, two turncoats of their order. Mirabeau was to be elected a deputy of the Third Estate and Talleyrand was to abandon the Church. They were almost of the same caste through birth and wholly of the same class through choice—the class of the outcasts, already sufficiently numerous to form a class by itself. They were attracted to each other through the agitation in ideas and projects; through the same passion for pleasures; through the same universality in attainments—Mirabeau was, like Talleyrand, a specialist in all branches of learning; through the same love of money and women; through the same impatience to satisfy their passions under cover of foreshadowed events, which they strove to hasten; and, finally, through the same astonishing diversity of occupations. They worked, intrigued, played, speculated, and ran after women as though they had nothing else to do. But they also repelled each other through that which attracted the one to the other. For, on the political stage, they were two stars who aspired to leading parts. Talleyrand, like Mirabeau, dreamed of becoming the Richelieu of a constitutional monarchy. Their omnivorous temperament exposed them to a less elevated and more precise rivalry: courting all women, they hunted on the same estates without being invited there. Moreover, these two "monsters" were not of the same species. If, in the menagerie of the Revolution, Talleyrand was a feline or a reptile, Mirabeau was the lion or the bull. They present a prototype of those false political friendships in which, on the footing of cordial distrust and watchful open-heartedness, "dear colleagues" seek each other's society while all the time they are despising each other, and who keep on good terms while all the time they are tearing each other to pieces. When Mirabeau wrote to Talleyrand, his junior by five years, he called him "my dear master", doubtless as an homage to the sacred character of his calling and his high family rank. Talleyrand replied with the assurance that he was "tenderly attached to him for life". Yet Mirabeau accused his "dear master" of "perfidy" and "held him in horror" on meeting him in Mme de Neyra's boudoir. He wrote of him in the following terms: "For money he would sell his soul,—and rightly so, because he would be exchanging his manure-heap for gold". However, their association was to be severed only by death, since they were accomplices.

In 1786, whilst Mirabeau was in Berlin,[1] whither he

[1] See the anonymous Court memoirs from the pen of Honoré Gabriel, Comte de Mirabeau, which were published in 1789, entitled *Histoire Secrète de la cour de Berlin, ou correspondance d'un voyageur françois, depuis le mois de juillet 1786 jusqu'au 19 janvier 1787. Ouvrage posthume.* This exceedingly rare book was printed at Alençon, but without the place being mentioned, and on its appearance attempts were made to suppress the entire edition. The work was publicly torn and burned by order of the Court of Parliament, an *Arrêt de*

had persuaded Calonne to send him on a mission, the Abbé de Périgord wrote to him expressing the hope that he would soon be appointed to the archbishopric of Bourges, the holder of which had just had an apoplectic attack. But, when the vacancy occurred, preference was given to another candidate. Received as a freemason a few months before, he did not find sufficient compensation for that loss in his elevation to the dignity of "premier superintendent" of a Parisian lodge which was later to be the origin of the Jacobins' Club. He did not obtain the see of Autun until 1788. His father, who was then very ill, wrote to the King and Queen to ask them to grant him that favour before he died. On the other hand, his mother was inconsolable at the thought of having contributed to making him a priest. Frightened on account of what his episcopal rank might add to so scandalous a life, she went secretly to the King to implore him to withdraw the promise dragged from him by her husband. Louis XVI, still confident in man's natural goodness and in divine grace, sought to reassure her and said: "It will serve him as a corrective".

The King signed the royal letters patent on November 2, 1788, just in time to give that satisfaction *in extremis* to the Comte de Talleyrand, who died two days later.

The new bishop made the customary retreat at Issy, in the Sulpicians' residence for novices. It was there he was consecrated by Bishop Comte de Noyon. When, on bended knee and his hand on the Holy Gospel, he swore to remain "for ever faithful to the Holy Roman Church, to our Holy Father the Pope", etc., the oath ought to have been doubly sacred to him, for that fidelity was already imposed upon him by the Talleyrand motto,

*la cour de parlement* printed on five leaves, small 4to, Paris, 1789, which itself is a scarce historical item.—Translators' note.

inscribed on his episcopal arms, in the Périgordian dialect: *Ré qué Diou* (Naught save God).

The new bishop was thirty-four years of age and possessed an official income of 52,000 livres, without counting his profits from gambling and stock-jobbing. Mitred, endowed, and regarded as one of the most able members of the clergy, Talleyrand at first carried out his duties to the measure his future interests exacted. On the morrow of his ordination he called upon the Archbishop of Paris, who handed him the badge of the pallium, since the Bishops of Autun, as successors of Saint Syagrius, were privileged to wear on their chasuble that band of white cloth woven in Rome with the wool of lambs blessed at the monastery of Ste-Agnès-hors-les-Murs. Then, to the inhabitants of his diocese he addressed his first charge, full of impressive eloquence, and a model of its kind. Having consolidated his rearguard in Paris, he set out for his new front, where he was not long in finding an opportunity for a fresh success. On March 15, 1789, he solemnly took possession of his seat in the Cathedral of St-Lazare, and, on the Holy Gospel, took the oath to treat the Church of Autun "in accordance with all the attentions due by a husband to his spouse".

The States General had been summoned for May 1. The first episcopal tour of inspection of the Bishop of Autun was to be an electoral one. He carried out his campaign according to the most modern methods: kept open table, was lavish with promises, addressed honeyed words to every presbytery by means of the young abbés whom he attached to his good fortune, and appointed, as liaison officer in Paris, his Vicar General, the Abbé de Renaudes, who was to become one of his most precious collaborators, one of the members of his "team".

In his profession of faith, exempt from the prevailing

ideology and phraseology (he ever more willingly sacrificed morality than good taste to his ambition), he declared himself in favour of the reforms then demanded by all enlightened people. On April 2 he was elected as a clerical deputy by a large majority. On Easter Day, the 12th, he called for his carriage and left for Paris without saying good-bye to the inhabitants of his diocese, whom he was never to see again. He had spent barely a month in their midst.

When, on May 4, before the opening of the States, fixed for the following day, the numerous deputies followed the solemn procession of the Holy Sacrament, headed by the clergy and followed by the nobility, whose brilliant dress formed a striking contrast with the sombre mass of the Third Estate, dressed in black—as though wearing mourning for its future victims amidst gala dress—the Bishop of Autun attracted universal attention. His fine air, his stature (five feet five inches and a half, according to the passport which was soon to be handed to him on the occasion of his journey to London), and his lameness quickened the curiosity aroused by his reputation, for history—nay, even legend—was already attached to his name. Supposing that he recollected that Richelieu opened his career at the States General of 1614, where, like himself, he was sent by the clergy of his diocese, he determined to follow other maxims than those of the Bishop of Luçon. The first of *his* maxims was to change them, should it be in his interest to do so. In one maxim alone was he never to vary: wisdom, in his eyes, consisted in taking part in certain follies in order to avoid worse. Or, as he says in his memoirs: "To yield before one is compelled to do so, and while one can still make merit by it". And again, still according to his memoirs: "Save what you are able to save", a formula which has been used a good deal since those days as an excuse for all capitulations while invoking "fatality", and in order to sacrifice all principles to private interests in the name of equally sacrificed public interest. Under the great Revolution, as on the occasion of all the revolutions that followed, "to save what one can" (*sauver ce qu'on peut*) is a free and flattering translation of "headlong flight" (*sauve qui peut*). Those with no other programme will only save themselves—and not always even then. Experience soon proves that, in troubled times, only the audacity of truth is an obstacle to the violence of error, concession having then no other object than to unbridle passions which one flatters oneself one can guide into given channels, and to hasten the loss of what one claims one can save. Talleyrand, however, was too modest: he was not to content himself with yielding; he was to take initiatives contrary to his convictions when his interest—his only law—engaged him to do so.

But how can we reproach him for assuming a mask, and even for changing it, in an Assembly which itself was a masquerade That "representation" of France was not the country's image; nor was it a caricature, for it bore no resemblance to it—it did not confine itself to the reproduction of essential features while exaggerating them; it substituted others which had nothing in common with its own. The legal country was the antithesis of the real country. As M. Pierre Gaxotte points out in his *History of the Revolution*, agricultural France was represented in the Assembly by members of the corporation of law clerks, who exploited it and whose interest it was to multiply conflicts which developed into lawsuits. The rural nobility, which, in its order, formed the majority as well as, in the moral and social meaning of the word, the quality, was represented by men of the Court. The clergy was represented above all by curés, readers of the *Encyclopaedia*

—a war-machine invented to destroy the religion of which they were the ministers.

And how can one reproach Talleyrand for abandoning the King when the King proved that he was false to himself? In his opinion, the Government committed a grave error in granting the Third Estate double representation, not because that assured a majority for reforms in which it had always been in favour, but because it delivered the Assembly into the hands of "barristers, a species of mankind whose habits of thought, the necessary consequence of their profession, generally made them particularly dangerous". After the fall of the Bastille, the Bishop of Autun saw salvation only in the dissolution of the States General and in fresh elections with another method of balloting. He was a partisan of the strong hand should there be fresh disturbances. He agreed with the Comte d'Artois in trying to persuade the King to show resistance. But, in his determination to give way, His Majesty was immovable. Discouraged, the Comte d'Artois told the Bishop of Autun: "As to myself, I am off to-morrow, and I am leaving France". Talleyrand strove to make him change his mind. Powerless to prevent him leaving, as he was to persuade the King to act, he concluded: "Well then, Monseigneur, nothing more remains for each of us to do than to think of his own interests, since the King and Princes desert theirs and those of the Monarchy."—"Indeed," replied the Prince, "that is what I advise you to do." Do not let us be more severe than Charles X, who confirmed those remarks, reproduced in Talleyrand's memoirs, which in themselves would not have sufficed to guarantee their exactitude.

The Bishop of Autun had little faith in the success of his efforts with the King. At the same time he saw to his security in the camp of the Revolution. It was ever his way to act like a gambler, who, having ostentatiously staked on one table, resorts to sleight-of-hand on another. In politics, the code of which is more indulgent than that of gaming-houses, that is not called trickery, but manœuvring. Far from being a disqualification, the "procedure" becomes a title to glory, provided that it is successful. On the occasion of the debate on the verification of powers, the Bishop of Autun made the clergy agree to that measure, not according to order, but at a general meeting. That was to the prejudice of the Third Estate, which had as many votes as the two others put together, and could count on numerous defections in the ranks of the nobility and the clergy. Talleyrand, it is true, reserved the distinction of the orders. But that reserve had the same object and was to have the same fate as all the reserves with which concessions of principle dragged from weakness were surrounded; they were forgotten as soon as they had made the incline towards the abyss sufficiently slippery. Talleyrand dispelled his scruples—presuming he had any —by this mental addition: "Continue to vote—it is of no importance, if the King adopts my bill for dissolution and electoral reform". On July 7 he demanded the annulment of the imperative mandates; an homage to the sovereignty of the States which, on June 17, had been transformed into a National Assembly. And on July 14 he received his recompense: he was elected, at the head of the list, a member of the Committee of the Constitution.

Then began for the Bishop of Autun a period of feverish activity. Amidst that fermentation of ideas, those he set forth were to be the boldest, if not the most fruitful, save from the point of view of his own career. In that new world which was in the melting-pot he was forging his future. On the stage of the Constituent Assembly he played with spirit; he tried his hand and succeeded in all parts; he treated all the most important questions, showed himself good at everything, and even ready for everything, in order not to lose any opportunity of placing stakes on all the ways towards power. When the Declaration of Rights was being discussed, Talleyrand, whose enemies already accused him of violating every law, divine and human, obtained the adoption by the Assembly of his definition of the law. He drew up the report on the question of the Portuguese and Avignon Jews, and concluded that their quality as citizens ought to be recognized. Judas in the pay of Israel, in the eyes of his enemies, he was none the less in favour in the Assembly. A few days later it entrusted him with the drawing up of an address to the nation, glorifying the work of its representatives. This composition was received with frenzied applause and had the honour of being posted up on the walls in the form of an invitation to the clergy to read it and comment upon it in their sermons. The Assembly showed him its gratitude by raising him to the presidency, in precedence to Sieyès, Barnave, and Mirabeau.

Talleyrand was also to be the author of an enormous Report on Public Instruction, in which he laid down principles which are at the basis of the modern school: the secularization of education, instruction in all its stages, for people of all ages, for both sexes, and for the whole of the population. One can find in it even the germ of the *école unique*. Being still a bishop, Talleyrand foresaw establishments for the formation of ministers of religion, but it was the Declaration of the Rights of Man and constitutional principles which were to compose "a new catechism for childhood". At the summit of the edifice Talleyrand placed the Institute, the idea of which originated in him.

But it was above all in financial questions that he

distinguished himself. Convoked to wipe off a deficit of 50 millions, the Assembly increased it in a few months to more than 300 millions. The treasury was empty. How could it be replenished? There was only one means of certain and, as people believed, immediate efficacy: to throw the possessions of the clergy into the gulf. It was the Bishop of Autun who made a proposal in that sense and obtained its adoption, on November 2, by 568 votes against 346. Those possessions were placed at the disposal of the nation, which, on its side, undertook to provide the expenses incidental to divine worship, the salaries of its ministers, and the funds for the relief of the poor. Those possessions, it was argued, did not constitute ordinary property; the clergy was only its guardian and administrator. It was a portion of the public fortune which had been specially appropriated. The State had a right to recuperate it, on condition that it respected that appropriation. Those possessions had been given to the Church, not to the clergy, who were only an instructional part of the Church. The Church was the assembly of the faithful. Now, the assembly of the faithful in a Catholic country was indistinct from the nation. Therefore, because France is a Catholic country the State had the right to despoil the clergy. Moreover, it was in its own interest. It would justify, "by the grandeur of its sacrifices", said Talleyrand, "the honour it formerly had of being called the leading order in the State. It was by ceasing to be a body—the eternal object of envy—that the clergy would become an assembly of citizens, the object of eternal gratitude."

Seizure by the State was thus to carry out the intentions of the donators, the wishes of the most enlightened ecclesiastics, and fill the coffers of the State. Finally—and this was another of the reporter's arguments—it would enable the State to indemnify those whom the suppression of tithes had reduced to poverty. Having abolished them amidst the enthusiasm of August 4, they began to see that the sacrifice was not borne by the privileged classes. It had resulted almost everywhere in transfers which assured the upkeep of hospitals or colleges, so that this reform, acclaimed in the name of humanity, progress, and knowledge, had had for its first result the privation of care for the sick and instruction for the children.

The revenue from these possessions being estimated at 150 millions, the sum set aside for the maintenance of the clergy could not be less than 85 millions, a figure which the ecclesiastical budget, awaiting its suppression, could never reach.

It was in vain that the opponents to the bill objected that the clergy could never be obliged to exchange its revenue as a landlord for the salary of a functionary: that the majority of the donations or legacies had been made, not to an assembly of the faithful but to such or such a religious establishment; that the sale of those possessions would enrich the State less than the middleman; that to destroy, without the consent of the interested parties, a property consecrated by the centuries, was to shake the foundations of all other forms of property and enfeeble religion. This last result was not the least aimed at. For the majority of the Assembly it was less a question of saving the State than ruining the Church, and still less, whatever Talleyrand might say, of procuring for the clergy a title to the gratitude of the nation than of shattering the principal instrument of its power.

The Bishop of Autun was too clear-sighted to be mistaken about the compass of a measure which was a veritable revolution. Even in the eyes of those who praise him for it, his glory would have been less unsullied if, as his English biographer, Sir H. Lytton Bulwer, points out, "he had not intrigued for office in order to obtain a recompense for having emptied the purse of his Order".[1]

Talleyrand was the author of a primary revolution, that which occurred when he induced the clergy to unite with the Third Estate in the debate on the verification of powers. That was a violation of one of the fundamental laws of the kingdom. A question of procedure, but the solution of which involved the future. The sale of the possessions of the clergy was another revolution in its character and consequences.

"Bankruptcy is at our doors", thundered Mirabeau from the rostrum of the Assembly. Impossible to avert it by means of loans, since the State was without credit. Equally impossible to realize the possessions of the clergy by sales on a grand scale. The only resource, therefore, was to discount their value by mortgaged bonds, which were very soon to be called assignats and, with forced market prices, to multiply in catastrophic proportions. One more revolution, in the confiscation of ecclesiastical properties, which was in the bud. The catastrophe was not only economic and financial: it was pregnant with a political and moral catastrophe. The poverty and cessation of labour which resulted recruited troops for rioting and brought forth from the streets those fanatics whom the clubs were to mobilize on days when the members assisted at a safe distance. All the purchasers of national possessions, having paid for them very cheaply with depreciated assignats, were interested in the maintenance of the new régime and the ruin of the clergy, whose counter claims they feared. In order to displace the responsibility of evils brought about by a foolish policy of inflation, demagogues

[1] *Essai sur Talleyrand*, par Sir H. Lytton Bulwer, traduit de l'Anglais par M. Georges Perrot. Paris, Reinwald, 1868.—Translators' note.

were to accuse the aristocrat and the foreigner, thus incit-
ing civil war and hostilities abroad. At the same time, in
order to renew the exhausted pledge of assignats, the
Revolution was to multiply pretexts for confiscations.
Hence, partly, the law relating to suspects. But, for the
crimes with which they were charged, confiscations were
too light a penalty and allowance was not made for unbridled hatred. Moreover, at a time when all the solid
foundations of social life were overthrown, why should
life be more sacred than property? Talleyrand, who protested with considerable force against the monetary policy
of the Assembly, arguing from the economic point of view,
failed to foresee its political consequences. When, after
calculations which were accurate and invoking reasons
which were also partly so, he placed the possessions of
the clergy at the disposal of the nation, he did not foresee that forced market prices would result and that the
*planche*—the plate—for the printing of assignats would
lead many of his friends to the *planche* of the guillotine.
Politics are more complicated than law or arithmatic—
even more complicated than the brain of a Talleyrand.

In revolutionary times there is a mighty gulf between
principles and their application. A few days after having
voted the seizure of ecclesiastical properties, the Bishop
of Autun, amidst the applause of the Assembly, set forth
his views on the administration of finances thus regener-
ated. He said: "In future, honesty must replace genius.
Side by side with the evidence of our calamities, we shall
have placed the evidence of the remedy. Everything must
be reduced to the simplicity of an account-book, sensibly
kept and safeguarded in good faith." These noble words
were a prelude to the dance of assignats, conducted by
folly and bad faith. As regards his personal book-keep-
ing, Talleyrand no more took inspiration from his own

declaration than the State did in the public accounts. Did
*he* not possess sufficient genius to release him from honesty?
At that period his coach-builder related the following dialogue with his illustrious customer, whose last order—a
magnificent carriage, which he used daily—had not yet
been paid. The purveyor, after numerous fruitless applica-
tions, presented himself at the Bishop's door at the very
moment when his equipage drew up there, and as soon as
Monseigneur appeared made him, hat in hand, a profound
bow. "Who are you, my friend?"—"I am your coach-
builder, Monseigneur."—"Ah! you are my coach-builder;
and what do you want?"—"I wish to be paid, Monseigneur."—"Ah! you are my coach-builder, and you wish to
be paid. Coach-builder, you will be paid."—"When, Monseigneur?"—"Hum!" murmured the Bishop. "You are
indeed inquisitive." Whereupon the equipage moved off
between two rows of idlers who respectfully saluted the
democratic Bishop. Not over-exact in paying his debts—a
middle-class failing—he willingly paid those of his friends,
after the manner of a great nobleman. For a régime which
did not pay its debts either, he would have been well
qualified for the office of Finances, a prospect of which
he was granted in a great ministry, where he may have met
Mirabeau, and which would perhaps have changed the
course of events had the Assembly not declared the incompatability between the duties of a minister and the
mandate of a deputy.

Unable to use Mirabeau whilst he was alive, he was to
make capital out of his death. Immediately he heard of his
malady he hastened to his bedside. "A confessor", people
said, "indeed worthy of such a penitent." Mirabeau
handed him his last speech, to be read at the Assembly
after his death—his political testament, which had for its
subject the right of making one's own will. He expired

amidst atrocious suffering, after saying to Talleyrand:
"Locusta did not forget me!" On the same day the Bishop
of Autun, appointing himself Mirabeau's executor, read
the posthumous speech in a solemn voice to the Assembly.
The words of the renowned orator who had just passed
into the great silence produced a deep impression. According to the *Moniteur*, it called to mind Raphael's funeral,
to which his last picture, "The Transfiguration", was
brought.

Talleyrand, who used Mirabeau's coffin as a jumping-
off ground, dreamed of being transfigured through filling
a plurality of parts, those of King of the Revolution and
Counsellor to the Court, in order to arrive at the salvation
of the monarchy through a directed Revolution. It being
current that the executor coveted the heritage, he was
accused of having hastened the opening of the succession
by poisoning his friend, through the agency of one of his
mistresses: an absurd accusation, for, though there may
have been a wardrobe for masks at Talleyrand's, there was
certainly no poison cupboard.

Later, when he was to have as much interest in confessing his errors as he had in committing them, he said:
"Here I do not fear to recognize whatever part I may have
played in that work, and that the civil constitution of the
clergy, decreed by the Constituent Assembly, was perhaps
the greatest political error of that body". Having made
that inevitable through his own initiative in regard to
clerical property, he feared its consequences and refrained
from taking part in decisions which aggravated it. When
the Assembly voted the civil constitution of the clergy
and made the oath of fidelity to that constitution obligatory, the Bishop of Autun, to use a well-known saying,
"hastened to abstain". But he took the oath as discreetly
as possible. A constitutional bishop, he was not to content

himself with "swearing without consecrating", after the manner of the Bishop of Orleans. He was to consecrate three new bishops; out of devotion, he said, to the Catholic Church, since elected bishops could only be invested with their episcopal character by those who were already so invested. Otherwise France, the eldest daughter of the Church, was exposed to the danger of falling, first into presbyterianism and then into protestantism. As to his adhesion to the civil constitution of the clergy, he was deserving of thanks, for he made it a pretext for a better defence of the unity of the Church of Rome. Therefore he deserved well of both Rome and France.

Such was not the opinion of Rome. By the brief *Charitas*, Pius VI declared Charles Maurice de Talleyrand suspended as regards all his episcopal duties and excommunicated after forty days if he did not repent. According to the newsmongers, his only reaction was to write to his friend Lauzun: "You have heard the news—excommunication. Come to console me and sup with me. Everybody will be refusing me fire and water, so that this evening there will only be frozen meats and iced wine." Cynicism worthy of the ex-Bishop, who, while consecrating new colleagues, pretended to transmit to them a character he had already renounced, for, on his nomination as an administrator of the Department of Paris, he had immediately handed in his resignation as a bishop, under the pretext that he was henceforth obliged to reside in Paris.

The flock of his diocese were no less severe on their lost shepherd. When he proposed the alienation of the possessions of the clergy, the canons of his cathedral sent him a protest. And when, having sworn to the civil constitution of the clergy, he addressed an apologetic charge to his priests, the "Reply of the Curés of Saôneet-Loire to Monseigneur the Bishop of Autun" was cutting. Apostasy, opprobrium, iniquity, shame, impudence were the mildest words in a phillipic which damned the sinner while presaging for him "infamy in this world and reprobation in the other".

Talleyrand's detestable reputation then reached its zenith. He was no longer excused on account of youth, and was not yet absolved by the services he was to render, nor by the crimes which others were soon to commit, and compared with which his errors were to appear but slight. This "monster" became an object of horror to his own family, and especially to the relatives of his parents, including his mother, who had emigrated. And he was also an object of scandal among those of his own circle. The Marquis de Travanet, a player of backgammon, always used to say when forming what is called the devil's point: "I make the Bishop of Autun's point". Anecdotes were rife which, though they may have been invented, nevertheless bear witness to the judgment of his contemporaries. Here are two examples.

One evening, in a Parisian café, Talleyrand heard a well-dressed customer relate the crime of parricide with which the Bishop of Autun had soiled himself when he cut his mother's throat in 1780. Whereupon the Deputy-Bishop addressed the company as follows: "Gentlemen, this gentleman knows only one part of the anecdote. In 1780 the Abbé de Périgord did far worse: he served up to a couple of his mistresses a hot pie made with the livers of his father, mother, and brothers. And he would indeed have added those of his sisters, if he had had any. This is all the more true since the Comte de Périgord died in 1788, since the Countess and her children are still living, and since *I* am the Bishop of Autun."

A certain Chevalier d'Antibes, who had a reputation

63

for candour, related that he had assisted at the circumcision of the Bishop of Autun, in the presence of the Dukes of Fronsac, de Liancourt, d'Aiguillon, and of MM. de Rivarol, de Chambreuil, and others. Rivarol took him to a masonic lodge. All those present were dressed as Jews. One of the Duc de Liancourt's footmen, who resembled Talleyrand, played the part. They enveloped him in woollen bedclothes so that "the rogue should not be stark naked". They took care to tell d'Antibes that the swathing of the lower part of the body symbolized the catechumen's infancy and that such was the procedure in the case of all adults who were converted to Judaism. After ceremonies impossible to describe, they gave d'Antibes a small piece of pork brought to counterfeit the operation, telling him to preserve it preciously, and that it would bring him good luck if he himself were converted to the law of Moses.

After his intervention in the confiscation of ecclesiastical property, Talleyrand ran greater risks than his counter-part, the Duc de Liancourt's lackey. There came an avalanche of anonymous letters containing insults, threats, and even calumnies. To shelter him, the Duc d'Orléans offered him accommodation in his house and one of his carriages with his livery. He refused. Fear was unknown to him. He accepted the risks attached to his conduct and would only take flight when there was some compensation for those risks.

The most memorable date in his career as Bishop and Deputy was July 14, 1790. The Assembly had decided to commemorate the fall of the Bastille by a solemn fête, the so-called Festival of the Federation,[1] because the federals

[1] A graphic description of the Festival of the Federation and of the part played there by Talleyrand, "the only person that could be found to say that famous High Mass in the open air, and which the

of the Departments were invited to it. At the same time
they were to glorify the unity of the French nation in that
love of the Revolution which was to shatter it, and that
national fraternity which was on the eve of demonstrating
it by twenty-five years of terrible carnage. On the Espla-
nade of the Champ de Mars, hollowed out in the form of
a huge basin, as though they were proud of washing there
all the dirty linen of the past, and enlarged by means of a
sloping embankment provided with seats raised one above
the other, as in the amphitheatre of a circus, as though the
people had been invited there to assist at a procession of
wild beasts, gladiators, martyrs, executioners and their
victims, without being yet aware of the bloody idyll, a
platform was raised for the principal personages surrounding an altar before which, assisted by the Abbés
Louis, Sieyès, de Pradt, de Montesquiou-Fézensac, and
one hundred and fifty Levites in white albs, attached by
tricolour belts, Talleyrand celebrated High Mass. Designated by the King for this part of Grand Chaplain of the
Revolution, it had been imposed upon him as he was the
great favourite in public opinion. Having forgotten the
liturgy, there was organized—according to the statement
of his friend Sémonville—a dress rehearsal with his com-
panions in debauch as assistants. At the foot of a chimney-
piece, which served as an altar, Talleyrand had as a chor-
ister Mirabeau, more competent than his "Bishop", owing
to the obligation under which he had been to attend
Mass regularly during his sojourns in prison. On seeing
Talleyrand, crowned with his mitre, assisted by such a
lay-brother, those present burst into roars of laughter,
heavens seemed to take a pleasure in drowning every five minutes
by torrents of rain"—is to be found in the *Recollections of Baron de
Frénilly*, 1768–1828 (edited with an Introduction and Notes by
Arthur Chuquet. London, William Heinemann, 1909).—Translators'
note.

and especially when, at the time for genuflexions, the Bishop's dog Pirame, barking furiously, rushed upon Mirabeau just as he was raising the tail of Talleyrand's cassock. On the Champ de Mars the laughter of his bosom friends was drowned by songs, an orchestra of twelve hundred musicians, the roll of drums, salvos of two hundred guns, the clamour of a crowd estimated at three hundred thousand persons, and by their frantic cheering when the King, surrounded by his family, the ministers, and the Assembly, took the oath of fidelity to the nation, and when Queen Marie Antoinette, holding the little Dauphin on high to the people, cried out: "Behold my son, who joins with me in the same feelings". After the Mass, Talleyrand lavished his benedictions on the Royal Family, on the Court, on his colleagues of the Assembly, on the eighty-three banners of the Departments, and then intoned the *Te Deum*, which the crowd repeated in chorus. The heavens had sulked at the festival. For the time of year the weather was icy and rain fell incessantly.

According to the testimony of Lafayette, who, surrounded by his staff, commanded the National Guard and rested the point of his sword on the altar, Talleyrand, at the moment when, adorned with his episcopal ornaments and aiding himself with his crosier, was ascending the steps, said to him in a low voice: "For goodness' sake don't make me laugh".

There was, indeed, reason for laughter, but less on account of the sacrilegious farce of which he was the hero than because of the illusions with which the stupid crowd was intoxicated. Talleyrand did not share them. He knew that that show—in the sense of a fair—was destined to be followed by sinister morrows. That festival had been conceived in hatred by occult powers which dominated the Assembly and saw in it a means of galvanizing the then languishing revolutionary faith. It drew from it fresh enthusiasm, which was soon to lead to the worst excesses. Two days after the adoption of a civil constitution for the clergy it had been called upon to celebrate its unity. The real object was the mobilization and concentration of the committees of the Departments—those federals who, fanaticized by the spectacle of collective frenzy, and subjected, during their sojourn in Paris, to brazen-faced preaching in the clubs, returned home in a revolutionary state of grace. The proselytizing of civilians was completed by the debauching of soldiers. All the regiments of France were represented on July 7, 1790, by delegates who, prompted by the clubs, were to become their agents in the army. A few days later the Eastern regiments— those on guard at the frontiers—mutinied. Only after a fratricidal battle was order re-established. This first-fruit of the enthusiasm blessed by Talleyrand was not to be the most bitter. Laughing in his sleeve, did he tell himself that the Champ de Mars was the gigantic source of an infection which was to become general—the cradle of a new religion —an idealogic Islam which, eager to spread, would soon cross the frontiers, threaten other States and combine them against France all the more certainly because, while disquieting them through foreign propaganda, they tempted them owing to the interior anarchy? When, amidst a storm of cheering, he ascended the altar—an altar which foreshadowed the scaffold—the Bishop of Autun was assisted by two spectres invisible to all save himself, two spectres which have more reality than all the remainder in that apotheosis of falsehood: the Terror and War.

After the constraint of such a ceremony as that, Talleyrand felt a need for relaxation. He found it in a gaming-house and broke the bank twice. In the morning, crowned with his mitre, he officiated; in the evening, at the house of one of his mistresses, he displayed his hat, into which he had poured the overflow from his pockets of gold louis and bank-notes.

"The mitred Alcibiades" merits that name, although he did not take everything as a model from the beloved disciple of Socrates. He was never to take refuge at Sparta and bend himself to Lacedemonian discipline so as to lead the Athenians more surely to victory; but he possessed great vices and great qualities, was eager for renown, adopted manners and ideas necessitated by circumstances. He profaned the religion of which he was a minister, just as Clinia's son parodied the mysteries of Eleusis after an orgy; but he venerated Mercury too highly to mutilate his statues.

He was a Gascon and all the more a French Alcibiades, the French being the world's Gascons. But he was a Gascon of Périgord, and the Périgordians are the Normans of the Midi. He possessed too great an acuteness and restraint ever to force the note. "Everything exaggerated is insignificant" was one of his favourite mottoes.[1] In no way a braggart, but undoubtedly a hoaxer, he took delight in astonishing people by his acts rather than by his remarks, and in intriguing much more than in scandalizing. "I wish", he confessed one day, "that for centuries to come people will continue to discourse on the subject of what I have been, what I have thought, and what I intended." That was already a way of telling us, of revealing to us, the solution of the enigma which he proposed to us. He wished to impose on his public the expectation of the unexpected, provided that the unex-

[1] Another, known as the "Talleyrand maxim", has also attained immortality: "With time and patience the roughest mulberry leaf is turned into smooth satin".—Translators' note.

pected always agreed with what he expected from it in his own interest.

Although he caused astonishment he was never astonished at anything; nor was he ever a dupe, though sometimes he feared being one, and that his cleverness would be defeated by his own success. Soon the unexpected was to surprise without astonishing him, and would weigh down but not overthrow him. Through having staked on two tables, the Monarchy and the Revolution, he was to lose on both provisionally. However, there was not yet an end to laughter. Throughout ill-fortune he was ever to retain his good-humour.

## CHAPTER IV

## STEEPED IN THE WATERS OF THE STYX

The United States have thirty-two religions and only
one dish.[1]                                                                   TALLEYRAND

IF the alternation of good and bad weather, of sun and
rain, is necessary to ripen man as they are to ripen fruit,
Talleyrand, who like many of his contemporaries was
rotten before he was ripe, was in some degree about to
rectify that misfortune. After the sweets of life he was to
encounter its difficulties and those trials which form the
character if they do not crush it. It was then the time—
and not, as he says in his memoirs, at St-Sulpice, where
he was happier—when he was to be "steeped in Stygian
waters". His Styx was to be the Thames.

The Constituent Assembly had been replaced by the
Legislative Assembly. Talleyrand was no longer either
Deputy or Bishop, and France was soon to experience
shocks of too violent a character even for that incomparable equilibrist. After the radiant period of the Constituent Assembly it was the season of rain and storm.
Then, once more, came a gleam of transitory sunshine
—his first mission to London.

At the end of 1791 war was believed to be imminent.
The Constituent Assembly had made it inevitable by
declaring peace to the world; that is, by requesting the
world to think similarly while offering it, as to the
French, liberty—as it understood the word—or death.

[1] Cf. "In England there are sixty different religions and only one
sauce."—Attributed to Prince Francesco Caraciolli.

70

War, particularly with Austria, the country of Queen Marie Antoinette and the stronghold of absolutism, was passionately desired by the clubs, the real holders of power, less in order to spread the Revolution abroad than to defend and develop it at home. It was a means of establishing a dictatorship, under the cloak of the country in danger, so as to enlist it in the service of their cause, which, in a nation weary, disillusioned, and even disgusted, was indeed in peril. It was to be an opportunity, after they had raised patriotism to a white heat, to finish with the King, who was accused of treason and communication with the enemy. As Talleyrand says in his memoirs: "the enemies of the monarchy desired war in order to lose it; the King would be made responsible for reverses which were inevitable, since they could refuse him the necessary supplies".

From the rostrum of the Legislative Assembly, Brissot thundered: "War is actually a national advantage, and the only calamity to be feared is not to have war". Nevertheless these bellicose humanitarians, being unable to break with entire Europe, desired to obtain the alliance, or at least the neutrality of the most liberal of the Great Powers, at that time the least disturbed by the Revolution.

Talleyrand was just the man for that mission. Was he not the successor to the presidency of the Diplomatic Committee and the executor of Mirabeau, the incarnation of the policy of an understanding with England? He was therefore sent to London, but on a semi-official mission, the Constitution of 1791 having proclaimed the incompatibility for a period of two years between the position of former member of the National Assembly and any official situation. He obtained the title of Minister-Plenipotentiary for the Marquis de Chauvelin, a young man of twenty-six, in theory his chief, but in fact his subordinate.

The Revolution desired to make with England what it styled a national alliance, because it supposed that London was liberal after the manner of Paris, and because that alliance would be in opposition to the family alliance linking the French Court with Austria.

Talleyrand had the best of reasons for accepting that mission with alacrity. It harmonized with the ideas he had held in 1786 when inspiring Mirabeau with his proposal for an understanding with London, a project which he was never to abandon and was to realize forty-five years later as the Ambassador of Louis Philippe to the Court of St James. Those who represent him as a man continually changing his ideas confuse the essential with the accidental, doctrines and régimes, programmes and parties. Just as in the field of foreign politics, where he always aimed at an English alliance, so in home politics, where his ideal was the constitutional monarchy which he outlined in 1789 and helped to establish in 1830, he set the example of continuity in his plans. Notwithstanding the deviations which circumstances imposed, there is not in the scheme of principles, unless it be in that of methods, a career which presents greater continuity than his, although there has been none so long. As regards France's relations with England, he was always inspired by two maxims, which more than a century later were to guide the policy of Delcassé: to settle colonial disputes in order to be able to collaborate in the sphere of general politics, and, in the economic realm, not to lose sight of the fact that "two neighbouring nations, whose prosperity is founded respectively upon commerce and agriculture, are designed by the eternal nature of things mutually to enrich each other". This dictum, showing the two countries to be complementary to each other, was held by Talleyrand from the day of his arrival in London in February 1792.

The mission was still more attractive to him because it enabled him to claim the merit of a neutrality from which England at that time had no thought of departing. The Anglo-French colonial dispute had been settled to France's disadvantage by the Seven Years' War. England was absorbed by a serious revolt in India, and, weakened by the American War, was forced to seek another market for her produce. In brief, the English thought that the Revolution was working to their advantage, which was only making returns to them, for they had worked hard for the Revolution. "The French", said Burke, "have shown themselves the ablest artisans of ruin who have ever existed in the world. They are doing our business for us, their rivals, better than twenty battles, such as Ramillies, would have done." Talleyrand, therefore, could not be other than successful in his mission, although his bad reputation having crossed the Channel, he was very ill-received by the King, and the Queen turned her back on him.

His mission had another advantage: it would prepare a refuge for him outside France on the day which he saw coming when he would find it more difficult to remain neutral in the midst of factions than to obtain the neutrality of England.

After June 20, the day which foreshadowed the early fall of the monarchy, the whole world in London turned its back on Talleyrand. France, delivered over to anarchy, might still possess diplomats, but she no longer had any diplomacy. Recalled to Paris to give an account of his mission, he was back there on August 10. He was entrusted to draw up the document which notified the Powers of the accession of a provisional government. In a passage addressed to the Cabinet at London he exhorted it "to remember that when the English people, in darker circumstances and after a still more terrible event, resumed its sovereignty, the European Powers, and France in particular, did not hesitate to recognize the new Government it had appointed".

That speech for the defence seemed the height of clumsiness. The man who made it forgot that with England the rule of all sound diplomacy is always to negotiate but never to plead; for, dominated by interest and sentiment, she is indifferent to reasoning, especially when the latter is juridical, facts for her being more important than law. He also forgot that it was better not to remind the English of the execution of Charles I, of which they were so far from being proud that they commemorated it by a service of expiation. But this apology of August 10 was, in the mind of Talleyrand, destined for home consumption. He desired to found a claim on the good-will of the Executive Council, which had refused him permission to return to London to pursue his mission, and from which he hoped to obtain a passport to enable him to deal with his private affairs. After August 10, the last brake—the survival of the monarchy—being destroyed, there remained nothing more to restrain the headlong rush to the abyss. On September 2, under the protection of Danton, Minister of Justice, assassins laid hands on the priests shut up in the prisons in the place of common criminals, who had been set at liberty. Danton, having glorified this butchery in a circular to the provinces, his "provincial brethren" as he styled them, organized similar slaughters in imitation of Paris. Talleyrand wrote to a friend that he remained "faithful to liberty, notwithstanding the mask of blood and mud with which atrocious blackguards have hidden her features". For the time being the liberty he most valued was flight from Jacobin methods of practising it.

What he sought in London was no longer a mission but a shelter for the moment and an alibi for the future. Never did he dare to leave off his travelling garments: "leather breeches and high boots, a round hat, with small dress coat and a pig-tail". In that garb they found him at night-time at the Ministry of Justice, ready to hasten away as soon as he had obtained his passport. And at last he got it. His object was attained: he was an *émigré* in fact, without being one officially; he was fleeing from the Terror without breaking with the Revolution. Had he not displayed a capacity for performing evolutions in more than two elements as the sequel was to show, he would have been regarded as a political amphibian. The equivocal character of his departure was paralleled by the ambiguity of his sojourn in London. At times he feigned to be a private individual, while on other occasions he boasted of some vague, self-appointed, yet judiciously planned mission. Its object was to establish between England and France a unity of weights and measures. This offered every possible advantage; it was profoundly peaceful, it unchained not a single passion, it did not expose him to any conflict either with his own Government or that of the English, and it allowed him to prolong his absence, since the metric system had not been adopted on this side of the Channel. In short, was this not for Talleyrand a programme, a symbol, an ideal; that of diplomacy which, as he conceived it, would bring peace to the world on the day when, in the realm of ideas, sentiments, and interests it had established among the nations a unity of weights and measures? No longer would there be mutual accusations—the source of war— that false weights were being used in order to obtain too good a measure.

Unable to carry out such a mission as that, Talleyrand

at any rate established in London, between a woman and himself, an understanding which, surpassing love and even tenderness, amounted to confidence. This understanding was reached with a woman possessing the least poise and circumspection of any in that period, little enough remarkable for those qualities; a woman who least resembled him, since she was as demonstrative and impulsive as he was cold and reflective. A favourable example, indeed, for the thesis of those who discerned in that unity, or unison of hearts, a result of their diversity or contrasts; an adaptation of two opposed temperaments. This work of sentimental and intellectual mosaic between Corinne (Mme de Staël), and the ex-Bishop of Autun responded to rare affinities, for it weathered, without the slightest injury, changes of residence or temperature, separations, and all the shocks of the Revolution. On the other hand, it was not subjected to that most searching test, life in common, and it was consolidated by an exchange of services which strengthened the bonds of sympathy by those of interest. For it was Mme de Staël who was to be the negotiator of Talleyrand's return to Paris. It was she who was to obtain for him the portfolio of Foreign Affairs under the Directory. She devoted herself to this with all the more zeal as the result flattered her pride while being a proof of her power. Talleyrand's diplomatic masterpiece was perhaps not so much the Congress of Vienna as the protracted serenity of his relations with such a woman of so tempestuous a character. Can it be that he never really loved her, since her admirers were to condemn her after their rupture with her with as bitter a hatred as if they had always loved her?

Talleyrand found a way into the heart of Mme de Staël by the broadest, shortest and surest road, that of literary ambition. She read him chapters of her treatise on *The*

*Influence of the Passions*. He declared that "never had he heard anything better thought out or better written". When, recalled by her husband to Switzerland, she expressed a desire to publish her *Reflections on the Queen's Trial*, Talleyrand found her a publisher in London, corrected the proofs, looked after the advertising, and himself wrote enthusiastic articles in the English journals. During their stay in London, Talleyrand, no longer possessing a carriage, was taken by Mme de Staël for drives in her barouche along with other friends. He occupied the box-seat, no doubt because, the inside being full up, he would have been unable to stretch his bad leg at full length. For it could not have been that he wished to play the footman and thus show his imperious lady-friend how far she had tamed him. Especially in London—where footmen preserved an hierarchical impassivity—would such a part have been incompatible with Talleyrand's habit (his impassivity was always strictly official) of turning round on his seat to take part in the conversation and gesticulating so excitedly that one day he broke the window. A strange preparation for diplomacy, which has been defined as the art of avoiding collisions and of mending broken window-panes.

A Talleyrand is never indifferent to politics. Activity being prohibited he consoled himself by offering advice when nobody asked him for it. Between his visits to Mme de Staël and the rides in her barouche he composed *On the Present Relations of France with other European States*, a memoir entirely in his own hand which was found among Danton's papers. Being for the time in safety he set himself not to flatter, as in his apology of August 10, but to serve. In this document, which is still worthy of perusal, he warned France against the disasters he foresaw, and which he would be called upon to repair in 1814, and announced the principles he would then seek to apply. To the madmen who were about to set Europe ablaze in order to force it to think as they did, he pointed out that "the real supremacy, alone useful and rational, the only one suitable for enlightened and free men, is to be master in one's own house and never to indulge the ridiculous claim of being master in other people's homes". He added that for States as for individuals, real wealth consists not in acquiring or invading the domains of another, but in improving the value of their own. He condemned "territorial aggrandizements, all those usurpations of force and cunning". He saw in them only the "cruel sport of political unreason". And, his tone becoming more elevated, he concluded: "France must therefore remain within her own boundaries; she owes it to her glory, her justice, her reason, her interest, and to that of the nations who, through her, will be free".

The greatness and security of France by the maintenance of a "territorial *statu quo*" which can only be disturbed to its detriment; risk of compromising this through ephemeral conquests whose sole durable result would be a rupture of the marvellous equilibrium obtained by the age-long effort of her kings; identity of her interests and those of Europe, both resting on this equilibrium, of which France must be the principal guardian since she is the principal beneficiary of it; harmony of her interests and her rights with her duty in a mission in which she has the privilege of simultaneously serving her cause and the cause of justice; benefit for France of an ideal, not of aggrandizement but of influence, binding her to menace none, but to tranquillize or protect the world at large, so that her frontiers, if she only overpasses them by her influence and prestige, will enclose her, but only to liberate her in assuring her the guarantees of peace and support in the world-wide part she is called upon to play through her clear and human genius. Such were the permanent conditions of a policy at once fruitful and sane. Imposed by history and geography, those fundamental data were ignored by the Revolution and the Empire. After having vainly restated them from the beginning of the drama, Talleyrand was to take them as his inspiration, so as to prepare, despite what seemed to be fatality, an issue which would preserve the integrity as well as the future of invaded and vanquished France. In that great drama the synthesis of his prophetic exhortations in 1792 and his work of representation in 1814 raised the former mitred Alcibiades and needy refugee of London to the rank of the chorus which alternately expressed the desires of men and the will of the gods, but with the added glory that in the Viennese Olympus he was destined to be the first of the gods.

But for the time being he was abandoned by the gods and considered by men of all parties as the vilest of the vile. While he was busy sending to Paris a document destined in his opinion to save the world, a discovery was made which his enemies were to exploit with the idea of hoisting him with his own petard. When searching in a hidden cupboard (a sort of iron safe) at the Tuileries, someone came across two documents which proved that the quondam Bishop of Autun had had secret relations with Louis XVI. On December 5 the Convention decreed "there are grounds of accusation against Talleyrand-Périgord. A seal will immediately be put upon his papers." Behold him now, in the eyes of the Revolution to which he had given so many pledges, an outcast, and officially an *émigré*, after having taken every step to avoid it. He had flattered himself that he had obtained all the advantages of the situation and none of its inconveniences.

Now he felt the inconveniences without the advantages, except that of escaping the guillotine. Nevertheless his life was threatened in London, where—O height of misfortune!—he was considered by the real *émigrés*, the thorough-going royalists, an object of execration. These had sworn their deepest hatred for the moderates, the constitutional royalists, the traitors whom they held responsible for all their ills. Among this small group of the accursed, Talleyrand, being the most prominent, the one who had played the most despicable part, was the most dishonoured. His enemies in Paris destined him for the scaffold should he return to France. His enemies in London reserved for him a less easy death: on the list of the great criminals of the Revolution which they were preparing, specifying the punishments to be inflicted according to degree of guilt, Talleyrand figured among those who were condemned to be broken on the wheel.

His abuse of the policy of assurance and counterassurance was a guarantee of security for him no longer. The superfine network of his cleverness being overstrained, broke. Both to right and left his life was in danger. The lucky gambler, who formerly broke the bank after having said Mass on the Champ de Mars, was now losing on both tables. And what made matters worse, that inhuman age would not even permit liberal England to extend the laws of hospitality to him. The murder of Louis XVI had stirred up in England fierce indignation. All Frenchmen implicated in the Revolution inspired a feeling of horror and were publicly denounced as assassins and cannibals. In vain did Talleyrand, following the example of the Court, Parliament, and people, go into mourning. In vain did he try to defend himself in London after his indictment in Paris: in London also he was the victim of his super-cleverness. It was said that he had instigated the decision of the Convention in order to put London on the wrong scent, and enable him to devote himself quietly to revolutionary propaganda there. Pitt then passed the Aliens Act, with the object of safe-guarding Great Britain from the contagion of revolution by empowering the Government to expel all foreigners under suspicion. Talleyrand, who was living miserably on what money remained to him from the sale of his library, desired to rejoin his friend Mme de Staël in Switzerland. But the Swiss Government considered him an undesirable. To complete his ruin, his enemies, *émigrés* in London or Jacobins in Paris, published spurious letters which they attributed to him. Nothing likely to injure him was omitted therein: insults to the memory of Louis XVI, a programme of revolutionary propaganda in London, a plan for landing on the Irish and English coasts. In January 1794 Talleyrand received an order to leave the kingdom within five days. He met the blow with a smile. So far from disheartening him, the mis-fortune lifted him above himself. Within that Epicurean, the Stoic was revealed. His few but faithful friends in London wept. "But", wrote Narbonne, "there was nothing to equal his calmness, and almost his gaiety." Recalling that crisis, Talleyrand says in his memoirs: "I felt a sort of contentment. It seems to me that in those days of well-nigh general misfortune, I should have almost regretted had I also not been persecuted." His stoicism was above all optimism. He did not lose courage because he did not lose hope. Fortune had showered on him too many of her smiles for him to doubt the return of her favour. When in Paris he enjoyed without scruple or restraint the pleasures which the most refined society showered on its favourites; he was forced with his friends to leave the banqueting-hall and to make room for intruders, every revolution being at bottom only a displacement of privileges. But his good humour did not flag. Though the horizon grew darker his face remained serene, alike in the struggle for his daily bread as on the occasion of those dainty suppers when he tasted "heavy dishes in the company of light women". This great sceptic, passionately in love with life, placed his faith in life alone. His last letter, dated from London, concluded with these words: "If Europe sinks in the future campaigns, I will prepare an asylum in America for all our friends".

His firmness was to be subjected to a ruder test. The American vessel in which he had booked a passage had scarcely gained the open sea than she was assailed by a terrible storm. With shattered rigging and partly dismasted, she drifted. The fury of the elements was above all to be feared because it exposed him anew to man's hostility. Aboard the *William Penn*, in great distress, he perceived on one side the coast of France, where if he landed he would run the risk of mounting the scaffold, and on the other the coast of England, whence he was banished. Finally English fishermen came alongside the ship and succeeded in bringing her into Falmouth. Whilst she was undergoing repairs, Talleyrand took up his quarters in a sailors' inn. There he noted a singular-looking person, taciturn and solitary, made inquiries and learnt that he was an American general of the name of Arnold who boarded in that hovel. His lucky star, Talleyrand said to himself, must have been responsible for bringing them together, for surely this table companion would give him letters which would open to him every door in the United States. But when, after the usual formalities, he asked for these, the only reply he received was: "I am the sole American who cannot give you letters for his country. All my relations with it are at an end. I must never return there." This general had sold his sword to the English during the War of Independence. We know nothing of the conversations which these two personages exchanged during their cohabitation. There was room for a dialogue on political philosophy between the general—an outcast from America, and not daring to show himself in the country to which he remained faithful—and the quondam Bishop of Autun, persecuted by the Revolution he had served and expelled from England, whose alliance with France he had always considered an ideal worth realizing. The example of General Arnold must have convinced Talleyrand that in troublous times, when it is difficult to know one's duty, the essential thing is to know one's own interests; that politics, for anyone not dominated by passion, seems to be a game in which luck is mingled with skill, a game which demands no other law than the absence of all scruples. Furthermore, that in the race for power there is only one rule: back the winner, since to back the loser is to betray oneself in betraying the winner, while to back the latter is not betrayal but foresight. Talleyrand's superiority consisted less in always backing the winner than in helping it to win after he had backed it.

After a voyage of thirty-eight days the *William Penn* touched port at Philadelphia. The first letter written by Talleyrand was for Mme de Staël. He congratulated himself on having made a good voyage. He had avoided "the English ships which stop American vessels and retain them in their colonies, the French who capture and pillage, and the Algerians who capture and sell". He made no mention of meeting an English frigate, in sight of which he donned a costume which is not exhibited in the show-cases of the Château of Valençay, where his

official dress-suits have been collected together; for, being afraid that the American vessel might be stopped and searched, and not over-anxious to be recognized, he borrowed from the cook an apron and a white cap.

Talleyrand did not reach Philadelphia with the same aspirations as Chateaubriand some years before. He did not pursue an ever-elusive object of desire in the virgin solitude of the New World; he did not transpose the key of his sighs, thrills, and lamentations into those of the forest in order to orchestrate his inner voices and amplify them by all the echoes of Nature. His sylph was not intangible although she might be double. The object he had in view was the rebuilding of his fortunes and perfecting his political education.

First of all: make another fortune, quickly and by any means. So he surveyed the country, not as a poet, after the manner of Chateaubriand, but like a man of business. Like René, he gazed upon the Niagara Falls, but with a different eye. If he says nothing about them in his memoirs, there is no doubt that he calculated their horse-power. On his arrival he wrote to Mme de Staël: "There is much money to be made here, but it is for the people who have it". And he asked his lady friend to help him. "If you know any people who want to speculate in land, I will look after their business willingly. Go a little into this." In another letter to the authoress of the *Discourse on the Passions*, he pressed her to be his go-between, to procure for him sleeping-partners and "commissions". Was she not the daughter of Necker? "If any of your father's friends are sending vessels to America, I am well placed to undertake the business of those persons who apply to me." His morale and feelings with regard to America varied with the ebb and flow of his undertakings. When he portrayed the United States as an Eldorado and declared his intention of settling there it was because he had carried out a good piece of business. But his luck changed and then he wrote to Mme de Staël: "A year here will kill me".

In the interval between two strokes of business Talleyrand continued (to use his own expression) his "course of political ideas", which are tinged with his principal anxiety, for it was chiefly a course of economic ideas. Scattered throughout his correspondence, they were to be condensed in his *Memoir on the Commercial Relations of the United States with England*, a lecture on which he delivered to his colleagues of the Institute at the meeting of April 4, 1797. His subject reflected the predominance, more evident than to-day, of economic over political problems in the United States. But, while entering into the details of the former with the experience of a business man, he had too great a grasp of them to fail to perceive the repercussions on the latter. Thus it was that he saw between the United States and their ex-mother country England, a profound and permanent solidarity which is to-day one of the essential facts of world-politics.

The thing which specially struck him among Americans was the coexistence of two often contradictory passions, which they reconciled as he himself did—the passion for independence and the passion for money. He slighted the generosity of the Americans when he said later on to his friend Barante: "Do not talk to me about a country where I found no one who was not willing to sell me his dog". On the other hand, he admired their spirit of toleration and attributed their welfare to the religious peace founded on the equality of creeds. When, later, he collaborated on the Concordat he applied the principles which had always been his, and the benefits of which he had verified in the United States.

The equality of races not being respected in the United States like the equality of creeds, Talleyrand did his reputation more harm there than by all the scandals of the past by parading about with a negress. However, she was so charming that he was not judged harshly for long. This was a way of preparing himself for the social and sentimental promotion soon to be his after his return to France through his marriage with the beautiful Creole Mme Grant. Similarly, by becoming a second-hand dealer when stock-jobbing did not pay, he prepared himself to carry on the same trade in a wider sphere where he would reap renown. Politician and journalist, he had already made a start in bartering opinions and sentiments. After pictures and works of art he was to be a statesman when he dealt in provinces, nations, and crowns.

At Philadelphia the tiny society of refugees centred around a person named Moreau de Saint-Méry, who for three days had been styled the King of Paris because he had presided over the electoral assembly of the capital. He kept a book-shop, and in the evenings, at the back of his premises, held receptions in which conversation took the place of refreshments. It appears that Talleyrand was the life and soul of the company. To chaff him, he was often styled "Monseigneur". He took his revenge by shaking hands in a peculiar manner. Seizing the person's hand with his steel-like fingers, in which, by some mysterious law of compensation, there was doubtless concentrated the whole force of his club-foot, he would compress the patriot' hand until the latter cried for mercy.

During the fine weather Talleyrand, accompanied by certain frequenters of the book-shop of Moreau de Saint Méry, made journeys into the interior of the State in old public vehicles, jolting over roads which were often impossible except on horseback. They passed the night in the log-houses of pioneers. One evening they were the guests of the Comte de la Tour du Pin and his young wife, whose maiden name was Dillon, and whom Talleyrand had known as a child. When they arrived, Mme de la Tour du Pin, with sleeves turned up and a small chopper in hand, was cutting with equal grace and care, as though she were trimming her nails, the bone of a leg of mutton preparatory to putting it on the spit; but for these French people who had fled from the Terror to the New World, the most succulent and cheering dish of all was a newspaper which had just arrived, announcing the fall of Robespierre and the 9th of Thermidor.

Very soon, the good news being confirmed, Talleyrand sent a petition to the Convention. After being entangled in London in his web of intrigue, he made use in Philadelphia of the remains, to tie once more the thread broken with France and the future. "I am no *émigré*", said he, "and I ought not to be treated as such." He reminded them of his mission to London, the pledges he had given to the Revolution and which had been the cause of his expulsion from England. His outlawry was an iniquity, for he had played his part in framing the new law and had suffered in a good cause.

In politics a cause is only good if the advocate entrusted with it enjoys the favour of power. Talleyrand's cause was excellent, for it was entrusted to Mme de Staël, to whom he sent his request. One of the first to return after the fall of Robespierre, she attracted to her salon at the Swedish Embassy all the men who counted for anything in the new régime, of which she was already the Egeria. She mobilized all her friends in the interest of Talleyrand, and with a zeal which would have been more touching had it been more disinterested. Her ambition played no less a part than her heart in that campaign. She dreamed of regenerating the Republic and, through the example of France, Europe, by adopting the American institutions that Talleyrand had had the opportunity to study, and which he would be better qualified than any other to establish and direct. In this race to power the ex-Bishop was a favourite of whom she was taking particular care, in order to make him, in the language of to-day, "her colt".

Marie Joseph Chénier was one of the most influential of the Thermidorians. Through the influence of Eugénie de la Bouchardie, a young woman with whom he was in love, Mme de Staël set him to work. Chénier had no sooner arrived at Eugénie's house than she sang to him—while accompanying herself on the harp—the ballad of the "Proscript". Then it was that, on September 4, 1795, Chénier mounted the rostrum and demanded Talleyrand's recall with a warmth inspired by his passion for Eugénie: "It is a question", said he, "of appealing to your justice on behalf of a philosopher whose unchanging principles have placed him among the founders of French liberty. I esteem it an honour to defend, in a republican assembly, the cause of a patriot of '89, honoured like ourselves by the hatred of tyrants and slaves. A republican at heart and by principle, it was to the land of Benjamin Franklin that he hastened to contemplate the spectacle of a free people . . . and he did not, like those unnatural children, the *émigrés*, turn a parricidal blade against the fatherland."

The philosopher, Talleyrand, whose sole and invariable principle consisted in neglecting no means to realize his own ambitions, and who, as far as liberty was concerned, esteemed that of returning to France above all else, had assisted Mme de Staël by sending her letters that might be shown, and the terms of which were designed to procure him the sympathy of the Directory. Chénier's oration was loudly applauded by the frequenters of Corinne's salon, and her proposal was adopted. Without discussion Talleyrand's name was there and then erased from the list of *émigrés* and the bill of indictment against him was cancelled. Not until two months later, on November 2, did Talleyrand receive the news. Whether it was that he awaited the summer, or whether, after causing himself to be forgotten he wished to make himself desired, he did not embark before June 13, 1796, on a Danish brig whose name *Den Ny Proeve* (The New Ordeal) was eloquent of either promises or threats.

## CHAPTER V

# TALLEYRAND AND THE DIRECTORY: THE 18TH OF BRUMAIRE [1]

Women must be made to obey.
TALLEYRAND

WHEN returning from America, Talleyrand, with the instinct of a migratory bird flying to its native land, ascertained his position towards power. He landed at Hamburg and there observed which way the wind blew: a well-chosen spot, for it was then a refuge for *émigrés* of all degrees. He met there, around Mme de Genlis, several of his former lady friends. Also the brothers Lameth, Dumouriez, and the Abbé Louis, who had assisted him at the Champ de Mars Mass on July 14, 1790, when he whispered to Lafayette, "Don't make me laugh!" The two accomplices must have had a good laugh together when they recalled that event after the horrors which had followed the Festival of the Federation.

He sported the tricolour cockade and, never in a hurry (he had belonged to the Church which makes patience a virtue), stopped a fortnight in Amsterdam, another centre of information, and then in Brussels, then the capital of a French Department. On reaching Paris he was fully acquainted with the situation.

[1] The second month of the French Republican calendar—from October 23 to November 21 inclusive. The 18th of Brumaire was the day on which Bonaparte overthrew the French Republic.—Translators' note.

The *Courrier Républicain* announced, as an official event, the return of the "former Bishop of Autun, a privileged *émigré*". He was, indeed, soon to become the man of the day. The new régime, aspiring to consolidation while growing more humane, recognized itself in this ex-leader of the Constituent, whose white priestly hands were unstained with blood, and who, they believed, had given it too many pledges not to be eternally attached to it. A sworn bishop, then an apostate—that fault was a veritable title to honour! But his chief qualification was his sojourn in America. He had suffered there for the good cause. Behold him, then, ranked among the saints of the Revolution, a somewhat martyred saint and all the better for it. He had done more than suffer there: he had completed his political education and acquired unparalleled experience. The United States were regarded in France as the high school of Liberty and the laboratory of Constitutions, each of the fifteen States having its own government. The Revolution, at last rid of the Terror, was seeking its definite form. It was its good fortune to be able to consult one of its most devoted children, who had had leisure to study every variety of free institutions in the New World. By qualifying him to return to the Parisian stage and play the premier rôle after Bonaparte, America was merely continuing to export anarchy to France in exchange for the independence she had received from her. The Revolution, before owing her a subtle Talleyrand ready for the struggles which were coming, owed her the myth of "the good savage" on which its entire mysticism reposed. It also partly owed her those two monsters which devoured the old régime: the deficit and ideology. The war against England had exhausted Louis XVI's treasury and cost him much dearer through the impetus it gave to revolutionary propaganda. After the myth of "the good savage"

America supplied us with that of "the good civilized individual", the citizen of the United States elevated to the position of an instructor of the human race and as a model of all the civic virtues.

Transposed in France, the American love of independence became the cult of Liberty; that is to say, hatred of all authority, a hatred which took its inspiration from violence, amidst which liberty perishes. "They wish to be free and know not how to be just", said Necker. They were just to so small a degree, without being more free, that, thinking they were imitating the republicans of America, they overthrew Louis XVI who had affranchised them. He was a victim of his greatest boon: his participation in an event which, in the twentieth century, was to contribute to the salvation of France and civilization; the most important event of the eighteenth century; more important than the Revolution, since it engendered and survived it. Though it also engendered Talleyrand's career, it did so only in a certain measure, with the collaboration of the interested party and with that of Mme de Staël.

Despite his listlessness, which was above all a means to an end, Talleyrand did not await Fortune. He hastened towards her and solicited her favours in every way. Profiting by the sympathy and curiosity aroused by his return, he kept the public on the alert and roved about without intermission. Hardly had he arrived than he attended a sitting of the Institute, to which, by a flattering anomaly, he had been elected whilst he was still in America and without any application on his part. His election was an homage paid to the author of the *Report on Public Instruction*, presented to the Constituent, and in which the plan for a national Institute was set forth for the first time. He charmed his colleagues, who selected him twice in succession for the reading of communications at public sittings.

With the anodyne title *Memoir concerning the Commercial Relations of the United States with England*, his first paper discreetly underlined his American qualifications. The "genius of the Revolution" still suffering from ideological prurience, the votes of the intellectuals were necessary to Talleyrand in order to impose himself on the Directors; he alone was not sufficient. A still surer means of conciliating them was to support their policy publicly. Such was the object of the Cercle Constitutionnel —the Constitutional Club—of which Talleyrand was one of the founders, and of a new journal, the *Conservateur* (conservative of the new régime), in which he treated questions of foreign policy. On July 3 he read at the Institute his second paper, entitled *Essay concerning the Advantages to be derived from New Colonies under Present Circumstances*. This communication, more expressly than his first, was his ministerial declaration. In colonies he appreciated above all the advantage of realizing the most earnest desire of the nation, namely, forgetfulness of interior disorders in a unanimous effort for exterior expansion. "The veritable Lethe, at the close of a Revolution, is in that which opens up for mankind the highways towards hope." Either in order to flatter the prevailing humanitarianism, or through one of those anticipations of the true statesman, he adopted the protectorate formula in the colonies: "Neither domination nor monopoly; always the strength which protects, never that which takes possession". A forerunner of Lyautey, Talleyrand claimed to be the continuator of Choiseul; "one of the men of our century", he said, "whose mind saw the clearest into the future—a man who already, in 1767, foresaw the separation of America from England and feared the partition of Poland". He recalled, in addition, that Choiseul contemplated the cession of Egypt to France. In stretching out one hand to Choiseul he extended the other to Bonaparte, and pointed out to him, by this evocation of the past, that he himself was not without a sense of future events. He proved it once more by inviting France to seek for tranquillity and prosperity in its colonial work and, in order "not to find ourselves behind events", to take up a position in view of that dividing up of the world which was to be the capital event of the following century. He concluded in terms which summed up the politics and psychology of colonials. He extolled "the pleasure of being able to attach to these enterprises so many agitated men who had need of projects, so many unhappy men who had need of hope". Thirteen days after reading this paper its author was appointed Minister of Foreign Relations.

The Institute, the Cercle Constitutionnel, and the *Conservateur* had created an atmosphere favourable to that result. But Talleyrand would not have attained it if he had not applied one of his maxims: "Under great circumstances women must be made to obey". The Directory—the most dissolute régime France has known—was the most accessible to feminine influences. The corruption of public morals reflected that of private ones. The Revolution not having changed human nature, the orgy of blood was, as always, followed by a frenzy of pleasure. The end of the Terror had given the signal for the dance. After the fear of death came the joy of life. Moreover, the past being destroyed and the future uncertain, people's minds were wholly concentrated on the present. Horace's *carpe diem* was the beginning and the end of all wisdom. Talleyrand, who had known the pleasure of living wholly in the present under the old régime, and who now knew the good luck of having survived it, was insatiable. A prey to checked ambition during his exile, he went hell for leather on the road towards Fortune, and to attain it employed every possible means. The Institute, a political club, a semi-official journal, and assiduous flattery earned for him Fortune's first smiles. In order to win her over entirely he was to avail himself of a woman, Mme de Staël, who in herself alone was an institute, thanks to her science; a political club on account of her salon; and a journal through her indiscretions. He had long since been accustomed to make use of her, and in that particular remained faithful. She was attached to him on account of the services she had already rendered him and because of the hopes she placed in him. She flattered herself that some day she might govern France through his instrumentality, without prejudice to her ambition inspired by a new favourite, Benjamin Constant. In politics—and sometimes in love—her chariot permitted at the very least double harness.

In order to obtain the first vacancy in the ministry, Talleyrand had to include the majority of the Directory in his designs. He knew only two members, his former colleagues at the Constituent Assembly, Rewbell and La Revellière-Lépeaux, both of whom were hostile to him. Rewbell, a sincere Jacobin and obscure provincial barrister, could not bear this great nobleman, whose patriotism appeared to him to be open to suspicion. As to the less solemn La Revellière-Lépeaux—the Pope of the new religion, that of the Theophilanthropists—the ex-Bishop of Autun had not been able to resist the pleasure of scoffing at him. Talleyrand's inner demon often played him a nasty trick by inspiring him with some jest or other which, in a minute of insolence, caused him to lose the benefit of a long-drawn-out sycophancy. One day La Revellière-Lépeaux, who was his colleague at the Institute and in the same section, that of Moral and Political Sciences, read there a paper on the laical religion he had invented. When the majority of the audience were congratulating him, Talleyrand remarked: "I have only one observation to make to you. Jesus Christ, in order to establish His religion, was crucified and rose from the dead. You ought to have tried to do as much." Another member of the Directory, the austere Carnot, said of Talleyrand: "He preserves all the vices of the old régime without acquiring a single virtue of the new one". As to the two other Directors: Letourneau de La Manche did not count, and Barras, the most influential of the five, combined all the vices of the new régime with all those of the old. That was his particular virtue in Talleyrand's eyes, for it enabled him to be understood. Moreover, Barras was of authentic though modest nobility, and consequently respected the heir of the Comtes de Périgord.

Therefore it was upon Barras, who was a familiar member of her salon, that Mme de Staël concentrated her principal effort. She brought her candidate to the Luxembourg to introduce him, and she sang his praises as a citizen and as a friend. "He is burning", she said, "to devote himself to the service of the Republic and Liberty. There is no more faithful friend. He will be entirely devoted to you; will go through fire for you. He is a being formed of the most delicate feelings, etc. etc."

When she stopped to take breath, her protégé bowed down to the ground and repeated: "Your respectful and grateful servant! Nothing save my admiration can equal my respect and gratitude."

Mme de Staël returned to the charge at the Luxembourg several times and had private interviews with Barras, who, pleading his colleagues' objections, resisted.

From those objections she drew her most telling arguments.

"They reproach him with having every vice. That proves they cannot reproach him with anything else. The virtuous imbeciles who surround you are inspired with base jealousy; that is the explanation of their wish to deprive you of such a collaborator."

"My colleagues of the Directory are unanimous in despising him."

"All the better for you, Barras. The worse he is in your colleagues' opinion, the more he will be exclusively devoted to you. Truly he is the most faithful dog you could have."

Meanwhile Talleyrand mobilized all his friends, male and female, with instructions to repeat everywhere that he adored Barras, was devoted to him in life and death.

However, Barras would not yet capitulate. With irresistible vehemence Mme de Staël made a final attack. Trembling, white-hot, and gesticulating, she entered the Luxembourg—and soon left, this time triumphant.

Shaking both of Barras' hands, she obliged him to sit down by her side. She was to win that race to power, not, as jockeys say, in an armchair but on a sofa. With swelling throat and breathless voice, she implored and threatened. "Barras, Barras, my friend, I count on you alone. Without you we are lost. Do you know what he said to me a short time ago? He said that he would throw himself into the Seine if you do not make him Minister of Foreign Affairs. . . . You must appoint him; otherwise I shall be in despair and I myself shall die. Really, I am at the end of my tether." Importunity to such an extent as that is a force as redoubtable as charm. In order to get rid of her (for, as he says in his memoirs, "never did I come out of such a trial more innocent and more pure") Barras ended by giving way. "Strongly urge your friend not to drown himself, for in that case it would not be possible to do anything with him."

Whilst his fate was in the balance, Talleyrand was not on the banks of the Seine contemplating suicide but in front of Barras' very door; he was sitting in Mme de Staël's carriage, musing over the fact that he had already borrowed twenty-five thousand francs from her, that he had not enough money to pay for a carriage of his own, and that, being infirm, he could not do without one. Maybe he said to himself that she was at that moment playing for a great stake as much to get her money back as (through an intermediary) to enter the Government. When, still all a-quivering, she came back to him, the contrast between the volcanic woman and her phlegmatic friend must have been perfect. A great actor, dispassionate and classical, and playing his part inwardly, Talleyrand must, while keeping back a smile, have suppressed the expression of his joy so as to limit that of his gratitude, observant not to give to such a cumbersome protectrice too heavy a mortgage on his future. Maybe, too, he made believe that he only resigned himself to accept power in order to be agreeable to her. For that is what he leads one to suppose in his memoirs when he wrote: "Mme de Staël's pressing entreaties and, more than all that, the feeling one has that to do a little good is not impossible, drove away all idea of refusing".

Barras was not at the end of his troubles. After Mme de Staël's onslaught he had to submit to his colleagues' recriminations. Those of Carnot and Rewbell were violent. But in the case of certain doctrinaires compromises can be effected. Already a republic of "comrades" existed. Rewbell introduced one of them for an office other than that of Foreign Affairs, so Barras obtained that Terrorist's vote for Talleyrand by giving his to the candidate in question. He entrusted Benjamin Constant, whom Mme de Staël employed as her liaison officer, to carry the good news to the new minister. Without a moment's delay Talleyrand proceeded to the Luxembourg and was admitted to Barras, whom he overwhelmed with thanks, and, as he kissed him, with words expressive of eternal devotion. It was late at night—the hour when Barras usually retired to rest. He was begged not to be embarrassed by his "humble servant", who was only "too happy" to be present at his nocturnal toilet. On leaving, Talleyrand showed a desire to embrace all the lackeys and he actually shook the door-keeper's hand effusively. This narrative, as well as the other—no less caricatural, but less improbable—relating to Mme de Staël's visits to the Luxembourg, is borrowed from the memoirs of Barras, whose protégé was soon to give him good reasons for speaking of him without the slightest excess of kindness.

As soon as he received notice of his nomination, Talleyrand proceeded to the ministry to enter on his duties. The remittance was made by the last holder of the office, Charles Delacroix, who was already accustomed to sacrificing himself for his successor, since Talleyrand before taking possession of his portfolio had already taken possession of his wife, by whom, in all probability, he had the most illustrious of his children, the great painter Eugène Delacroix.

What was the new minister's programme? We know not whether he unbosomed himself as regards that while Barras was undressing, or whether he merely assured him, with hand on heart, of his zeal in the service of the Republic and Liberty. But in the carriage which took him to the Luxembourg, seated behind Benjamin Constant and Boniface de Castellane, his former colleague at the Constituent Assembly and one of his bosom friends, he was more explicit and yet more sincere. With hands trembling with joy he gripped their knees and kept on saying: "We hold the fort. We must make an immense fortune . . . an immense fortune . . . an immense fortune."

Awaiting something better, there was hardly anything more such a man as he could do. He possessed just sufficient power to turn it into cash—not enough power to direct events. All authority being concentrated in the hands of the Directors, who appointed and dismissed ministers, the latter held office only nominally. They were not members of a Cabinet; they took no part in Councils of State; and they were not permitted to speak at assemblies. They were nothing more than clerks. Talleyrand was much above his office, but circumstances did not allow him to increase it to his stature, nor to put his ideas into action. Gaudin, when offered the Ministry of Finances by the Directory, refused it with the words, "Where there is neither money nor the means of making it, a Finance Minister is useless". Had Talleyrand been as disinterested as Gaudin he might have said, "Where there is neither diplomacy nor the means of creating it, a minister is useless". There was then neither diplomacy nor the means of creating it largely because there was no money. The golden age promised at the dawn of the Revolution displayed itself by the flight of gold. The louis d'or was worth 60,000 paper francs. Having borrowed at 100 per cent to pay the most urgent expenses, the Government failed to find further credit even at that rate, and was reduced to forced loans which failed. All their dragooning was powerless to dislodge money. Only one resource was left—War. This policy possessed every advantage: it justified a strong hand, was an excuse for punishing every enterprise against the régime as an outrage against the imperilled country, it reflected glory on the country in lieu of its lost liberty, and, while keeping the generals busy abroad, it guaranteed the security of the Governors. Above all, it had the advantage of filling the empty coffers. In those happy days war not only nourished itself, it nourished the Directory, awaiting the time when it suppressed it. But it nourished it on the condition that it was victorious. That was the position, thanks to Bonaparte. Forced taxation in Italy yielded infinitely more than forced loans in France. In the case of the Revolution, which had declared peace to all the world, war—alimentary war— became an industry of prime necessity.

Talleyrand was a man in favour of peace, and during his long career the invariable axis of his policy was alliance with England. Now there was war— and war with England! Moreover, his pen could do nothing more than countersign the decisions of the sword. He was merely the registrar of History.

Talleyrand thought that, though his pen was a slave, his pocket was free—and empty. So he made haste to fill it, because of the uncertainty of the future. With a zeal inspired by jealousy more than by indignation, the virtuous Barras in his memoirs recapitulates what he calls the "diplomatic tips" of the Minister of Foreign Affairs— his "gifts", as the special agents whom he entrusted with such negotiations phrased it. They were inspired by a noble feeling: the anxiety to assure his independence and the dignity of his old age. The Prussian Minister, Sandoz Rollin, wrote to his sovereign: "Talleyrand loves money and openly declares that, on relinquishing office, he has no desire to have to ask an alms from the Republic".

Talleyrand dazzled Paris with his luxury but he himself was neither dazzled nor enervated by it. Ever on the lookout for opportunities for consolidating and increasing his fortune, he was like a great, insatiable feline prowling about at its ease through the political jungle. His keen senses detected every noise and every breath. Especially did he scent with unerring instinct the fair wind to Power, and thus hunted in the right direction. He turned away from the Directory, which, even for a sense of smell less fine than his, was now exhaling a strong odour of decomposition. Vomited by the country, which at the last elections had elected only adversaries of the Government, it aimed at making the country obey while violating all the principles of the Revolution; so as, it said, to preserve its results, but in reality to preserve its creatures; that is to say, to preserve itself.

It was the 18th of Fructidor,[1] the time of the electoral operations, annulled by decree and in virtue of that fundamental unwritten principle of the Revolution that its divine law took precedence of the national will. The latter was only sacred if it remained faithful to the Republic. In virtue of other decrees the leaders of the opposition were deported and the Terrorist legislation re-established; independent journals were suppressed and their editors sent to the hulks. This "police operation", which was, above all, a piece of brigandage (the "rotters" of the Directory having no other ideal than to enrich themselves out of the plunder of the State), was encouraged by Talleyrand and carried out with the troops which Bonaparte placed at Barras' disposal. Both played the game of the Directory with the ulterior design of favouring their own, since the technique of a sudden deviation from constitutional order involved the confidence, and, as far as possible, the assistance, of its victims.

Bonaparte's and Talleyrand's ambitions met and drew

[1] The twelfth month of the French Republican calendar, from August 18 to September 16.—Translators' note.

them together before they actually knew each other. It was then that the strange and natural conjunction of their two planets took place: "the meteor which consumed itself while dazzling the world" before its extinction in the west, and the star which was ever subject to eclipse, coming in or out of the shade according to the state of the sky, and the double property of which was ever to submit to the rising sun and, sometimes, to cause it to rise.

In 1798 the rising sun was Bonaparte. A rising and already brilliant sun, his rays, which bore the names of victories, confounded the Powers, illumined the horizon of France, and revived the agonizing Directory, awaiting the moment when they were to reduce it to ashes. The Government, indeed, owed its life solely to the millions plundered by the commander-in-chief of the Italian army. In exchange he was allowed an entirely free hand to govern his conquests as he liked. He was getting his hand in to govern France. He created all the organs of a complete Government: administration, finance, diplomacy. Without referring to Paris he negotiated with Austria and concluded the Leoben preliminaries. Caesar was revealed in the Proconsul. His rivals, Jourdan and Moreau, were beaten in Germany. He alone was victory, glory, order, and money. France—persecuted and exploited in the name of immortal principles by a band of profiteers— turned with immense hope towards the young general who was revealing himself to be as great a politician as he was a general; towards that god of war who was also the god of peace. Peace he needed to consolidate his victories and respond to the desires of France, whereas the Directory, whose divorce from the nation was more and more complete, needed war in order to last; war which would keep Bonaparte at a distance and, through victory, make good the exhausted credit.

Talleyrand strove to become indispensable to the indispensable man. He enveloped him on all sides; he flattered and served and directed him. No sooner had he become a minister than he wrote the general, whom he did not know, a private letter informing him of the fact, and in terms so well turned as to seduce him.

"Justly alarmed by duties the perilous importance of which I fully realize, I need reassurance through the feeling of what your glory ought to contribute as regards means and facilities in the negotiations. The very name of Bonaparte is an auxiliary which ought to remove all difficulties.

"I shall hasten to send you all the views which the Directory instructs me to transmit to you, and Renown, which is your ordinary medium, will often deprive me of the happiness of communicating to it the manner in which you have carried those views out."

Joséphine, who had decided to rejoin Bonaparte in Italy and who knew the Minister of Foreign Affairs, sang the praises of citizen Talleyrand. Consequently the general wrote to the Directory to congratulate it on its choice and at the same time sent an amiable reply to the new minister, encouraging him to keep up direct correspondence. Talleyrand did not wait to be asked twice. He wrote him especially a letter giving an account of the 18th of Fructidor, using a formula which has been used since then "Momentarily we have deviated from the Constitution but there has been a return to it—I hope for ever". And when Bonaparte signed the Treaty of Campo-Formio, the minister congratulated him in a lyrical manner, concluding with the words: "Farewell, General and Peacemaker. Farewell—with my friendship, admiration, respect, and gratitude."

On December 5, 1797, the conqueror of Rivoli was

back in Paris. He went to live in the house where he had known Joséphine and which he had just purchased, in the Rue Chantereine, which, through Talleyrand's courtesy, had been renamed Rue de la Victoire. This change was the object of a decree justifying it, as much out of the propriety of suppressing "a sign of royalty" as through the desire to consecrate the glory of the armies of the Republic. Now, the name Chantreine was derived from *raines* (frogs), which swarmed—and croaked—in a neighbouring marsh. A fact unknown, in the swamp of the Directory, to the frogs who were clamouring, without being aware of it, for an Emperor.

Bonaparte's first visit was to Talleyrand. Whereupon there were outbursts of tenderness, an exchange of confidences, and reciprocal advances. Addressing a great nobleman and one who was a former Bishop of Autun, and whose secret thoughts he divined, the hero of the Republic showed him discreetly that they were made to understand each other and had points of view in common—especially a mutual disdain for revolutionary fanaticism.

"You are", said Bonaparte, "the nephew of the Archbishop of Rheims, who is now at the side of Louis XVIII." Talleyrand was quick to notice that, already consecrating his successor, Bonaparte did not say, "at the side of the Comte de Lille". "I, too, have an uncle", continued the general, "who is an Archdeacon in Corsica; he it was who brought me up. In Corsica, you know, that is the same as being an Archbishop in France."

The fact that they were both nephews of archbishops was not their only reason for associating their careers. Since the time when, at St-Sulpice, the Abbé de Périgord —consumed by ambition, keen to know all and possess everything, isolated, gloomy, taciturn, and meditative like the young military pupil of Brienne—played "the little Bonaparte", events had created fresh bonds between them. Both had traversed those events rather than lived them, adopting the colours of the day, but without feeling its passions and only in order to prepare for the morrow. In that position, above parties, they were able to hold out their hand to each other and collaborate in such a way as to conciliate the views of those parties. Amidst civil discord they both possessed the arbitrator's vocation and could give themselves up to it all the more willingly since it served their ambition, while responding to the most imperious needs of France. The country's other profound aspiration—peace—was also theirs. Bonaparte, who during his Italian proconsulate had acquired a taste for power and felt himself worthy of it; Bonaparte, who over the head of the Directory had made peace with Austria, conceived a dream which exceeded the glory of a conqueror. In order to realize that dream he had to satisfy, not a condemned Government, which was at peace only in the midst of war, but a public opinion which demanded that peace with all the more ardour because, through the conditions under which it had been concluded, it assured France, in addition to repose and prosperity, her natural frontiers.

Bonaparte, who prided himself on intellect rather than on the strength of the sword, and who did not wish to risk the reproach of instituting a government of soldiers, enlisted assistance among civilians. Where could he have found more precious assistance than with the most intelligent and most pacific civilian? Temperamentally and professionally Talleyrand was pacific, since vanity —in default of humanity—inspires diplomats with that love of peace which restores to them their importance, usurped by generals in war-time. The antinomy of the

general and the diplomat, which was to declare itself later
between them, was momentarily solved in a community of
views and interests, on a double—home and foreign—
plan. Coming from such different horizons, the planet of
the little Corsican soldier of fortune and that of the great
nobleman who had gone over to the Revolution (but only
in order to make it an ally) had passed through the same
phases and followed the same orbit. Not only at St-Sulpice
and at Brienne. The Italian campaign, which in the eyes
of the Directory had the advantage of being a form of
deportation, was a consecration which brought the young
conqueror near to power. During his sojourn in America,
when he had been banished and where it looked as though
he was doomed to definite oblivion, Talleyrand found his
own Italian campaign. He returned from it with that halo
of liberty of which the United States was the home and
the school, just as Bonaparte returned from Italy with a
halo of glory. Liberty . . . glory—magic words which fill
all hearts with enthusiasm and rapture, especially when they
are united. In the same way as Bonaparte, in a fit of discouragement, was at one time about to leave for the East—
not as an emulator of Alexander but as a mere instructor for
the Turkish army—Talleyrand had had a plan for establishing himself definitely in business in America or in India.
Three days after his return from Italy, Bonaparte occupied
himself especially over his election to the Institute. He
was anxious for his renown among the intellectuals; like
Talleyrand, who, on his return from America, canvassed
among his learned colleagues for the honour of addressing
them in public. Talleyrand, who, in order to cover the
ground without stopping, had abandoned as cumbersome
baggage his caste, his order, and his mitre, was to have
nothing to reproach Bonaparte with when, without even
informing the Government, he abandoned his army in

Egypt before the enemy, so that he might return precipitately to France, where, instead of being shot, as any other general would have been, he was to be raised to supreme power. The exceptional destinies of those two men evaded the common rule and were subject to no other law than their fatality.

Finally Bonaparte knew, as Talleyrand did, how "to make women obey". It was Joséphine who, by an exchange of favours with Barras, hooked for him the command of the army in Italy. The minister and the general were not, therefore, lacking as regards affinities—nor in subjects of conversation. Besides, they were attached to each other by their dissimilarities as well as by their similarities. The mind of the one, ever in a state of fermentation and semi-agitation, was enlightened and improved through union with the most clear mind of the other. Their association was a certificate of liberalism and "intelligence" for the soldier, and one of patriotism for the civilian. Talleyrand's experience—that of a man sixteen years older than Bonaparte—was of inestimable value for the hero of twenty-eight; a consummate experience of home politics, of the "legal country"—a ground sown with snares and precipices especially for a young general, who was awaited and acclaimed by the country itself; an experience also of foreign policy, and of their mutual reactions, for Talleyrand, initiated by his past into all the problems of the national life, knew how to leave his speciality in order to dominate that life and apply to the management of affairs that synthetic mind without which a man is not a statesman. Certainly Bonaparte revealed in Italy and in his negotiations with Austria astonishing diplomatic gifts, but he had much to learn from a Talleyrand who, through family tradition, had the manner and language of the old Courts, and who, through practice, was acquainted with their means of action and tendencies. For Bonaparte (who dreamed of reconciling the Past and the Future) Talleyrand (who owed his formation to the old régime and his position to the new one, who was in contact with all classes of society, and who had used all parties without being a slave to any) was an incomparable liaison agent inside and outside the country. In addition, the minister's interest which bound him to the general guaranteed the latter his devotion until further orders; his discretion encouraged him; his prudence reassured him; his tact and shrewdness charmed him; his high birth over-awed him and made his caresses more flattering. Bonaparte took a fancy to Talleyrand, somewhat for the same reasons which had had weight with him in Joséphine's case. His bosom friend—soon to be his accomplice—and his wife were both of them aristocrats by birth and, through their adventures, of the upper *demi-monde*. Politics had no more secrets for the one than love had for the other. Both instructed that indefatigable reader in those things—the most useful—which are not to be found in books. Between instructor and instructress Bonaparte contracted tastes and feelings which perhaps forearmed him against serious errors. In contrast with them the little Corsican became Gallicized and the General of Vendémi-aire,[1] who saved the Revolution by cannonading the reactionaries opposite the Church of St-Roch, "de-jacobinized" himself. We tremble at the thought of the catastrophes of which France would have been the victim if Bonaparte had chosen as a mentor the man who was then the most in view with Talleyrand—Sieyès, a Jacobin aggravated by philosophy, and, as his Egeria, Mme de Staël, a foreigner intoxicated with Germanism, but whose

[1] The first month of the French Republican calendar, from September 22 or 23 to October 21 or 22.—Translators' note.

repeated attacks were shattered against his conjugal passion. Talleyrand, older than Bonaparte, like his wife, was to become, on the political plane, his Joséphine, thanks to his greater experience. A union equally delightful at the beginning, then stormy and adulterous; for the minister was no more faithful than the wife. But he was less sterile. That union gave Bonaparte a child who was to have a splendid future and an illustrious posterity—the 18th of Brumaire.

Already their household held forth hopes, especially the one nearest the heart of France—the hope of peace. In the same way as Joséphine brought her husband nearer to the old nobility, Talleyrand sought to bring him closer to the ancient Courts, beginning with Austria, which was the Faubourg St-Germain of Europe. And Bonaparte had just concluded peace with her. In order to consolidate that peace and make it bear all its fruits, no one was better qualified than the Minister of Foreign Relations, who had been educated at the school of the old régime, the diplomacy of which was founded on the alliance with Austria.

At the solemn reception which the Directory gave Bonaparte, Talleyrand accentuated the word Peace. It was the signatory of the Campo-Formio Treaty they glorified. Talleyrand, Minister of Foreign Relations, was invited to introduce him preferably to the Minister of War, so as to throw into the shade as much as possible that military glory, the dread of the Government; that glory which it was necessary "not to extinguish, but to illumine and direct", as Barras expressed himself in his verbal instructions to Talleyrand, who replied, "I know what soldiers are, Citizen Director".

When the day came Talleyrand put on gala dress, expressive at one and the same time of his official and personal feelings: a tricolour costume with poppy-coloured trousers, jacket with blue lapels, the whole made of iridescent silk and, says a spectatress, "of changing colour". A sword at his side and on his head a black hat adorned with three flame-coloured feathers, he it was who rendered "to Bonaparte the honours of France and to France the honours of Bonaparte". Salvos of artillery followed (they could not quite forget that Bonaparte was a soldier), but moderated by an orchestra which played "the favourite airs of the Republicans" and by the choruses of the Conservatoire singing the "Chant du retour", a song with words by Chénier and music by Méhul in which the warriors were ranked with old men, bards and young girls, who, in the final stanza called on the soldiers to take their well-earned rest:

> Tu fus longtemps l'effroi; sois l'amour de la terre,
> O République des Français!
> Que le chant des plaisirs succède aux cris de guerre,
> La Victoire a conquis la paix.[1]

Before the altar of the Fatherland the former Bishop of Autun celebrated a laical Mass. Since the Festival of the Federation, when, before another altar, Talleyrand whispered to Lafayette, "Don't make me laugh ", he had learnt how to keep a serious face at all the political Punch and Judy shows. In a grave tone and strong voice he harangued Bonaparte, who, by bringing peace, "recalled, despite himself, the innumerable marvels which had produced so great an event". After this discreet allusion to his victory the orator added: "When I think of all he has done to obtain pardon for this glory, of that simplicity worthy of the ancients, of his love for abstract sciences, etc. etc., ah! far from fearing what people may call his ambition, I

[1] "O Republic of the French! long wast thou the terror, be now our love on earth. Let songs of pleasure replace thy warlike cries. Peace has come through Victory."

feel that it will perhaps some day be necessary for us to solicit him, in order to drag him from the charms of his studious retreat".

Bonaparte replied in a few very modest words. In his eyes true eloquence on that occasion resided elsewhere than in official speeches; it lay in the frenzied acclamations of the crowd which rose towards him—and him alone.

Having fêted Bonaparte publicly and by command, Talleyrand desired to fête him on his own account at a grand reception which he gave at the Ministry of Foreign Affairs. He knew that the surest way of touching his heart was to flatter Joséphine's vanity. So, faithful to his principle "to make women obey" he gave a fête in honour of "Madame Bonaparte". This was also an opportunity for him to show his patriotism. The invitation card bore the request—to which everybody conformed—to exclude from the toilettes everything which might come from England. This prince of cosmopolitanism was thus the first who gave the watchword: "Buy French Goods". And it was this future artisan of the English Alliance who, at supper-time, proposed a toast to the success of the invasion of England; that is to say, to the success of his guest, Bonaparte, who had just been appointed to the command of the "Ocean Army", prepared for the operation in question.

The luxury, good taste, and tact of the host made such an impression on Bonaparte that in his *Commentaries* at St. Helena, he recalled that fête. More than through the audacity of the new fashion for "veiled nudities" or through the grace of the new dance, "La Bonaparte", both of which were launched at that soirée, it was memorable on account of the meeting between the young general and Mme de Staël. Talleyrand attached less importance to services rendered than to those which were expected. He was not, therefore, disposed to compromise the latter by importuning his new friend to be agreeable to his former protectress, who, unable to count on him for an introduction, took the arm of a person of no importance and forced him, willy-nilly, to carry out her wish. It was her dream to form, with the emperor, a couple who would rule the world. Was Bonaparte not the only man on earth worthy of her, and was she not the only woman on earth worthy of him? He was dominated by ambition—just as she was; and like herself he possessed genius. Their souls were sisterly; their brains were fraternal. Disappointed over her liaisons with men less virile than herself, but a woman all the same, this female tyrant aspired to be dominated by someone. Tyrannical with Benjamin Constant—perhaps through vexation at not finding a master in him, or out of a desire to awaken a masterful spirit in the slave, by exasperating him—she sought a master in Bonaparte. Therefore she had no right to be offended when the general cut the conversation between them short by replying to her question, "Who, in your opinion, would be the first among women?" with the curt words, "She who bore the most children, Madame".

That affront, which a smile made less discourteous but all the more mortifying, caused not the slightest remorse to the host. Talleyrand considered that he owed nothing to the woman who had introduced him to Barras, since the services she rendered her friends were, above all, for her own benefit. Self-love was centred in them, and thereby she pushed herself to the front. One day Bonaparte asked him, "What sort of a woman is she?"—"An intriguer", replied Talleyrand; "and to such an extent that it is thanks to her I am here."—"She is, at any rate, a good friend?" inquired Bonaparte.—"A friend? She would throw her friends in the river, so as to fish them out afterwards with a line". The essential point, with Talleyrand, was not to cause the slightest displeasure to the master of the day.

At the same time he took care to be useful to him under all circumstances. On January 21 the Directory celebrated by a fête the anniversary of the execution of the Tyrant, Louis XVI. In his position above parties, the absence or the presence of Bonaparte would have been equally unseemly. Talleyrand found a solution: the general was present at the revolutionary show in his capacity as a member of the Institute—an anonymous spectator in the midst of his colleagues.

A fresh service of another order. After an inspection on the Channel coasts, the Commander of the "Ocean Army" discovered that England was more vulnerable elsewhere. During his absence Talleyrand, whose "Essay" on the colonies had suggested to Bonaparte the idea of the Egyptian expedition, completed several reports to prove to the Directory that, since Egypt commanded the road to India, it was there the most sensitive blows might be struck against our chief adversary. Cairo would be the shortest way, not from Paris to London, but from the former Rue Chantereine to the Luxembourg. It was under Talleyrand's auspices that Bonaparte embarked for the East, the cradle of the gods, of civilization, and of empires.

At the same period the General—who, after feeding the Government and enriching our museums with the *spolia opima* of Italy, was penniless—may have had recourse to Talleyrand's purse, only too happy as he was to establish that fresh title to Bonaparte's gratitude.[1] If that was so it

---

[1] At the time of the Egyptian expedition Talleyrand spontaneously lent Bonaparte ten thousand francs "needed to remove the obstacles placed in his way by secret enemies". See the *Mémoires de Mme Rémusat.*—Translators' note.

doubtless explains Napoleon's indulgence towards that taste for diplomatic "presents" which his minister was to retain after he had made his fortune.

During the Egyptian campaign the general-in-chief was, without doubt, kept acquainted with the situation in France by the man who, having staked on his good luck, had now become his trainer. It was through him, it is said, that he was informed "when the pear was ripe". It ripened quickly. Poverty and anarchy reigned at home, and many of the Departments were in a state of insurrection. There was also persecution of the Catholics, and a sort of neo-Terror was established owing to fear; fear of the basest kind, that of profiteers; the "rotters" who trembled at the idea of being obliged to relinquish their prey—France—and disgorge. The neo-Jacobins, sanguinary but with less fanaticism than the earlier type, were more abject and hypocritical. They did not re-establish the guillotine, but they deported their adversaries and brought them to their death through ill-treatment. They were a combination of cruelty, cowardice, and greed.

Abroad, the destruction of the French fleet by Nelson at Alexandria was the signal for a fresh Coalition. France lost the majority of her conquests and Alsace was threatened. The Directory, who saw the time drawing near for leaving the banqueting hall, was more engrossed over taking double mouthfuls than in beating the enemy. Amidst this state of rottenness the Empire germinated.

Brooded over by Talleyrand, who had nothing else to do, the Empire hatched on the 18th of Brumaire. Not being in the habit of waiting until the house came crash before leaving it, he had sent in his resignation on the pretext of violent newspaper attacks against his policy and person; campaigns which were doubtless encouraged by certain members of the Directory. He was especially exposed to the animosity of Rewbell, who called him "a powdered lackey of the old régime", while adding that he only lacked being "better legged". In playing tricks upon him he was pitiless. One day, in the presence of his colleagues, he put a number of questions to him and insisted on an immediate answer. The Minister of Foreign Relations excused himself as follows: "Citizen Director, I am not prepared, and even if I were I should not consider myself sufficiently strong to maintain any discussion with Citizen Director Rewbell, whom everybody recognizes as possessing the best head in Europe in diplomacy, as well as in administrative matters. I would, however, ask you to permit me to withdraw to the ministry to meditate there; and to-morrow I shall have the honour to bring you a satisfactory reply. As regards the things I know best, I need to reflect and be some moments alone."—"If you only need to be alone to fecundate your genius," replied Rewbell, "I'll supply you with a means of fecundating your genius." Whereupon the Director proceeded to shut Talleyrand up. But after an hour or so he liberated him and repeated his questions. Talleyrand remained calm and complained of having a headache. Then Rewbell dismissed him triumphantly with the words: "Off to bed with you, Basile; you are decidedly feverish".

Napoleon's friend was soon to have his revenge. Free, he was in a better position to serve him. He was on good terms with Sieyès, who had now placed Rewbell in the Directory, the president of which, in rotation, he had become, and who, during his recent embassy in Berlin, had had every reason to praise his minister. Now, Sieyès, of whom Talleyrand said, "he makes magnificent coats, but they never fit", was planning a Constitution and even thinking of applying it. This man of intellect, seeking an

rm and a sword, had fixed his choice on Joubert; he had
made him commander-in-chief of the army in Italy, where
e was to find an opportunity of distinguishing himself
nd strengthening his titles. But Joubert was defeated and
illed at Novi. To whom was the sword to be given?
Bonaparte had just landed at Fréjus. At the very moment
when the wear and tear of institutions gives individuals
heir chance and demands an appeal to a soldier, he
eached Paris as though to reply, "*Adsum!*" Sieyès and he
ot knowing each other, neither wished to take the step of
evealing himself to the other. So Talleyrand brought into
he business his rancour, ambition, tact, and social capital.
He established contact between Sieyès, the "tailor" of
onstitutions and "manufacturer" of strokes of policy in
tate affairs, and that serious customer, Bonaparte. He
resided over the tryings-on and suggested alterations.
The headquarters of this conspiracy were at his own
house in the Rue Taitbout. And there he distributed the
arts, without forgetting his companion, Mme Grant.[1]
He counted on her putting the emissaries of the Directory
n the wrong scent, which she did with reassuring can-
our, for she knew nothing. During one of the nights
receding the 18th of Brumaire, Talleyrand received a
visit from Bonaparte, who came to settle with him the
nal measures to be taken. Suddenly they exchanged an
nxious look. From the paving-stones of the street came
he clatter of a detachment of cavalry and it stopped op-
osite the door of the house. There could be only one

---

[1] Catherine Noël Worlhée (1762–1835), born in India at Tranque-
ar, then a Danish colony, who married Georges François Grant,
om whom she was divorced. She married Talleyrand on September
, 1802. See the memoirs of Mme de Rémusat, vol. ii. p. 183,
ose of Mme de Chastenay, vol. ii. p. 52, and Remacle's *Agents de
ouis XVIII*, p. 103. Also *The Recollections of Baron de Frénilly*, pp. 87,
n. 1, 153 (William Heinemann, 1909).—Translators' note.

explanation—they were about to be arrested by order o
the Directory! . . . Having blown out the candles they drew
near to a window, whence they saw the horsemen move
off and disappear. It was only a company of *gendarmes* who
were escorting the *cagnotte* (that portion of the stake
which is set aside for the authorities) of a number of the
gaming-houses of the Palais-Royal, and whose progress
had been impeded by a blockage of the traffic, due to
carriage accident. After having, perhaps, trembled, Bona
parte and Talleyrand burst into laughter. However, they
knew the Directory too well not to have felt the wind o
death blow past them. Both of them gamblers, they must
have seen in that nocturnal encounter with the Govern
ment *cagnotte* an invitation to precipitate the ending o
the great game in which they were engaged.

On the 18th, at dawn, Talleyrand was at the Rue de l
Victoire. He swore on a crucifix, it is said, to observe
secrecy regarding the decisions taken. In order to clear the
ground he was entrusted with the task of bringing about
the resignation of the most important Director after
Sieyès, namely Barras. Calling upon him at the Luxem
bourg, he urged him to withdraw provisionally, in his
own interest, in order to avoid any appearance of opposi
tion to Bonaparte. The principal scene was being played
in the wings. There could be heard the clamour of
crowd, the roll of drums, the sound of trumpets, an
cheering. And on opening the windows, behold the troop
placed under Bonaparte's command marching to the
Tuileries amidst the enthusiasm of the people! The argu
ment was so decisive that Talleyrand is alleged to have
kept to himself another argument with which Bonapart
had supplied him, to wit, a few millions intended as
recompense for Barras' disinterestedness. But, with tear
in his eyes, he kissed the Director's empty hands raptu

ously and thanked him in the name of the Country and Liberty. That evening he supped "at the house of an angel", that is to say, at the house of Mlle Lange, Barras' favourite. And a few days later he was once more Minister of Foreign Affairs.

Henceforth there existed between Bonaparte and Talleyrand the fraternity born of ambition, of risk and success, a fraternity which no rivalry poisoned, since these two stars played wholly different parts. In the prologue which governed the whole of the Napoleonic epic, Talleyrand played the leading part behind the scenes. Together they had conspired. For a few days there had been no secret between the one and the other, and neither one nor the other had had any sense of shame. When Bonaparte was crossing the Rubicon, it was Talleyrand who extended his hand and guided him towards the opposite shore. Between them there was at least one corpse, that of the Directory. Those are things which are not to be forgotten and which explain others. To those who are astonished at his forbearance towards Talleyrand's treason, Napoleon could have replied: "There was the 18th of Brumaire". At St Helena the two most sacred relics of Napoleon—those the sight of which brought tears to his eyes and made his heart beat faster—were two ringlets: one from the head of the King of Rome, the other from that of Joséphine. Despite his faults, despite the divorce, she remained his real wife, and his only mistress. She it was who revealed to him love. Talleyrand served his other passion, his passion for power. Despite everything, despite the divorce, after terrible household scenes, Talleyrand remained his master. Napoleon insulted him and cast him aside, but he did not succeed in shattering him. The first raptures he had felt on being all-powerful enchained him like those awakened by the voluptuous charm of

Joséphine. When, at St Helena, the fallen Emperor called to mind his honeymoon with France, he could not refrain from a certain feeling of indulgence towards his eminent go-between, Talleyrand, who in the meantime was playing the same part for others.

## CHAPTER VI

## TALLEYRAND AND THE EMPEROR

He signed his name to events; he did not bring them
about.                                    CHATEAUBRIAND

JOSÉPHINE initiated Bonaparte in the art of love and taught
him that which is often the same thing—resignation.
Talleyrand initiated him into power and desired to teach
him that which is often the condition of its duration—
moderation. Like Joséphine, who was a royalist, Talleyrand, who had been one, who was to become one again
as soon as it was to his interest, and who incarnated the
old régime through the Revolution, was to Bonaparte—
impatient as he was to base his personal power on national
reconciliation—a precious bond between parties and
classes, between the Past and the Future. Bonaparte, who
declared his solidarity with the whole of our history "from
Clovis to the Committee of Public Safety", and who
flattered himself on having raised the "French Party" on
the ruins of the factions; Bonaparte, who began with a
"succession of Edicts of Nantes", could not have found a
better collaborator. The former Bishop of Autun, having
lent himself to all parties without giving himself to a
single one, knew them sufficiently well to despise them,
and had always been too independent to fear them. He
had known how to be their accomplice without remaining
their prisoner. He embraced the "French party" with all
the more ardour because he identified it with his own
interests. In order to remain faithful to the one, he told

himself, and especially to the other, he would separate himself from Napoleon when he judged that the imperial cause and national cause were irreconcilable. Meanwhile he had another claim to the confidence of the First Consul: temperamentally and professionally he was a man of peace. Now, Bonaparte, suitor for the hand of France, wished to add to the wedding-presents, in addition to peace at home, that peace abroad which she desired no less ardently. On that account the choice of Talleyrand as Minister of Foreign Relations was a programme. It was an olive-branch held out to Europe. Again like Joséphine, but more efficaciously, Talleyrand was to be associated with the stages of a prodigious ascent. Napoleon was to see in him, as in her, a sort of mascot, with, later, a slight feeling of fascinated aversion.

Talleyrand left nothing undone in order to strengthen through inclination that union, already justified by reason. He realized the paradox of imposing upon Bonaparte by his impassibility and of conquering him by his sensibility. We know nothing of his effusions in private and secret conversations, but we can guess their fervour by that of his correspondence, where, however, it must have been moderated through a fear of ridicule and through prudence. Now, his letters, in which flattery is enveloped with solicitude, abound with tender and even impassioned expressions which, coming from Joséphine's pen, would have intoxicated Bonaparte. Before Marengo he wrote to him: "I dare to say that your absence being still prolonged, I should not only feel the desire to be near you but I should feel an urgent need". And after Marengo there is this compliment which contains the double perfume of adulation and temptation: "Under what auspices your return is promised us! No empire has been established save on the marvellous, and in this case the marvellous is reality."

When the Minister of Foreign Affairs went to Bourbon l'Archambault for his annual cure, the separation was heart-rending. He resigned himself to it (he wrote to Bonaparte) only because his health was necessary to serve him the better; and he concluded his letter as follows: "Permit me to repeat that I love you, that I am most impatient to return to you, and that only with life will my devotion end". During his cure he was more preoccupied over the health of the General—whom he affected to believe was suffering—than over his own. "I cannot bear the idea of seeing sorrow draw near to you, first of all because I love you and then . . . I don't like your library—you remain in it too long, you who were for the heights." Having been offered a candidature for the Senate by one of the Departments, he declined it because he intended to owe nothing to anyone save Napoleon. That was love. Nay, even adoration. When communicating to the Emperor more or less well-founded rumours of a plot to kill him, he wrote: "It is essential that Your Majesty should know everything; and who can have the courage to say it to him if not those who adore him?"

However, we do not say everything to beings whom we adore, especially when that adoration is not disinterested. In the worship he rendered his idol, the ex-Bishop of Autun did not reveal certain mysteries of the vestry. Secrets were connected with his coquetry. For instance, he did not tell Napoleon how he acted to give him the impression of indefatigable zeal (for he sometimes did show zeal) and of perspicacity never in default. In his room at the ministry, in the Rue du Bac—where he kept near him a little strumpet who was expert in the art of sealing letters— his bosom friends sometimes surprised him in a strange reversal of their rôles. Faithful to the principle that, in order to retain his intellectual liberty the minister ought never to undertake jobs which could be done by subordinates, Talleyrand drew up few documents, and himself wrote still less. So as not to have the appearance of being his own secretary, this great nobleman is said to have dictated a few notes from which his "hacks" took inspiration when interpreting his thoughts in the official style. But he resigned himself to be the secretary of his secretaries when, under their dictation, he copied out a report intended to be placed under the Emperor's eyes. Likewise, when the Emperor rendered homage to the astounding accuracy of his foresight, his minister did not tell him that, by an artifice worthy of an extra-lucid clairvoyant, he purchased the breach of faith of foreign couriers, who thus supplied him with the substance of his prophecies.[1] On the other hand, when the First Consul's brother-in-law, Leclerc, was killed during the San Domingo expedition, Talleyrand did not leave him in ignorance of the fact that if the diplomatic corps wore mourning at his receptions it was in accordance with the suggestion of the minister himself, who, however, displayed as much disdain for the foreign representatives as he did respect for the master of the day. "If I have any difficulty," he said, "it will be to prevent them having hired mourners." In addition to being a director of mourning, Talleyrand was also an organizer of pleasures, which he

[1] Referring to Talleyrand's fine perception of character and of the indications of coming change, Macaulay wrote: "Neither Theramenes in ancient, nor Talleyrand in modern times, had a finer perception of all the peculiarities of character, and of all the indications of coming change, than some of our countrymen in that age. Their power of reading things of high import; in signs which to others were invisible or unintelligible, resembled magic. But the curse of Reuben was upon them all: 'Unstable as water, thou shalt not excel'." See the essay on Sir William Temple, and for other references to Talleyrand the essays on Hallam's *Constitutional History* and on Lord Holland.—Translators' note.

arranged in such a way as to serve political ends. A perfect host—and one who was then unique, inasmuch as no other had such fine manners and so much money, this upstart of the old régime gave magnificent fêtes, which, forming part of a vast rallying-plan, marked all the more progress for that "French party" which the First Consul strove to assemble around him. It was on those occasions that the majority of the noblemen who were to become his chamberlains were introduced. There, too, that for the first time he met the members of the Bourbon family. By bringing Bonaparte, the members of the Revolution, and the *émigrés* around the supper-table Talleyrand smoothed the highway to the Empire.

The "Grey Eminence"[1] of the 18th of Brumaire, Talleyrand played the same part during the succession of *coups d'état* which were soon to raise Bonaparte to the summit of power. Having divined the immensity of his ambition, he applied himself to the task of exploiting it to the profit of his own. Of the three consuls whom he named *Hic, Haec, Hoc* (masculine for Bonaparte, feminine for Cambacérès, and neuter for Lebrun), he desired to know only *Hic*, the sole male element in the triumvirate. He wished to work only with Bonaparte, and so advised him to occupy his two colleagues with judicial and administrative affairs, and to reserve government for himself. Bonaparte was thankful to him for a piece of advice which corresponded with his own secret thoughts. "He is a man of great understanding", he said. "He is quite right: one can walk quicker when alone." At the first opportunity Talleyrand suggested to him a means of finishing with the survivals of parliamentarism and of organizing absolute power: the withdrawal from the Tribunate, where the opposition had

[1] "*L'Éminence grise*" was Père Joseph de Tremblay, the Councillor of Richelieu.—Translators' note.

taken refuge, of the knowledge of delicate questions and their submission to the Senate, whose complacence was boundless. This was the institution of the Senatus-Consultum, a sort of Decree-Law (or Order in Council), much more a decree than a law, since the "Upper Chamber" was at the orders of the Executive. The best manner of obtaining all rights was to legalize despotism. The Senatus-Consultum, an instrument invented by Talleyrand, permitted, by means of improving the Republican Constitution, its suppression until the day when the Senate, ever faithful to itself, was to beat its own record for baseness by declaring the dethronement of the vanquished Napoleon.

Anxious to consolidate the advantages acquired through the new régime, Talleyrand was not content, on Bonaparte's behalf, with the Consulate, which was first of all decennial and then, from 1802, for life. If he were killed in war (he had already had a narrow escape), if he were the victim of an outrage (there had already been several), what would become of France? asked Talleyrand. And, said he to himself, what would become of my endowments? The salvation of the State and that of its most faithful servants necessitated the guarantee of heredity. The Minister of Foreign Affairs made himself its champion, notwithstanding the one chiefly interested, who, being childless, preferred to sweep aside the idea of death and not have to choose an heir in a family already insupportable and which would then become impossible. Talleyrand inspired the municipalities with the idea of addresses in favour of heredity. He declared himself in favour of the title of Emperor as being more military than that of King, exempt from the discredit which this had in the eyes of republicans, more humiliating for the execrable Habsburgs, and more in conformity with Bonaparte's cult for ancient Rome, as well as with the extent of his conquests and dreams. But the humbug who was ever awake in him entrusted Berthier to propose the title of King to Bonaparte, who forthwith treated him as an imbecile. When, on May 18, 1804, the day on which the Empire was proclaimed by Senatus-Consultum, according to the system he had imagined and following on the campaign of petitions he had inspired, Talleyrand rushed to St-Cloud to congratulate Napoleon and display marks of the most profound respect, the descendant of the Comtes de Périgord doubtless thought that if the protocol had only permitted it, that would have been a good occasion to transpose the legendary reproach of his distant ancestor to Hugues Capet by saying to his august master, "Who made thee Emperor?"

In 1812, when they detested each other, Napoleon confessed to Caulincourt: "Talleyrand was one of those who contributed the most to the establishment of my dynasty". In the early years he also contributed to strengthen it. Having, until fresh orders, bound his future to the new régime, he strove to stabilize it and encouraged Napoleon, in accordance with his own words, "to cast anchor". He had approved of the creation of the Legion of Honour, a levelling distinction, since it is accessible up to its highest grades to all citizens, assures the recruitment of an *élite* from the masses, bestows upon the nation a moral framework, not a social class, thus respecting the principles of the Revolution while "cleansing it from stain", as Napoleon boasted of doing. According to a saying worthy of Talleyrand, it was "the Phrygian cap cut into little bits" with which to supply honour within the reach of all the virtues. When, later, still to stimulate merit by rewarding it, Napoleon by an extension of heredity added to the moral framework of the Legion of Honour the social framework of a new nobility, Talleyrand, on being consulted, gave his commendation. Was not the institution democratic when it was represented as destined to "uproot" the old nobility? Was it not even demagogic, since Napoleon justified it by his desire "to give lustre to the best of the nation"? And did not Napoleon, adding example to precept, wish that his first duke should be the most "common" of his marshals, Lefebvre, Duc de Dantzig, whose wife had been a washerwoman? In Talleyrand's eyes the new nobility was a useful *savonnette à vilains*,[1] for it attached them to a new régime. It added nothing to his consideration for those bedizened upstarts who, he said, "knew not how to walk properly on a parquet". It in no way deprived him of the consideration he had for himself, or for his own titles, which he considered were superior to those of the old *and* the new nobility, since he prided himself on belonging to a dynasty anterior to that of the Bourbons.

When Bonaparte let go that most powerful anchor of societies, the anchor of religious peace, Talleyrand put his hands to the rope, but not until the end.

A strange spectacle, displaying a lesson in tolerance which should never have been lost: the altars raised up again by a Government composed of a military philosopher, in the irreligious sense of the word, the most absolute leader that France has ever had—therefore naturally hostile to the Church, which at first appeared to him as the limit and the bridle of the State—and of two ministers, the only ones who counted: Talleyrand, an exbishop, and Fouché, an ex-priest of the Oratory, the more apostate of the two, although he had not been ordained, for the other had abandoned God without abjuring Him

[1] An expression formerly applied, disparagingly, to those offices which were purchased to ennoble the holders. Literally: "villeins' soap-ball".—Translators' note.

and bore Him no grudge. In religious matters his natural tolerance, strengthened by his sojourn in the United States, agreed with his political judgment in order that he might become a sincere collaborator of the First Consul, so long as it was merely a question of reopening the churches, of putting an end to the persecution of refractory priests, of reconciling all Frenchmen by reassuring all consciences, of turning to the advantage of the State, which might find there a support still more than a limit, the immense force of a moral ideal, of social order, and of even military discipline which the teaching of Christ and Catholic organization had accumulated for centuries past. But when it was a question of liquidating, by negotiations with the Holy See, the schism created by the civil constitution of the clergy, and of regulating, by a Concordat, the relations between Church and State, Talleyrand, who was not in the habit of forgetting himself, feared the consequences as regards his personal situation. However, in the presence of the open conflict between the parish priests who, having taken the oath, were in possession of the churches and those who had not sworn but who retained the confidence of the faithful, liberty did not suffice to establish a religious peace. This conflict, which was a cause of anarchy and presented the danger of civil war, was insoluble without the assistance of Rome. On the other hand, a Concordat had to decide regarding those priests who had abandoned the ecclesiastical state and married. That was centring attention on the most glaring case of all, that of Talleyrand, Minister of Foreign Relations, and, in that quality, the negotiator of the Concordat. When scandal is general, particular scandals no longer exist. Talleyrand, who enjoyed that immunity, was perfectly aware that it was incompatible with the restoration of discipline. He was not yet married. Either because he felt that he was destined to be married some day, or because he wished to be admitted to the lay communion without any reserve, he did everything to obtain that result, and to such a degree that the fate of the Concordat appeared to be dependent upon that of his personal concordat—upon what an ecclesiastical historian has called "the Madame Grant clause".

The Holy See having suppressed in the project submitted to it the article relating to married ecclesiastics, Talleyrand strove to oppose and even wreck the negotiations.

Seeking for peace with Austria and England, he concluded it, they said, on land and sea, but not in Heaven. Assimilating the wives of ecclesiastics with national estates, he declared that the consecration of the one was of as much importance to public peace as the consecration of the other. The instructions he sent to Rome were impregnated with a Gallicism which exceeded that of Bossuet. He laid a trap for the Curia by proposing, so as to bring about liberty of choice and an appeasing mixture of the two elements, that both those prelates who had emigrated and constitutional bishops be invited to resign their seats. This was another assimilation in which he sought from the Pope a tacit absolution which Napoleon himself did not fully grant, since he wished "to surround the constitutional riff-raff with real priests".

Nevertheless the Concordat was signed on July 15, 1801. The question which interested Talleyrand the most was not mentioned in it. Affecting the interior discipline of the Church, it was not a subject for negotiations with the civil authority. Despite all the entreaties of the First Consul and his minister, the Pope, with inflexible gentleness, maintained his *non possumus*. However, a month later, by a brief which was an act of his sovereign clemency, Pius VII absolved the members of the secular clergy who had married, but the benefit was extended neither to the regular clergy nor to the bishops, who were considered to be bound to duties more rigorous than those of simple priests. Their marriage was a bigamous act since they were spouses of the Church.

Talleyrand soon returned to the charge. Not having been able to enter the fold with the flock of stray sheep, he negotiated for his secularization as an individual. Special treatment, he said, was indeed due to the minister who, after having, through the part he took in the civil constitution of the clergy, been the principal author of the schism, had done more than anyone else to repair it, and who retained, thanks to his ascendancy over Bonaparte, so many means of serving the Church or harming it. On the occasion of this second campaign he mobilized canon law and ecclesiastical history to find arguments and precedents in support of his cause. He mobilized Mme Grant, whom he placed at official dinners next to the papal nuncio, but who received from him merely commonplace marks of courtesy. He mobilized the First Consul, who threw himself into the controversy as though it were a battle, with an impetuosity which indeed bore witness to the favour his Minister of Foreign Affairs then enjoyed. Doubtless the faithful were scandalized to see the man who had re-established religious peace retain an outlawed bishop as his principal collaborator. But that was only one more anomaly in a situation in which almost everything was unprecedented.

There was no proportion between that paradox and the trouble the First Consul gave himself to put an end to it. In his correspondence with the Curia, the nuncio Capara pointed out "the extraordinary importance which Bonaparte attached to it". In his eyes it was "a State affair". He vouched for his minister's repentance. Talleyrand addressed to the Holy See a humble and prudent petition, in Latin—humble since he begged the Pope's pardon for the very serious errors of his past, *erribus gravissimis a se commissis*; prudent, since he did not mention marriage, but confined himself to requesting the grace of absolution and, what was the essential point for him, the annulling of his vows. The Pope replied by a brief which was a model of gentleness and earnestness; he sent him his apostolic benediction, but laid down such conditions that the nuncio judged it preferable not to communicate anything to Talleyrand. The First Consul grew impatient, wrote personally to the Pope renewing his entreaties, and, to show that the secularization of his minister was indeed a State affair, instructed his representative at the Holy See, Cacault, to take it in hand. At the same time he sent him instructions prepared by Talleyrand, and in which were cited all the favourable precedents regarding secularization from the origins of the Church, including the period of the Borgias, which was not perhaps very opportune. Simultaneously, Talleyrand stimulated the zeal of the nuncio by caressing and threatening him alternately. Having recalled all he had done and could still do in the interest of the Church, he pointed to the ruin of religion in France and in all countries under its influence should Rome persist in what he called its uncompromising policy. At a reception at the Tuileries, the First Consul, primed by his minister, resumed the same thesis in a conversation with the nuncio and gave him a lesson in ecclesiastical history in order to prove to him that they were not asking anything exceptional. Caprara acquiesced, smiled, gave his promise in Paris, moaned and supplicated in Rome. "The protectors of religion and the Church have been the First Consul and M. de Talleyrand. But if the latter is rebuffed, for what can we hope?"

To the Holy See principles were more sacred than they were to Talleyrand. Its attitude, which united suppleness with firmness and benevolence with dignity, aggravated the impropriety of the pressure brought to bear upon it. Animated with the greatest spirit of conciliation, it was disposed towards all concessions compatible with its essential duties; but it refused to bow down before the exigencies of power when these wounded the Christian conscience; a power, in its eyes, superior to all the powers on earth. Not one of the precedents quoted by Talleyrand being valid, the Pope did not authorize Talleyrand to get married. But in his long-deliberated reply this point was passed over in silence, so as to spare his susceptibilities. The Pope confined himself to taking note of his submission to the Holy See and to welcoming him in "the communion of the laity". However, to ward against an abusive interpretation of this silence, the Pope added to his brief a letter to the First Consul—a letter written in Italian, in order to give it a more personal character. While rendering homage to the services which Talleyrand had rendered religion in France, he expressed regret at not being able to satisfy "his desire to take a wife", the laws of the Church being opposed to this; laws which, during eighteen centuries, had not suffered a single derogation. The Pope's delicacy, if understood, went unrewarded. Doubtless because his letter was of a personal character. Officially, the First Consul took no notice of it. By his order the negotiations were completed ambiguously. The papal briefs not being allowed, by virtue of organic laws, circulation in France without the authorization of the Government, the First Consul requested the Council of State to register the one concerning Talleyrand. On the following day the *Bulletin des Lois* published a consular decree declaring that the papal brief by which citizen

Charles Maurice Talleyrand, Minister of Foreign Relations, was restored to secular and laical life *would have its full and entire effect*. The public was so thoroughly convinced by this extensive formula that even the higher ranks of the French clergy shared its error. The nuncio would not have dared to dispel it and the censor took good care not to allow the rectifications published by Rome in the foreign gazettes to filter through.

Thus it arose that Monseigneur d'Aviau, Archbishop of Bordeaux, wrote: "Talleyrand is divested of orders and de-mitred; so he may marry". Moreover, in 1814 it was the Holy See itself which, over the same question, set the example of ambiguity, but in favour of Talleyrand and even of Mme Grant. The latter, on becoming civilly Princesse de Talleyrand, got the Prince to hand a letter to Cardinal Consalvi, who represented the Pope at the Congress of Vienna. Was this not a trap? Did not the Princess flatter herself, in connivance with her husband, that she would occasion a reply which would complete the brief of 1802, be brought to light and perhaps published triumphantly  This was a cruel perplexity for the Secretary of State, who was on the best of terms with Talleyrand, and who occupied, thanks to him, a place of honour at the Congress. Silence was an affront, courtesy an imprudence, orthodoxy a provocation. Consalvi asked for instructions Cardinal Pacca replied: "Write to Mme de Talleyrand— only, do not let the address be in your own handwriting do not seal the letter with your arms; and in that way no one will have the right to say that you approve of the name and title borne by this lady". Talleyrand, who had become a minister of His Most Christian Majesty, had right to attentions in the present and in the future. He also had that right as regards the past, at any rate for a part of that past. The Holy See did not forget that the former

Bishop of Autun, who had consecrated constitutional bishops, had since then rendered great services to religion, as much in Italy as in France, and that, in spite of everything, he was the negotiator of the Concordat, the only one of the constitutions which lasted more than a century from the time of the fall of the monarchy.

The former Bishop of Autun, on becoming Minister of Foreign Relations, was qualified to compare and settle the respective points of view of the Church and civilian society. When Bonaparte, surpassing Charlemagne, imperiously asked the Pope to come and crown him at Notre Dame, Talleyrand made himself the advocate of a project against which the cardinals raised strong objections. The journey *ad limina* in a contrary direction exposed Pius VII to the appellation "the Chaplain of the Emperor of the French". Was it expedient to bring the Holy Father into the presence of a minister who had profaned his sacred character by contracting the bonds of marriage? In his despatches Talleyrand enumerated all Napoleon's titles to the gratitude of the Holy See; and among those titles figured the recession of Benevento by the kingdom of Naples. When the Pope came to be deprived of it in favour of Talleyrand, it was still the Pope who ought to be grateful. "That was in order to pacify Italy", the minister was to write to Cardinal Consalvi. Service was rendered the Holy See by suppressing that bone of contention with the kingdom of Naples. It was the old story of the oyster and the suitors over again. When the Pope's journey was decided upon, Talleyrand advised the Holy See "to bring for the ladies a multitude of rosaries". And, doubtless, in his mind Mme Grant was one of those ladies. However, Pius VII laid down as a condition of his journey "that he should not be introduced to that dame". Nevertheless Talleyrand, Minister of Foreign Relations and Grand

Chamberlain, paid the honours of Fontainebleau to the august visitor. The sight of that notorious "infidel" was doubtless more painful to him than that of the Mamelukes which the Emperor supplied as his escort. This was a splendid opportunity for Talleyrand of establishing a fresh record—that of coronations. After having assisted at the coronation of Louis XVI, he played his part at the coronation of Napoleon, before playing another at that of Charles X: in all, four coronations, counting that of the Revolution at which he had himself presided when celebrating the Champ de Mars Mass at the Festival of the Federation.

This quick-change actor played still another part in a vaudeville which formed a prelude to the liturgical pageantry in Notre Dame. On the eve of the great day, in the course of the first visit the Pope paid Joséphine, she confessed to him that she was not married according to the rites of religion. After this confession, made in view of another sacrament, the scenario proceeded as she foresaw it would: refusal to crown her on the following day unless her case was immediately set right; ultimatum from the Holy See to the furious but disarmed Emperor; and the celebration—*in extremis* and clandestinely—of that "forced marriage" in the private chapel of the Château by Uncle Fesch, with Talleyrand and Berthier as witnesses.

After being a witness of the marriage, the ex-Bishop of Autun was to be one of the originators of the divorce. He advised it, just as he advised the proclamation of the Empire, and for the same reason. What was the good of the principle of heredity if there were no heir? Heredity did not suffice to consolidate Napoleon's conquests and the gains acquired by his minister, especially as the Emperor's life was at the mercy of an attempt upon it, or of a mere accident on the battlefield. Once more an "anchor" was let down. On the present occasion it was a double anchor—one for time, in the hope of a son; the other for more elbow room, in the hope of the Austrian alliance, which, it was believed, would guarantee peace on the Continent and overawe England. At the Council meeting of January 21, 1810, which deliberated on the subject of the choice of a wife, Talleyrand doubtless repressed a smile when Napoleon said that, if he had only been able to follow his own inclinations, it would have been among the young pupils of the Legion of Honour, among the daughters of the heroes of France that he would have chosen his companion. That would have made a most magnificent Epinal colour-print. But Talleyrand, in agreement with the one most interested, conceived a great historical picture. Its subject was not Napoleon's marriage with France—already consummated and renewed every time that, by an almost unanimous referendum, the nation threw itself into his arms—but the marriage of Napoleon, who was the Revolution personified, with Legitimacy, and, through it, with Europe, a Europe of kings reigning by Divine Right. That was, as it were, a second coronation specially for foreign consumption, and it was also an absolution which, to be complete, could be given by Austria alone. Such for France were the winnings of the game when the new Empress, having barely arrived, made her first appearance at the whist table, as Napoleon remarked, with two regicides, Cambacérès and Fouché. The hand of that Austrian lady, who was supposed to be a messenger of peace, effaced the blood of the other Austrian, whom they made responsible for the war and the blood of Louis XVI. "Oh, that I were my grandson!" exclaimed Napoleon when, at the summit of his glory, he aspired to the duration of his dynasty. Behold him, on entering the Habsburg family, at least on a level with the Bourbons, and on becoming the nephew by marriage of Louis XVI and Marie Antoinette, who, godfather and godmother of Marie Louise (whose name was composed of theirs), appeared to be those also of her august husband.

Another reason put forward by Talleyrand to justify the preference given to an Archduchess rather than to a Grand Duchess was that Austria was the only power which was capable of continuity. Its Government was a Cabinet, dominated by the interests of the State, whose policy survived the sovereign. The Government of Russia was a Court whose policy was as inconstant as the intrigues and passions which ruled it. When a Tsar died, the event was a revolution; when the Emperor of Austria died, it was only an occasion for mourning. However, at St Helena, when the dying Emperor dictated to Montholon his last wishes, he addressed the following supreme advice to his son: "That he should look for a Princess of Russia, the only Court where family bonds dominated politics". The fate of the Aiglon—his Eaglet—made clear to the disabused son-in-law of the Emperor Francis that State interest—and under its most cruel aspect—which Metternich incarnated at Vienna, where the State had ever dominated family bonds. As far as he was concerned, his marriage with Marie Louise had been a means to an end—grandeur and the domination of the world; in the eyes of the Viennese Court it was the thin end of the wedge leading to revenge. On the one side, a glorious solution; on the other, a shameful manœuvre. Marie Louise was offered to Napoleon, wrote the Prince de Ligne, "as one sacrifices a fine heifer to Minotaur". Above all things, gain time; neutralize the adversary while awaiting a better opportunity. To Napoleon, Marie

Louise was a lightning-conductor. And she was indeed that, but for the sake of Austria. That was what Talleyrand had foreseen. "By passing the nuptial ring through the monster's nose", he pulled it in his own direction. "My secret motive", he confessed in his memoirs, which are sincere as far as that point is concerned, "was that the preservation of Austria depended on the step the Emperor was going to take." The preservation of Austria; that was, then, the trump card in Talleyrand's hands. Above all, in that matrimonial affair, was he anxious not to rupture his marriage with Fortune.

It was perhaps through the part he played in Marie Louise's marriage that Talleyrand had the greatest influence on the foreign policy of the Empire: a transient and limited influence, which did not turn that course of events, which was stronger than mankind, which at the most slackened it, but not without deviating a part of it from his own mill. On the whole, Chateaubriand's words, "He signed his name to events; he did not bring them about", are correct. On the other hand, as regards home politics, we have seen that this Minister of Foreign Relations did bring about the most important events without signing his name to them. The greatest diplomatist of his time could not display all he was capable of doing in the presence of the greatest conqueror of all time. In those days, peace, even when it was not signed on a drum, was always dictated by the sword. Treaties were promulgated rather than negotiated. They were imperial decrees, the diplomatic form of which was derisive, the "high contracting parties", save one, always the same until its downfall, being merely capitulating parties. Talleyrand conducted those negotiations but did not direct them. Those labours were not his work, for the plan, traced by fatality, escaped him and nothing remained of it apart from results absolutely contrary to those for which Napoleon and his ministers were seeking.

Talleyrand's activity during that period appears in a mass of documents exceedingly interesting from a technical and even an historical point of view, but without any connection with his rôle as a constructor, which only began after the fall of the Empire, and perhaps without any connection with his inmost thoughts. Those official despatches were not acts, action being reserved for soldiers; they were not opinions, for they reflect a conformism which, especially under a régime of absolute power, was the administrative equivalent for the instinct of preservation; they were, therefore, hardly anything more than attitudes commanded by that instinct. Private letters, even the most intimate in appearance, were often nothing more than that. In connivance or not with the receivers they were indited with a view to their communication to third parties, so as to produce immediately, or at the right time, such or such a useful effect: a test, an alibi, a feigned and flattering adhesion, or a bait for confidences. They constituted what fencers call a feint.

Talleyrand who, in his celebrated portrait of the perfect Minister of Foreign Affairs, painted him with "the faculty of showing himself open whilst remaining impenetrable, of being reserved but with all the appearance of openheartedness", made use of everything—even friendship and even love—to attain political ends. It was his own portrait he was painting when he added: "He must not cease for a moment, during the twenty-four hours, to be the Minister of Foreign Affairs".

Talleyrand did better than that; he did not cease to be effectively the minister when he no longer held the post officially.

When—in semi-disgrace—he was replaced by the honest Champagny, who "was acquainted with the practice of diplomacy, but did not know its secrets", he transformed his dismissal into promotion, raised himself to the position of a super-minister who abandons trifles—mere detail work—to a subordinate, in order to devote himself wholly to great politics. Minister or not, he was above all the man of ambition who must never for a moment cease to be one. In that double capacity, Talleyrand, the spurious idler for tactical reasons and out of coquetry, one who converted his indolence into a weapon and a charm, was never wholly at rest. Feline-like, he always slumbered with one eye open. This great nobleman considered that he was on the decline if he became congested over scribbled paper. The slightest effort was to him an inelegance, smacking of the plebeian. But he worked all the time, while playing among men and women; he worked even during his "distractions", which—it is still he who tells us this—the perfect minister must choose skilfully. We may, without temerity, conclude that he remained faithful to that method when penning his familiar notes and that the sincerity of his correspondence suffers from it. Nothing is more easy than to make him appear in contradiction, not with himself, but with one of his numerous rôles. Nothing is more unjust than to overwhelm him by taxing him with incoherence, since his most divergent remarks converge towards his own interests. Nothing is more vain than to wish to discover political thoughts in texts where there are, above all, personal and ulterior designs, *ad usum delphini*, the dolphin—that constellation of the Northern Hemisphere—being indifferently Napoleon, the Emperor of Russia, the Emperor of Austria, Metternich, or the future Louis XVIII. He himself did not always discern it. When the objective was too distant to be visible, his shooting was guess-work; when that objective was too dispersed to be aimed at, he fired so as to cover a fixed zone and the entire field of possibilities.

If, incessantly watching over himself, he did not reveal—even in his effusions—those wholly calculating thoughts of his, we nevertheless know what this thought was, for it became a doctrine. After having formulated it in 1792 he applied it in 1815 and in 1830. It was the doctrine of peace by means of an equilibrium—a Continental balance of power by means of an alliance with England, without prejudice to an alliance with Austria—that is to say, alliance with the two most conservative Powers. Such a programme not being compatible with that of the Revolution and the Empire—which had only one programme, for the Empire, especially as regards its foreign policy, was "the executor of the Revolution"—he put it to sleep, under the reserve of reawakening it discreetly when he believed in the possibility of being able to announce its realization. But, having no taste for useless sacrifices and battles lost in advance, he did not feel disposed to wage them in order to try to impose his programme. Even in his moderation he showed a sparing spirit, and we cannot but admire the uncompromising nature of his opportunism. Was not that the surest means of being mindful of the future—his own future, but also that of his doctrine?

He extended to politics the following maxim of an Oratorian, Père Thomassin, whom he quoted during the Concordat negotiations: "Nothing is more in conformity with canons than their violation when the result is a greater benefit than that arising from their strict observance". He had no remorse when violating his principles so as to safeguard himself as their defender.

In the early years he worked without reserve for a

PBdQ3
Survey

eace which Napoleon desired no less ardently than he
did. Already at the time of the Directory it was the conqueror who was pacific. Politicians wished to prolong
the war, since it kept generals at a distance and brought in,
through taxation, more than it cost. From the point of
view of the orthodox revolutionary, these "rotters" were
as pure as crystal. Fierce "die-hards", they demanded the
deposition of the Habsburgs and the proclamation of a
republic at Vienna. In order to calm them down, Bonaparte threatened to resign. Later, on becoming Emperor,
he was to say to Fox, before the rupture of the Peace of
Amiens, "Those who would rekindle war between Euro-
peans, members of the same family, desire civil war", an
utterance reproduced since then in many a pacifist speech
but without mentioning its author. Nothing was more
sincere and more natural than this aspiration of Napoleon
towards peace. He judged it as necessary for the stability
of his power as for the prosperity of France. His pride
accorded with his reason in order to demand it. Peace was
to allow him to display all his gifts and accomplish his
destiny to the full. The strongest ambition is when
talents are felt before they have been yet satisfied. A commander-in-chief with a capacity for becoming the head of
a State, he aimed at adding the glory of a conqueror to
that of an empire-builder. A great actor, he took a delight
in playing all the leading parts which were within his
range, in showing the public that his compass was as
extensive as it was brilliant. "I have had enough", he said,
"of the profession of a general. I am going to resume that
of a Prime Minister, and once more turn my attention to
my great business reviews."

In the eyes of Talleyrand, a professor in the art of
moderation, Napoleon was not therefore a bad pupil. If he
profited only slightly by his lessons, that was due less to

his inner demon than to an exterior fatality. He was the
prisoner of his origin. They had raised him to the throne
in order to defend the conquests of the Revolution; civil
and military conquests. Between the nation and himself
there was a pact sealed by the most solemn oath, on the
gospel, on the day of his coronation at Notre Dame. His
fate was bound up with that of France's natural frontiers
which he had sworn to preserve. He knew full well that
the return of France to her old frontiers meant the return
of the Bourbons. Now, as regards those conquests,
Europe would never sincerely recognize them. During
the Revolution and the Empire all the peace treaties
were merely truces, stratagems of war—a unique war.
Napoleon was both its hero and its victim; he was not the
responsible author. For the Republic declared and imposed that war on Europe, a war of revolutionary propaganda, the logical conclusion of which was to be the
establishment of a universal monarchy. At that price only
was victory to be definitive. During that period history
did not recommence, for it was unprecedented; but it
engendered. From the day on which a Minister of Foreign
Affairs, Delessart, was imprisoned and then massacred by
the Republic because he wished for peace, until the final
catastrophe, the succession of events was implacable. The
germ of Waterloo was not at Austerlitz but at Valmy. In
order to guard Belgium and the left bank of the Rhine,
Holland must be dominated and England more completely alienated. So as to neutralize her natural ally on the
Continent, Austria, they must dominate both Germany
and Italy. But that was not sufficient to conquer England,
entrenched on her island, "a fortress raised by Nature";
England, which possessed a double dominion—the sea and
subsidies. Hence the necessity for a Continental blockade,
a gigantic manœuvre to ruin her commerce and starve her

out: an illusory manœuvre, unless the whole of the
European states, from Portugal to Russia and including
the states of the Pope and the Grand Turk, were united.
But in that case it was an impossible and dangerous manœuvre, bound to end in a coalition of all nations, not
against England, but against France. Thus the orgies of
Liberty developed into an orgy of blood in the struggle
between two tyrannies: the tyranny of Napoleon on land,
and on the sea the tyranny of England—another form of
universal monarchy, that of Commerce; easier to defend
because less visible, and easier to support because it
affects only interests while striving to consolidate them;
whereas the Grand Army, having conscription and immortal principles in its baggage, was a menace to body
and soul.

To that advantage England could add another after
Trafalgar, the advantage of being able to rule the waves
more completely than Napoleon had ruled on the
Continent.

This huge war was essentially a duel between two
besieged strongholds. On the one side England, more or
less closely blockaded on her island; on the other, France
with her natural frontiers, who, in order to protect them,
was ever multiplying glacis and exterior fortifications
beyond her advance guards. Vassal states, feudatory
kingdoms, protectorates, such was the character of the
dependencies of France which bastioned the French Empire, face to face with England. In addition there were the
custom-house stations to keep an eye on the blockade.
Napoleon stretched the circle of investment to the very
confines of Asia without being able to break it, for England consolidated it from time to time. From the point of
view of the frontiers he had inherited, his conquests were
defensive, his expeditions merely audacious sallies from

the garrison, never decisive even when triumphant. Each of them drew him still further away in pursuit of a peace which escaped his grasp. This god of war, from whom miracles were demanded, thus dragged the cannon-ball of victory to all the capitals so as to spare France—such as she was when he received her—an invasion, driven back to Moscow, but only to enable it to flow back again as far as Montmartre. His genius remained lucid, but, dominated as it was by the "genius of the Revolution", it could illumine nothing save the road to the abyss. Against the force of circumstances, Talleyrand, however great his talent, could not be hand-rail for that double-headed genius. All he could do was sometimes to slacken its fatal progress, without ever, while acting as a brake, exposing himself to being crushed.

The Treaty of Lunéville, signed on February 9, 1801, confirmed for France possession of the left bank of the Rhine and a dominant position in Italy. On those two points, Talleyrand, if he had been in a position to impose his own views and set a greater value on interest than on passion, would have forearmed French policy against disastrous deviations.

The occupation by France of the left bank of the Rhine realized the objective of the old monarchy, but with a departure from its method, and this made the occupation precarious and consequently dangerous. Through not being definitive, it became a provocation, and then a justification for Germanic enterprises against her own territory. The ancient monarchy, patient because it counted on centuries, advanced slowly but surely: a "knife-grinder" policy, but the gains from which were acquired for ever. Step by step it approached a goal which the Revolution reached at a bound; but in its tradition it found a guarantee for its conquests, while the Revolution found in its ideology the principle of its ruin. The Treaty of Luneville traced between France and Germany a precise limit and, while leaving the towns on the right bank of the Rhine to Germany, stipulated that they should be dismantled. In a treaty, the imprecision of frontiers, like that of texts, being to the advantage of the stronger or more skilful party, the policy of the old régime saw there a help rather than an obstacle, especially in its relations with Germany. The immensity of the Germanic chaos and the tangle of rights, as well as of frontiers, countenanced that. After organizing that state of anarchy by the Treaties of Westphalia, it cultivated it as the best guarantee of European order and French independence. On the other hand, the Revolution strove to bring that chaos to an end, whereas it was more necessary than ever to safeguard its conquests. The military dismantlement of a few German fortresses could not be a substitute for the political dismantlement of the whole of Germany.

The Treaty of Lunéville provided for certain necessary changes assuring compensation to princes who had been dispossessed through the French conquest. This was an excellent occasion for applying the revolutionary doctrine: the secularization of ecclesiastical estates would provide for the emergency. Thus Protestant Prussia, which annexed a great part of that territory, was favoured at the expense of Catholic Austria, whose customers were the ecclesiastical princes. At the same time, the number of German States was reduced from 360 in 1792 to 82. They flattered themselves that Germany would be grateful to them for having transformed her from a state of feudal subdivision to that of a modern State, for having created her in their own image, "One and Indivisible", like the French Republic. They congratulated themselves on that "simplification", which was to be the origin of a few complications later on. The victory of France was thus crowned by an event which was soon to be its destruction.

By aggrandizing Prussia and preparing the unity of Germany, the Revolution was steering its direct traditional course. All its learned men were full of admiration for Frederick II, the king-philosopher. The Prussian Alliance was one of their most sacred dogmas, and to such a degree that in 1792 they offered the command of the French army to the Duke of Brunswick. This dogma was still more sacred from the time when, on absorbing the ecclesiastical States, the kingdom of Prussia became the principal purchaser of national estates. Meanwhile, loaded with favours by France, that enlightened State preferred an alliance with Russia. In France's case it was glad to receive but not to give; its policy was that of hands as full as you like, but free.

Talleyrand preferred an alliance with Austria. Unable to establish it on the organization of Germany, where revolutionary orthodoxy was opposed to the idea, he wanted to facilitate it through the organization of Italy. Pleading the bad example that had been set by those badly brought-up daughters of the French Republic, the Batavian, Helvetian, Ligurian, and Parthenopian republics, he proposed, instead of increasing the number by the creation of a Cisalpine republic, to call upon an Austrian prince to reign over a part of Italy, while maintaining there other States, including those of the Pope, so as to assure an equilibrium in conformity with our interests.

To his mind this was not giving Italy to Austria; but it was giving Austria to peace. This calculation has since been justified in countries where foreign dynasties have been rapidly nationalized. It was justified above all in the countries where Napoleon founded thrones for his brothers, who soon raised against his will "the rights of their peoples". But, in the face of "liberal" and Protestant Prussia, Austria incarnated Absolutism and Catholicism. Any condescension towards her would therefore have been as heretical in Italy as in Germany. The very shadow of the Habsburgs must be driven from Italy in order to unify and "regenerate" it, after which they had not the slightest doubt she would throw herself into France's arms to form with France and Germany a Triple Alliance which would guarantee European peace, or rather a Federation which would resuscitate the Western Empire as it existed under Charlemagne. This system, indeed, ended three-quarters of a century later in a Triple Alliance, but directed against France and against peace. This was what Talleyrand, the realist, who based his policy not on the gratitude of nations but on a calculation of their interests and strength, foresaw from the year 1797 in a report to the Directory. Already he discerned that Italian unity would draw her into an alliance with Austria against France. "Gratitude", he said, "is not a virtue of nations. Proud of her strength, emancipated Italy would seek to free herself from our influence. Austria would then, perhaps, be struck with the good idea of offering her an alliance, under the pretext of protecting her against our ambition."

In politics Talleyrand showed more constancy than fidelity. He renounced his ideas when it was to his interest to do so, but he always returned to them. After Austerlitz he again extolled an alliance with Austria and set forth a vast plan which, according to Thiers, would have changed the face of the world had it been adopted. France and Austria were to take no further interest in Italy, which until then had been their biggest apple of discord. Austria being not a nation but a State whose body could be any-where because her heart was nowhere, they would graft on to her southern territory certain members to replace those amputated in the north and west, in Germany and in Italy; and these new members—Valachia, Moldavia, Bessarabia, north of Bulgaria—would place her in contact and in conflict with Russia, which for a long time had coveted them. By organizing this Austro-Russian antagonism, the two chief Continental adversaries of France would be neutralized one by the other, and they would guarantee, after having made allowance for fire, the integrity of the Ottoman Empire. Russia was pushed back into Asia, where she would come into collision with England. By deflecting Austria's ambitions towards the East, an end would be put to all opposition of interests between her and France; she would become our ally and be detached from England, who, abandoned by her Continental soldier, would then be compelled to make peace. Thus the Danube, becoming Austrian along the whole of its course, would guarantee the French Rhine, and the superiority of influence of the Napoleonic Empire would be pacifically established on an immovable basis.

In its main lines that was the manœuvre accomplished by Bismarck after Sadowa; an easier manœuvre for him, for Prussia could find an ally in the conquered enemy from whom not an inch of territory had been taken away. Austria, not having other allies, there was no question of abandoning them: the independence and unity of Italy was too strong to be brought into question again and leave to Austria perspectives for territorial extension elsewhere than in the East. Above all, Bismarck, between a sovereign and nation equally docile, had more elbow room than Talleyrand between Napoleon's ambition and the more redoubtable ideology of the Revolution. His plan was chimerical for the precise reason that it was reasonable, politics, especially in a revolutionary period refusing to be formed into a syllogism. "I work", said

Napoleon, "on the human skin . . . it is ticklish." Talleyrand worked on the parchment of Chancelleries . . . and that is a much better material. His system could not change the fate of the world unless he first of all changed the heart of the world. It was equally unacceptable by France and Austria because he took no account of passions, which are the great forces of history. Austria, the great victim of the Revolution and the Empire, was their implacable enemy; the amputations she owed to them were of too recent date for her wounds to have become cicatrized; she could not give up hereditary and Catholic provinces in exchange for new and schismatic provinces, the possession of which implied war against her Russian allies to the benefit of the Corsican "Ogre"; possession moreover precarious, like all the upheavals of that period. The ambitions and hatreds of the conqueror were no less opposed to Talleyrand's plan than the resentment of the conquered, for Napoleon, Roman before he was Corsican, and haunted by the glory of the Caesars, had not put on the crown of Italy merely in order to lay it aside. Though he himself might be capable of moderation, this was forbidden him as regards Austria because of the antinomy between that Power and the Revolution, whose work he was continuing. His fresh victory was therefore to mark a new stage of his domination over Italy and Germany, and at the same time it facilitated a new stage in the direction of the unity of these two countries. His domination was to come to an end, but unity was to remain.

The great plan which Talleyrand was later to describe as political romance was to become true in later days, but to Germany's profit. It would be puerile to conclude, from our present standpoint, that he had any other object than to establish for himself a title to Austria's gratitude and to prepare a personal alliance with that Power. It would be

doing him an unmerited honour—or an injury—to hail in
that attempt to reconcile the victor and the vanquished
the dawn of Locarnism. There are, moreover, some
differences between the two systems. France having then
gained the victory, not with the assistance of a coalition
but over a coalition, her mansuetude appeared as an act
of generosity rather than as a weakness; that generosity
being shown towards a conservative power disarmed and
conciliated her, whereas in the case of a revolutionary and
insatiable Power like modern Germany the same policy
has a contrary effect. Locarnism, essentially, is the accep
tation of English arbitration in our relations with Ger
many, whereas the advantage to Napoleon of reconcilia
tion with Austria would have been to find in it an aid in
imposing peace on England and French arbitration on the
Continent. Apart from the exclusively personal side of
Talleyrand's plan, he showed himself to be a disciple of
Choiseul, a partisan of an Austrian alliance against Eng
land, and not a precursor of Briand.

Talleyrand did not insist. He had liberated his con
science in Paris and safeguarded his position in Vienna.
That sufficed. He was never the man to make himself the
advocate of lost causes. More willingly would he be the
devil's advocate when the devil was sure of winning his
suit. A case in point was that trial whose victim was to be
the Duc d'Enghien, if it is permissible to apply the word
trial to an outrage in which legal forms were no more
respected than the principles of law. To a friend who re
proached him with not having—like Chateaubriand—re
signed to show his reprobation, Talleyrand replied: "If
Bonaparte has been guilty of a crime, that is no reason why
I should be guilty of a piece of stupidity". But to what
extent did he consider that non-participation in the crime
was already a blunder? The letter which, according to the

testimony of Chateaubriand and Baron de Méneval,[1] he sent to the First Consul advising him to arrest the Prince, and in which these words are found, "policy demands punishment without exception", does not settle the question. A letter from Talleyrand, when it does not raise the question of authenticity, invariably raises that of sincerity. In his estimation a signed document was above all a cloak for the time being, but when the wind changed it became a burden. To understand the part he played in the Vincennes drama thoroughly, one would have to know his private conversations with Bonaparte. All that we know is that, at the Council of March 10, when the arrest of the Duc d'Enghien was decided upon, he remained silent, leaving Cambacérès the task of declaring himself to be against that step. He may have said nothing because he thought that that was the best means of getting Cambacérès' opinion adopted, since this regicide was more qualified to defend successfully the cause of a Bourbon than the ex-Bishop of Autun, who was innocent of the crimes of the Revolution and suspected of being in sympathy with the old régime. Why should he expose himself to the loss of the Master's favour without any chance of saving the Prince's life, since the most powerful intercession of all—that of Joséphine—was to be in vain? In Bonaparte's eyes nothing could prevail against the reason of State. "It was", he said later, "a necessary sacrifice to my security and grandeur." Necessary in order to terrorize the royalists and, by striking terror into their hearts, more surely rally them around him; above all, necessary in order to make the Jacobins accept the idea of a new monarchy

[1] See *The Memoirs of Baron de Méneval*, translated from the French by Robert Harborough Sherard (Hutchinson & Co., 1894. 3 vols.). Baron de Méneval was Napoleon's secretary, and his recollections throw valuable light on the whole of the Napoleonic period.—Translators' note.

by placing the irreparable between the future Emperor and the old dynasty. It was when thinking of the Vincennes drama that Talleyrand in his memoirs quoted the following passage from Machiavelli: "A usurper cannot consolidate his power until he has taken the lives of all the members of the family which reigned legitimately". Previous to the coronation by the Pope the blood of a Bourbon supplied the First Consul with the holy anointment of the Revolution and the only purple it could defend and share.

Talleyrand was not a sanguinary person, and we must not forget that he was Minister of Foreign Affairs. In his conscience he could not but blame Bonaparte for complicating France's diplomatic task by throwing at monarchical Europe, as though it were a challenge, the head of an innocent Bourbon. The fusillade at Vincennes awakened a profound echo there and foreshadowed the greater tragedy of war. But as Talleyrand's well-ordered solicitude began with himself, he was capable of showing the most zealous conformity, while soothing his conscience—less exacting than his prudence—with the hope that his zeal would be profitable to him without causing any harm to the unfortunate Prince whose destiny was irrevocably fixed. Did he also desire to conciliate his conscience and prudence, or his prudence and foresight, his position with Bonaparte and his chances in the case of a Restoration, by secretly giving the Duc d'Enghien the alarm in a letter addressed to his friend the Princesse de Rohan, a letter which is said not to have arrived in time to be useful? That would have been somewhat after his manner which permitted of a double game—unless it was a triple or a quadruple one.

## CHAPTER VII

## TALLEYRAND AND THE EMPIRE

I have remained faithful to a given person only in so
far as that person was faithful to the rules of common
sense.                                    TALLEYRAND

IT was soon to be a double game and in a struggle that involved no longer merely the fate of a Prince but the fate
of crowns and nations. Empires, thrones, and nations
were above all to be the pawns on Talleyrand's personal
chess-board. However, though he might first of all think
of himself, he did not become indifferent to France, his
partner through the force of circumstances; he could not
increase his winnings unless, amidst the ruination of the
Napoleonic system, her stake was saved. In order to save
his own, this lucky yet cautious player gradually withdrew his money before the run of luck broke. Speculating
on a rise, on the 18th of Brumaire, he settled his political
affairs very discreetly and at the highest quotation, at
Tilsit and Erfurt, which marked the zenith of the Empire.
After that he speculated for a fall.

At Tilsit, Napoleon would not have been human had he
escaped the intoxication of power. He had crushed
Prussia at Jena; that Prussia whose army from the days of
Frederick II had been esteemed the finest in the world;
and he had beaten the Russians at Friedland. His beautiful
and haughty enemy, Queen Louise, in whom he saw
"Armida," in her distraction setting fire to her own

palace",[1] humiliated herself at his feet and implored him in vain. She must, however, have been a most touching figure, since her grace and majesty, in the midst of sorrow, drew tears even from Talleyrand. There was a triumph more intoxicating for Napoleon's pride, for the conqueror captivated his adversary of the previous day—Alexander, Emperor of Russia, who fell into his arms and swore eternal friendship. In his tent at Tilsit they united to impose peace on England and share the world between them.

Behind the scenes Talleyrand saw the other side of the picture: he saw Alexander's duplicity; England's tenacity; the complicities she would encounter on the Continent while awaiting the time when she could again find alliances; the impossibility of an enterprise which aimed at universal domination; the rancour of a subjugated but agitated Germany, which formed the habit of awaiting the salvation of a mutilated Prussia, but which alone preserved an appearance of independence; the hostility of nations wounded through their children because of conscription—wounded in their interests through taxation and the Continental blockade, in their traditions by revolutionary ideology, in their religious conscience by the conflict between the Pope and the Emperor; and finally the first signs of the weariness and disquietude of a France which, after the efforts and superhuman sacrifices of fifteen years, was beginning to give way under the burden of the Empire.

[1] Armida is one of the prominent female characters in Tasso's *Jerusalem Delivered*; a beautiful sorceress with whom Rinaldo fell in love. After his disenchantment and escape, she set fire to her palace, rushed into the midst of a combat, and was slain. Napoleon's witty remark was made when, in 1806, he learnt that the young queen of Frederick William of Prussia, who had declared war against him, was riding about in military costume to arouse the soldiers' enthusiasm.—Translators' note.

In Napoleon's policy Talleyrand perceived a series of *fatal* contradictions in the double sense of that word—inevitable and mortal.

There was a triple contradiction between the Russian Alliance—which after Tilsit became the pivot of the whole system—and Alexander's character, the feelings of Russia and the principles of the Revolution, whose crowned soldier Napoleon was. Alexander, inconstant and visionary, was a sincere man with a warped mind, and consequently he was more prone to deceive. When, at Tilsit, Napoleon proposed the alliance to him, but to the exclusion of Austria, he said: "I have often slept two in a bed, never three". It appears that Alexander found that witty remark charming; but he had only an innocent flirtation with France in view, his serious relations being ever with Austria. He saw merely an expedient for disarming the conqueror by means of an agreement in which Napoleon sought for a faithful partner in his struggle against England. Had he been tempted to go beyond those mere trifling preliminaries, his family, Court, and people would not have permitted him. The most absolute sovereigns are sometimes the weakest, because they cannot share their responsibility with anyone. Alexander's mother, who dominated the whole imperial family, held France and Napoleon in horror. The aristocracy and the nation had the same feeling. All classes cursed the Continental blockade, which deprived them of English articles to which they were accustomed and prevented them exporting the produce of the country. The Franco-Russian Alliance ran counter to the principles of France no less than to the feelings and interests of Russia. In the sphere of home politics it ran counter to dogmas, not practice; the Revolution having had recourse, so as to save itself, to the military dictatorship of Napoleon. The paradox was more notorious in the realm of foreign policy. Alexander would not have been able to take the alliance seriously and overcome the opposition of his associates had it not opened up to him the road to Constantinople. Now Napoleon did not wish to hear of a concession which would ruin France's interests in the Levant and hand over to a doubtful ally the keys of the East, where he himself thought of striking decisive blows against England. Nevertheless, in order to maintain the fiction of the alliance as much as possible, he had to resign himself to doing nothing for Poland. That unfortunate country was to be twice the victim of the Revolution, which theoretically ought to have saved it. On the contrary it was Poland which saved the Republic. Cut up in 1793 and in 1795, she figured in the grand bull-fight of Europe as the horse of the picador who wears out the fury of the bull and draws it away from its adversary. Her executioners despatched her while France was proclaiming the rights of man and the rights of nations. Through sealing the alliance with Russia, after Tilsit, Napoleon sealed his own doom.

The contradiction between France's ideal and the means taken to realize it was conspicuous everywhere. It was a double ideal and binding upon everyone: a guarantee for her natural frontiers and the enfranchisement of the human race. The second point was not less "natural" than the first and was derived from it, the peaceful enjoyment of our conquests only being assured in a Europe united through a hatred of tyrants and the worship of liberty. Liberty engendering fraternity, the sole hindrance to the sacred trilogy was the rupture of equality in favour of France, who, extending beyond the limits of ancient Gaul, would exercise an incontestable superiority of power. But was not that advantage due, as author's rights, to the great nation which, through bringing about the Revolution, had accomplished the happiness of humanity? Europe not being of that opinion, France, in order to retain her natural frontiers, embarked on unnatural conquests and Napoleon constructed an edifice which set the laws of equilibrium at defiance.

It was an edifice the floors of which grew broader and broader until it resembled an inverted pyramid. To Belgium and the left bank of the Rhine were added the vassal States, Holland, Germany, Switzerland, Italy; then allied Russia; then, after Tilsit, in the clouds of dreamland, Egypt, Persia, and India, where England was to be destroyed. In the moments when he believed in Alexander's sincerity, Napoleon lost the sense of what was possible, and universal domination appeared to him no longer as a means of conquering England, as a war-map the elements on which were negotiable things, but as a goal. It was then that Talleyrand, echoing the words of Madame Mère, said: "Really, this little one is not at all reasonable".

The system, threatened with ruin through its form and enormous size, was also threatened with an explosion because of the interior ferments which were gradually undermining it. There was an absurd contradiction between the principles of the Revolution and the necessities of war. After suppressing liberty in France so as to give it to other nations, they proceeded to suppress liberty in those nations in order to try to conquer England. Moreover, the nations had not the same idea of liberty as the ideologists of Paris. Above all, they appreciated the liberty of choosing their own master. Now, Napoleon was a foreign master, and he enslaved them for ends which were foreign to them. The obligation to pay heavy taxes, to march to their death on battlefields, and to give up a lucrative commerce with England was a form of liberty which disenchanted those who had most enthusiastically saluted the French flags. In Germany the western empire formed an imposing façade. The new Charlemagne, the "regenerator of the Germanic Constitution", governed—under cover of the Confederation of the Rhine, of which he was the protector —all the territories which stretched between the Rhine and the Vistula. But in Berlin officers were sharpening their swords on the French Embassy steps and uttering cries of death against the French. The universities were the hotbeds of this national movement, which had its apostles everywhere, and which was soon to have its martyr, that young student who attempted to assassinate the "Tyrant" Napoleon. This stirring-up of the German people with his powerful hand united and disciplined them; it was to develop in them ferments which raised the principle of political liberty, propagated by the Revolution, to the status of national independence. When Napoleon was appointed protector of the Confederation of the Rhine, the Prince-Primate Dalberg gave orders that the room at Ratisbonne, where for three centuries the inoffensive Diet of the Empire had assembled, should be closed and the throne of Charles V be removed. He suppressed every trace of the past. . . . What the future held forth was the throne of William I, who was proclaimed Emperor of Germany in the Galérie des Glaces at Versailles.

A contradiction between principles and acts on religious grounds is no less dangerous than on diplomatic ones. Napoleon, the man who had restored religion, was to be drawn into persecuting the Pope[1] in order to force him

[1] Pius VII (Gregorio Barnaba Chiaramonti, 1742–1823), who, on refusing to recognize Joseph Bonaparte as King of Naples and to be present at his coronation at Naples, aroused the open enmity of Napoleon. The results were another occupation of Rome by French troops (February 2, 1808), the incorporation of the papal cities, and shortly after of Rome itself, with the kingdom of Italy, and the

to observe the Continental blockade. He was to occupy his States, lay hands upon him, and be excommunicated at a time when the spiritual authority of the Holy Father was more necessary to him than ever. It was necessary in France, where the catechism, drawn up by his order, enumerated, after the duties towards God, *the duties towards the Emperor*: "love, respect, fidelity, military service, and the payment of taxes"; duties obligatory "under pain of eternal damnation". Authority still more necessary outside France, in all parts of the Empire—Rhineland, Southern Germany, Belgium, and Spain—in order to inspire fidelity or resignation among ardently Catholic populations. And thus Napoleon, who had come forward before other people as a "Liberator" and a "Messiah", cut the figure of a despot and Antichrist.

In brief there was contradiction, or disproportion, between the growing exigencies of an Empire exceeding lawful bounds and the decreasing resources of the nation. It is to the honour and wretchedness of the nations, and especially the French people, that the recollection of that glory is more living than that of the sacrifices it cost. But contemporaries felt those sacrifices cruelly. Glory—a dazzling state of mourning for liberty—was paid for by innumerable humble but most acute afflictions. Already, when Napoleon returned to Paris after fresh triumphs, he was no longer received with the unanimous acclamations which had greeted his early victories. Amidst the unresponsive crowds he might have heard the sobbing of mothers. Already the "annuity of one hundred thousand

arrest of the Pope (July 6, 1809) and his confinement in Savona and afterwards at Fontainebleau. In 1814 he was released and restored to the possession of all the papal territories except Avignon and Venaissin in France, and a narrow strip of land beyond the Po.—Translators' note.

men" no longer sufficed for him and he was living on the capital of the country. From 1805 the Emperor, who first of all had incorporated only part of the contingent, enrolled entire contingents, recalled to the colours demobilized contingents, and raised new ones, one to two years in advance. The contingent of 1806 was called up in March 1805, and so on.

Talleyrand anticipated the call of destiny. He did not wait for clearer warnings to divide the risks in the investment of his political fortune and to liquidate a portion of his Napoleonic securities. He sold out with an enormous profit. In August 1817 he abandoned the office of Foreign Relations, while remaining, through his prestige with the Emperor, a consulting minister—an admirable combination for retaining authority while declining responsibility.

At the same time he became a great dignitary of the Empire with the title of Vice Grand Elector: "the only vice in which he was wanting", said Fouché. The Grand Elector was the Emperor's eldest brother, Joseph, King of Naples, and he was always absent. Therefore his deputy concentrated in his hands the entire responsibility of the post, which, its object being theoretically the control of the elections, was, under a régime which had almost entirely suppressed them, practically a sinecure. The only election worthy of his care would have been that of Napoleon's successor.

It was not with a feeling of professional duty that Talleyrand, who for a long time had been on bad terms with Fouché, was soon to be reconciled with him so as to consider the steps to be taken if the throne became vacant. Who can say whether the heir of the Counts-Sovereign of Périgord, who, though possessing so much mental restraint, showed none whatsoever in his greed of power or money, did not dream of becoming the Emperor of the

West, while knowing full well that he was merely dreaming? A grand dignitary of the Empire, he was also from 1804 a grand officer of the Palace, in his quality of Grand Chamberlain; a post which, with a sovereign like Napoleon, was *not* a sinecure. Finally, from 1806, he was Prince and Duke of Benevento: a triple dignity (without counting that of Grand Eagle of the Legion of Honour) which perhaps inspired a satirical heraldist in the choice of the new armorial bearings which were attributed to him, and in which figured *three lions rampant and crowned with gold*.

Talleyrand was not more faithful to the Empire of which he was a prince than he had been to the Church of Rome of which he had been a bishop. On the contrary, when he became Minister of Foreign Affairs *in partibus infidelium*, he profited by his liberty to stress his opposition. Being no longer obliged to accompany the Grand Army, he re-established contact with the two forces where, above Napoleon, he detected the secret of the future and the potentialities of his ambition: French public opinion and the foreign Powers. This official semi-retirement revived his personal activity, while restoring both his liberty and his health, which had been weakened by camp life. During the imperial epic he was less sensitive to grandeur than to woes and horrors, such as cold, hunger, insomnia, and the mud in which his carriage sometimes remained stuck for hours, despite the vigorous —and symbolic—efforts of the soldiers who pushed and tugged at the wheels "to unearth diplomacy", while cursing in their not over-diplomatic language the cumbersome civilian inside. Amidst the wounded and the dead the odour was such that, in a letter to d'Hauterive, he congratulated himself on the intense cold which preserved the unburied corpses.

He recouped himself in Paris by putting a spoke in the wheels of the imperial chariot. Other and more comfortable campaigns he undertook; and during these this great constable of intrigue exercised supreme command. What was his objective? He aimed at adapting himself to all possibilities, without excluding those most favourable to the Emperor. Who were his allies? All the discontents and all those who had "an eye to the future". What were his weapons? His authority, which increased the more errors Napoleon made; his experience; his deep knowledge of Europe and the secret springs of politics; his wit and common sense; his pomp and charm of manner; his friendship and an excellent table; his discretion and indiscretion (he sometimes made use of confidential remarks without revealing the identity of those who had made them); his silence and his utterances; an acquiescence which said more than words; a word which he let fall from on high as though he were an oracle, or which he whispered in the ear of some foreign diplomatist; a word which was to produce a current of opinion in well-chosen circles, or which, transmitted by some special courier to other capitals, would give the right direction to certain decisions there. It has been said of Talleyrand that he believed himself to be the leader of parties of which, in reality, he was only the confidant. But, besides being also the inspirer, a confidant of his quality is all the more a leader when he avoids the appearance of being one.

The fact that Talleyrand's salon became the centre for a secret—and all the more redoubtable—opposition did not prevent him from practising the worship of Napoleon and even celebrating it in his quality as Grand Chamberlain. But faith was no longer in him. An expert in the art of detaching himself without entirely breaking off relations, he remained the friend of his mistresses though he had cast them aside. In that respect he treated them as he did the Powers and governments. That was his "in-case-of-need" system, in which, politically, Napoleon remained the one most worthy of consideration until fresh orders. He did not cease to collaborate with him, to be consulted, and even employed on great occasions. His abilities inspired the Emperor with more confidence than his character caused him distrust.

Therefore Napoleon took Talleyrand with him to Erfurt, where he had made an appointment with the man whom he thought was his only great friend, the Tsar Alexander, thus bringing together two great unfaithful men whose agreement was to hasten the infidelity of Fortune.

The Emperor had already taken too unfair an advantage of Fortune not to have wearied her. It was in Spain that she abandoned him. What was Talleyrand's responsibility in that disastrous adventure? The denials he exchanged with Napoleon do not enlighten us on that point. Nor do we get much more help from the letters he sent him; letters which, according to Chateaubriand, he removed from the Archives of the Tuileries in 1814. They may have been compromising at that date without having the least influence on the Emperor's plans in 1808. It would be necessary for us to know their secret conversations, though these would not have thrown light on the degree of authority which our professor of moderation retained over his more and more intractable pupil. Thiers has described both of them as they were at that time—eternally in private conversation at Fontainebleau: the Emperor holding forth vehemently and at great length, while "he walked up and down in the spacious galleries, sometimes slowly, sometimes with a rapidity in pace with his thoughts, and thus putting to torture the infirm

M

courtier who could only keep up with him by immolating his body, just as he immolated his soul when flattering the fatal and deplorable impulses of genius". Here, soul is a false window for the sake of symmetry. Talleyrand's soul had encountered many another tricky situation and it possessed more power of resistance than his leg.

It is most probable that Talleyrand, in order to retain, or once more obtain, Napoleon's favour, endeavoured to divine his thoughts so as to flatter them, rather than to communicate his own thoughts, and all the while conciliating his interests and scruples under the conviction that another attitude, dangerous for him, would have been unprofitable for his interlocutor, who was impelled by force of circumstances—not by the impulses of his genius—along the path to the abyss into which he was destined to fall. Fatality and his inner demon were in agreement to precipitate him therein. The Continental blockade would be a fiction if the Peninsula escaped him— and it would escape him, despite all treaties of alliance, if it remained under the government of the Bourbons. The chain of events, from war on England, via Tilsit and the Russian alliance, to the deposition of Charles IV and the Spanish war, was inevitable. Napoleon, who had already dethroned the Bourbons of Naples, followed the logical reasoning of his system by dethroning those of Madrid. Consequently, when Charles IV and his son Ferdinand fell into the Bayonne trap, how could he resist the temptation of conjuring away his crown? The Emperor's ideology blinded him to the consequences of his system and made that decision as legitimate as it appeared to him to be necessary. He believed that the French flag, within whose folds was justice and liberty, would be acclaimed by a united nation, intoxicated by love and gratitude. Yet that was far and away the most atrocious war of the

Revolution and the Empire. In order to undertake it Napoleon had stronger reasons than the mere imitation of Louis XIV. Talleyrand laughed at the Emperor when he invoked the example of the Grand Roi. He knew quite well that the throne of Madrid was then vacant, and that its last occupant had by testament appointed the Duc d'Anjou as his successor. Nor was he unaware that Louis XIV, at the time he accepted Charles II's testamentary wishes, was at peace with the whole of Europe and had not disturbed it through distributing, by decrees, as Napoleon did, crowns to members of his family. The two situations were entirely different.

A new crown being vacant, Napoleon, who conceived the organization of Europe as a universal monarchy, with the Emperor at its summit and the other sovereigns as lieutenants, began to move kings here and there. His brother Joseph was promoted from Naples to Madrid, and replaced at Naples by Murat. The Empire, with its 130 Departments and feudatory States, then stretched from Gibraltar to Hamburg, but as it extended it grew weaker. Already Napoleon's thoughts—when it was not himself in person—went backwards and forwards from one end to the other of this Penelope's web, in order to weave it afresh as soon as it broke under the stress. That web was to be rent to pieces in Spain. The French expedition kindled there a huge Vendée infinitely more terrible than the civil wars in that Department during the Revolution; it offered a Continental battlefield to England, and inaugurated there that era of national wars which was soon to set Austria, Russia, and Germany ablaze. The "imponderables" changed their camp. Liberty, after being Napoleon's ally, outstripped the Saxons of Leipzig and turned against him. The Spanish war also ushered in defeat with the capitulation of Bailen. On learning of this,

Austria mobilized. In Prussia, Stein wrote to Frederick William to urge him to conclude an alliance with Napoleon: "a mere blind to hide the measures which will be taken to dispel it". And while perils were on the increase, Napoleon's resources were on the decline. Young men avoided conscription by taking refuge in the mountains or the woods. An ever-increasing number of deserters formed an army given up to brigandage. "Cowardice", wrote Fouché, "turns a deserter into a rebel and destitution makes him a brigand."

It was under these by no means favourable auspices that Napoleon met the Tsar Alexander at Erfurt. "In war as in love", he said, "it is necessary, if one would make an end of it, to meet each other face to face." And he thought it was the same in the case of diplomacy. He counted on his powers of seduction, on man-to-man conversations, looking straight into each other's eyes, so as to revive recollections of Tilsit and obtain more efficacious assistance from Alexander. The object was to neutralize the Continent, and especially to guard himself against an Austrian attack in the rear while he was occupied in Spain, where, in order to re-establish the situation, his presence was necessary. If Alexander showed his teeth to the Emperor Francis II, Napoleon's private interview with Spain would not be disturbed.

Alexander showed his teeth; but with a most engaging smile. Of the three emperors, the one who was not invited to Erfurt, Francis II, was to be the best served. While promising Napoleon his help against Austria, Alexander assured Francis II of his faithful friendship. Nothing, however, had been neglected to dazzle and tempt the Tsar. At Erfurt, in the centre of Germany, chosen so as to make a deep impression on all his vassals invited to this spectacle of his power and his intimacy with the Emperor of Russia, Napoleon domineered like a demi-god on a parterre of kings, a parterre which, in the opinion of an eye-witness, was above all a mere border. The intellectual kings of Germany he also received there—Goethe, Wieland, and their contemporaries; intellectual kings worthier than the others, and whose homage was probably more sincere. In that theatre where, before the new Augustus, Talma played *Cinna*, the staging was more brilliant than at Tilsit. But the other side of the picture—Spain—bore a darker aspect. In vain did Napoleon abandon Finland and the Danubian provinces to Alexander, besides opening up to him the prospect of the partition of Turkey. Alexander, "a crowned Hamlet", cherished a more grandiose dream. He possessed the indecision and duplicity of the Prince of Denmark, but to these he added presumption. He believed that his genius, like his Empire, was limitless, and that Providence had selected him to save the human race. Willingly would he cry out with Hamlet, but while changing the essential words, the words "O cursed spite!"—for he cursed not the chaos of which he flattered himself he was the luminary: "The time is out of joint: O benediction! that I was born to set it right!" Talleyrand found no difficulty in coming to an agreement with him when, on proposing to him, not an alliance against Austria but an alliance with Austria against Napoleon, he said: "Sire, what are you here for? It is for you to save Europe, and you will only succeed by resisting Napoleon. The French are civilized, but their sovereign is not; the sovereign of Russia is civilized, but his nation is not. It is therefore manifest that the sovereign of Russia ought to be allied to the French nation."

Before setting out for Erfurt, Talleyrand had been present at the rehearsals of *Cinna*, side by side with Napoleon, who keenly appreciated, as an apology for the

execution of the Duc d'Enghien and also for the special
benefit of his crowned guests, the passage on "those State
crimes which are committed for the sake of the Crown".
The Prince de Bénévent's personal policy, with a view to
bringing Russia and Austria together, was not, if they
thought it so, a crime committed for the State against the
Crown, for he considered it was favourable to the Crown
as well as to the State. It was necessary, in order to save
Napoleon from himself, to set Europe in opposition to
ruinous allurements, and thus save both France and
Europe. France first of all, since Talleyrand considered
himself a better Frenchman than Napoleon, who was
guilty of sacrificing France to the Empire. All he would
have betrayed would be the Emperor's passions, but to
the profit of his real interests. Such is Thiers' opinion.
But the majority of historians do not make that distinction, and some of them attribute to him the Tsar's defection, the new war with Austria, and all the catastrophes
which followed.

At Erfurt, Talleyrand saved neither France nor Europe,
but he did not lose the Empire. Europe saved herself and
the Empire lost itself without his aid. France alone owed
him gratitude when, after the downfall of the Empire, he
contributed to her salvation, thanks to his "treason",
which gave him on Alexander a mortgage by which his
country was to profit in the days of defeat. Meanwhile,
above all he marked certain special points in his personal
game. Perhaps he was deluded in that respect, for even
the most perspicacious diplomatists unwittingly consider
themselves to be the authors of events of which they are
really only spectators. He applied himself, as Albert Sorel
has said, to "detaching the ally and preserving the enemy".
Now, "the ally" Russia had never been attached, and the
enemy Austria had never ceased to be an enemy. From

April 11, 1805, the Tsar had concluded with England a convention which, according to its ostensible part, left France her natural frontiers; but the secret clauses of the agreement brought her back to those of 1789. Through the effusions of Tilsit and Erfurt that engagement expressed Alexander's real thought. In 1808, when France was engaged in the war with Spain, he had no need of Talleyrand for persevering in that thought. Russia, indignant at the treatment inflicted on the Bourbons of Madrid, was more than ever hostile to any form of collaboration with Napoleon. France's Ambassador at St Petersburg, Caulaincourt, who, in spite of the Tsar's efforts to prolong, so as to exploit, the fiction of the alliance, was isolated through "the drawing-room blockade", wrote to say that the adoption of the French alliance would be equivalent to "a change of religion" for the Russians. In a country which was an autocracy limited by assassination, the people who were unaware of Alexander's real intentions were indignant at his interview with the "Antichrist" and talked of annihilating a Tsar who was on the point of betraying Holy Russia.

Against those public threats and the secret engagements with England and Austria, the alternate violence and caresses of Napoleon could not prevail. It was in vain that, at Erfurt, he threw his hat on the ground and stamped on it in the course of a discussion with the Emperor of Russia, who, looking at him fixedly and with a smile, remarked after a silence, and in the calmest of tones: "You are violent, but I am stubborn; and anger means nothing to me. Let us talk, let us reason, or I go." It was in vain that, with too great a show of solicitude after too great a display of temper, Napoleon, with the help of Talleyrand—who in his position of Grand Chamberlain reigned over the theatrical world—sent Mlle

Georges to Alexander with the object of inducing him to set aside Mme Narichkine, whose political influence they feared. Alexander's infidelities constituted the triumph of his constancy and, on her side, Mme Narichkine made it a principle, according to Joseph de Maistre, "to pay no heed to distractions". In politics Napoleon's coquetries were merely a distraction, above all with the object of diverting the adversary, and Alexander asked the serious ally to pay no heed to it. To the Austrian representative at Erfurt, von Vincent, he declared that he was "engaged on his honour to preserve Austria from any attack whatsoever".

The stakes were now on the table. The problem with Talleyrand was how to slip away from his seat while apparently still playing his hand. He concluded not only his own private peace but an alliance with Russia and Austria, that is to say with Europe, so as to be able to stand before her, on the day of liquidation, as the only French statesman who, having foreseen, understood, and above all prepared everything, was the only one qualified to arrange everything. But the fashion being then, as it invariably is, to disguise calculations under the colour of principles, he spoke only in the name of civilization, Europe and France. For he did not forget France. In one of his conversations with Alexander he abandoned the Empire, but so as to defend France and her natural frontiers the better. He committed a double error: a psychological error as regards Napoleon, if he considered it possible to save part of the conquests while sacrificing the others. It is wiser on our part not to slight his common sense by believing in his sincerity. At Erfurt he could no more reveal the whole of what he thought to foreign interlocutors than he could reveal his thoughts in his memoirs to posterity. In both cases his language was calculated to conciliate the proprieties and his mental reservations. At Erfurt he did not occasion events, and he did not even sign his name to them, for it was Champagny, the nominal minister, who signed; what he did was to anticipate those events. As though with the object of emphasizing the personal character of his policy, Talleyrand, who was entrusted with the duty of discreetly sounding Alexander on the subject of a marriage with a Grand Duchess—a marriage the impossibility of which he realized—indiscreetly yet successfully asked him, on behalf of his nephew Edmond, for the hand of the richest and most captivating heiress in the whole of Russia, the daughter of the Duchess of Courland, who, under the name of the Duchesse de Dino, was to become a collaborator in his policy and a consoler in his old age. After the "Madame Grant clause" in the Concordat, a clause in favour of Dorothée had to be seen to at Erfurt.

In lieu of being the author of events, as he prided himself on being, and as people accused him of being, Talleyrand set to work to precipitate them. Speculating on a fall, he manœuvred to accelerate it by keeping Vienna and St. Petersburg informed. We cannot attribute to him a preponderant rôle in the result without refusing to acknowledge the entanglement and multiplicity of causes. The progress of events is ruled by too many currents, and they are sometimes accompanied by terrible eddies, for the effect of each of them to be discernible. More rapid from their source than at any other period of history, they assumed, as they mingled on nearing the catastrophe, a torrential course which swept along both governments and nations, shattered or kept afloat the aspirations of humanity.

Barely three years elapsed between the birth of the King of Rome—which appeared to assure the duration of the Empire—and Waterloo. At last Napoleon had an heir;

yet he lost the heritage. Once more, after Wagram, he entered Vienna as a conqueror, to cull there an archduchess and fresh provinces. He won too many battles not to find, soon, that he had lost the war. Each fresh victory increased his burden and the perils of his position. The Empire, which was already double the size of that of Charlemagne, further annexed, beyond the Adriatic, the Illyrian provinces, and these were excrescences rather than extensions. From Portugal to the Balkans and from the Straits of Gibraltar to the Baltic Sea the structure of the Empire, with its long coast-lines in all directions, called to mind that of a marine monster, stretching out its tentacles as though to embrace all the seas and smother England. Still more monstrous as regards its composition than it was in its structure, its very heterogeneity was the cause of its fragility. Napoleon exhausted himself in vain efforts to smelt it into a single block, to make it watertight and obviate all the leakages which, despite the blockade, were feeding England. While he was caulking at one point, leaks appeared elsewhere. In such an Empire, which though born only yesterday included all races, all religions, and all the languages of Europe, the blockade, which ought to have been a seamless dress, was but the parti-coloured garb of Harlequin.

While the blockade was stirring up a revolt as regards interests, the tyranny it involved provoked everywhere an awakening and a revolt of national feeling. At the same time, the Pope's imprisonment—another result of the blockade—mobilized religious feeling against the Emperor, and at a time when he needed it more than ever to maintain obedience among ardently Catholic nations, and to give to his power that spiritual support he had sought at his coronation, so as to impose on the conscience of Christianity the pre-eminence of the man who, high above the heads of kings, incarnated, as the Roman Pontiff, the principle of unity and universality. In agreement with the Pope, Napoleon, the anointed of the Lord, would have been able to stand before the nations as the very envoy of God. But now he was nothing more than a scourge. The whole of Spain, fanaticized by 190,000 priests or monks, rose against him, as formerly, in the days of the Reconquista, it had risen against Islam. Henceforth the better observed Catechism was no longer that which, in France, prescribed military service and the payment of taxes under pain of damnation, but that which, in Spain, was in the hands of every child, and which dealt forth instruction as follows: "Who are the French?"—"Former Christians who have become heretics."—"Is it a sin to put a Frenchman to death?"—"No, Heaven is our recompense when we kill one of those heretical dogs."

While facing this crusade in the West, Napoleon, in his gigantic effort to dominate the sea by land, was preaching another crusade in the East. It was indeed a crusade, that expedition to Russia whither, in order to impose his will on Alexander, who had become England's ally, and also on the Muscovite barbarians, he dragged at the tail of the Grand Army the contingents of all nations. When, in the name of civilization, the Russian hordes had been driven back, the ways were to be free towards the mirages which had incessantly fascinated him—Constantinople, Persia, and India. But the Colossus of snow, which had not melted in the sun of Austerlitz, was still more solid in his own country. Before long, as a consequence of one of the most extraordinary vicissitudes in history, the Cossacks were to devastate French towns and country places. By penetrating in the direction of Asia, Napoleon the conqueror, peace-maker, and organizer, was, after having been Caesar, Augustus, and Charlemagne, to become an Alexander; but only to draw Atilla into France.

In Paris, Talleyrand awaited Atilla without the slightest fear, and he even prepared a lodging for him in his palace in the Rue St-Florentin.[1] He read the bulletins of the Grand Army with the same state of mind as he did the Stock Exchange quotations, when the Bourse confirmed his previsions. He smiled when he compared Napoleon to Joshua: Napoleon, who thought he could prevent the snow from falling; or when, on noting that his officers attributed disaster to the elements, he compared him to Artaxerxes, who had the sea flogged to punish it for having disobeyed him. He had long been of the opinion that the game was lost. He decided that the best thing to do was to put an end to the expenses. In brief, treason became the most sacred of duties—and the surest of investments.

Napoleon had no illusions as regards Talleyrand's feelings. Yet he did not render him incapable of doing him further injury. People have expressed astonishment at such gentleness, especially after the famous scene of January 28, 1809. Riding his horses to death, the Emperor had just returned to Paris with lightning rapidity in order to strike down those who, profiting by his absence in Spain and under Talleyrand's instigation, were coming to an agreement as to the choice of his successor. In the presence of the other grand dignitaries of the Empire assembled for that execution, Napoleon assumed his most stormy expression and in a thundering voice insulted his Grand Chamberlain in the following terms: "You are a

[1] The Hôtel de l'Infantado, where "Talleyrand, the Harlequin" entertained the Powers. "Talleyrand, the Harlequin, who, on climbing from the street to the *entresol*, jumped to the first-floor when the ladder had been removed from under him." See *The Recollections of Baron de Frénilly, loc. cit.*—Translators' note.

thief, a coward, and a faithless man; you have deceived and betrayed everybody; nothing is sacred to you; you would sell your own father. . . . What do you want? What do you prefer? Dare to say it. You deserve to be shattered by me like a glass, and I have the power to do so; but I have too great a disdain for you to take so much trouble. Why did I not hang you on the Carrousel gates? But there is still time for that yet. . . ." Then, after the most ribald threats and insults, came the crowning stroke: "You did not tell me that the Duc de San Carlos was your wife's lover". To which the Prince, who had remained imperturbable, replied: "That is indeed so, Sire. I did not think that that report could have the slightest bearing on the glory of Your Majesty or on my own." And as he withdrew with dignity he let fall the words: "What a pity that so great a man should have been so badly brought up!" [1] On returning home he went to bed. Was that because he had maintained impassibility only at the cost of extreme nervous tension and that, alone with himself, he shed "that hard and polished exterior on which insult and disdain glided off without penetrating"? Or else did he stretch himself out for a while out of coquetry, so as to be fresh and more brilliant a little later in the salon of his friend, the Vicomtesse de Laval, where he smilingly related the terrible scene, without omitting a single word of what the Emperor had thrown in his teeth? The next day he appeared in the Court circle as usual.

Talleyrand was not destined to be hanged on the

[1] This episode reminds one of the fact that Napoleon was well aware of how useful Duroc, Murat, Berthier, and especially Talleyrand had been to him, as regards feminine society, whilst on his campaigns. For all of them undertook to satisfy the Emperor's passing fancies. "Talleyrand", said Napoleon, "had always plenty of mistresses." See the *Mémoires de Mlle Avrillon*, vol. ii. p. 282; and Frédéric Masson's *Napoléon et les femmes.*—Translators' note.

Carrousel gates. The Emperor was satisfied when he had deprived him of the Grand Chamberlain's key, leaving him his dignities and prebends. Doubtless he was unaware of the Prince's conduct at Erfurt. But had he been acquainted with it he probably would not have treated him otherwise. When Fouché, who was much more guilty, was taken in the act of secret negotiations, not with an ally like Russia but with the most implacable adversary, England, Napoleon confined himself to depriving him of his post as Minister of Police. Queen Hortense said of him: "He humiliates too much and does not punish enough". Punish? That absolute sovereign had not the power to do so. He would have had to strike down too many people, and those who were in too high a position. Among his associates there was no longer any faith in his star. All of them were either intriguing or whispering. Had he applied sanctions, nobody, said Mollien, would have considered himself or herself safe. Could he shoot Murat and his sister Caroline, who were accomplices and eventual beneficiaries in the Talleyrand-Fouché plot? That powerlessness of his was accompanied by a certain timidity, inherited from the very origin of his throne, the recollection of the help of those who had placed him there, and a feeling of his fragility. When there are "daggers in the air", as Fouché expressed it, without counting Austrian cannon-balls and Spanish bullets, is it not the duty of the servants of the State to watch over its stability? In Napoleon's indulgence there was also this demi-god's profound contempt for humanity. To the amnesty of disdain was added, in Talleyrand's favour, a triple immunity. Napoleon was the greatest sportsman of all time. His epic was a series of extraordinary performances, the final uselessness of which the more often consecrates their beauty. When he had no more illusions as to the future of the Empire, when he foresaw that all that would end badly, he nevertheless held his ground, an incomparable champion whose ideal was to surpass himself, to beat his own record, after having beaten all those of history, and without any other object than that of pleasing himself and engraving his name on the memory of mankind. That splendid captain knew that he could not have won so many games, that he could not have gained the world's championship without his team, and, even when it did not play the game but played that of the adversary, he did not break away from it. Now, Talleyrand was the "ace" of his team. When he felt that his luck was abandoning him, he exclaimed, "Ah, if only Talleyrand were here!" He looked upon him as one of those fetishes with a double purpose which certain players awaiting either luck or bad luck, praise and blame alternately rather than ever break them to pieces.

To that add the fact that Napoleon's government was one of high functionaries, very limited in number, who felt their solidarity, even when detesting each other, and every one of whom thought that, as far as he was concerned, he was the State. In that quality they enjoyed greater immunity in fact than immunity from the legal standpoint, which under another régime was to protect parliamentarians. There was a more complete immunity for Talleyrand than for any other, for he was also a great dignitary of the Empire, and great dignitaries participated in the majesty of the throne and the inviolability of the imperial family. When Napoleon bestowed a principality upon him he treated him on the same footing as his brothers. And reciprocally Talleyrand betrayed him as they did; but not to so great an extent.

That was not all. In Napoleon's attitude towards Talleyrand there was a sentimental element and even, in consequence of an alternation of brutality and weakness, a passional one. After his quarrel with the Prince the Emperor forbade Marie Louise to let him join her whist parties. But on two occasions he insisted on offering him the post of Minister of Foreign Affairs. He vilified and praised, threatened and consulted him. Admiration and gratitude were mingled with his disdain because between them, as we have seen, there was a corpse on which the imperial throne was built—the corpse of the Directory, the recollection of the 18th of Brumaire; and above all there were those people who were living, all the dreams of power and glory born from that corpse and partly realized with the help of Talleyrand, who, however, had no faith in them. Both had been comrades, accomplices, and even cronies, as for instance on the night preceding the coronation when the religious marriage of Napoleon and Joséphine was patched up in order to enable the Pope, on the day following, to anoint their foreheads with the holy oil. There were also other bonds. The Emperor's bulletins, to which, not without reason, he attached great importance, since they were often manifestoes laying down lessons to kings and nations, were revised by Talleyrand before being published. Who knows whether, in order to retain his hold on Napoleon through one of the strongest of feelings—literary pride—he did not take care to preserve that first sketch which he was clarifying? To him the Emperor had laid bare his heart, like his mind, when he made use of him in the early days of his love for Marie Walewska.[1] He had displayed before him his physical

[1] This was not an *amour* of the moment, like Mme Fourès in Egypt and Grassini at Milan before Marengo, but a lasting connection at Warsaw and at Finkenstein in 1807, and at Schoenbrunn in 1809. Mme Walewska was Napoleon's left-handed wife—known as his "Polish wife". See Frédéric Masson's *Napoléon et les femmes*.—Translators' note.

misfortune when at Strasbourg, on his way to Austerlitz, he had an epileptic attack. Alone with Rémusat in his bedroom, Talleyrand had heard his moans, saw him foaming at the mouth, and writhing in the midst of his convulsions; he had undressed him and rubbed him with eau-de-Cologne. Their intimacy was such that some-times—after having worked together far into the night and they were worn out with fatigue—they slept side by side on the same sofa.

Talleyrand was the only person who had authority over Napoleon and the only one whom Napoleon never intimi-dated. He took the liberty of displaying a respectful im-pertinence which would not have been tolerated in the case of any other person. Many instances—more or less authentic, like all the witticisms attributed to Talleyrand—of this have been given. But if we lend only to the rich, we borrow from them still more, and, on the whole, chronicle restores to them only a part of their wealth. "Talleyrand, where have you made so much money?" asked Napoleon.—"Sire, I bought Government Stock on the 17th of Brumaire and sold it on the 19th." That was a familiarity dating back to the beginning of the Consulate. On the day when the First Consul was waiting feverishly for news of the signing of the Treaty of Amiens, Talley-rand called upon him with the signed treaty in his pocket, and, without saying anything about it, entered into a lengthy conversation on secondary matters. Just as he was taking leave of him, Talleyrand remarked: "By the by, I am going to give you a great pleasure. The treaty has been signed—and here it is!"—"Well!" exclaimed Bona-parte, "why didn't you tell me so immediately?"—"Ah! because you wouldn't have listened to what I had to say about all the other things. When you are happy, there's no getting near you". Often he kept back important documents until Napoleon was in a frame of mind which would make him receptive of his advice. In the case of such an impulsive man as he was, it was urgent to wait. Napoleon forced him to marry an adventuress whom he "attached to his neck like a sign-board", thus discrediting him, so as to break him in and enslave him. Having, on the day following the legal confirmation of the union, convoked him, Napoleon said: "I hope that Citoyenne Talleyrand will forget Mme Grant and be an honour to you". The new husband replied: "Citoyenne Talleyrand has only to take Citoyenne Bonaparte as a model".

Apart from that conjugal resemblance and certain analogies already noted in their formation, everything else was contrast between the two personages. On the occasion of official ceremonies, between a double row of bent backs and bowed heads which often served to hide ironical faces, and amidst a hum of curiosity, noisy flattery, and whispered sarcasms, Talleyrand at the height of his reputation used to hobble slowly along, but with the most lordly air in the world. Between his flowing locks and the folds of an immense silk-muslin or lace cravat, his impassible face was lit up but not made clear by an enigmatic look and smile. With a sword at his side, he wore a red velvet coat lined with white silk, and a cloak to match; facings, collar, and lapels of embroidered gold cloth, and a white silk scarf worn with a gold fringe slung over one shoulder; white knickerbockers, and a black felt hat with upturned brim, ornamented with white feathers. He supported himself on a combined stick-and-crutch, which like a halberd, struck the parquet rhythmically as he proceeded along. One might have said that this ex-bishop was his own beadle and that an invisible master of the ceremonies preceded him to ward off the crowd, while announcing, "The Prince!"

Most simple, in the uniform of the Chasseurs de la Garde, without a trace of gold embroidery, without any other ornament save the Star of the Legion of Honour on his breast, and wearing a black hat on which only the tricolour cockade shone forth, as befitted a great nobleman who, disdaining luxury for himself, leaves such adornments for his servants, another still more extraordinary man, sweeping the crowd of courtiers with his eagle-like glance—that "devouring look" of his—advanced with rapid step. This was "The Man", as his soldiers called him, walking hand in hand, as it were, with his most faithful companion Glory, preceded by the God of War and the God of Fortune. That procession, more brilliant than the whole Court, threw into the shade even the Prince himself on those solemn occasions when, carrying out his duties as Grand Chamberlain, opposite the suddenly opened folding doors, he announced in a loud voice, "The Emperor!"

The moral contrast was greater than the physical one. Talleyrand, a man of the old régime, represented the past, which paid court to the future, but in order to profit by the present. Napoleon represented the future which, in order to master the present, took its inspiration from the past. That was the serious reason for their collaboration. But as regards method they belonged to two different species. At St. Helena Napoleon described the first intoxications of glory by the following lyrical metaphor: "I saw the world flee beneath me as though I had been carried through the air". Talleyrand's lameness forbade such a flight as that. He was an essentially pedestrian genius. We cannot help seeing in him the Sancho Panza of a formidable Don Quixote who was riding a chimera, a Sancho Panza who carried wisdom to the point of associating himself with folly if it appeared to him to be inevitable, but without ever leaving the earth. Such a domestic squire as that was ready to learn how to ride on horseback, but on the back of a little horse which could follow only far behind the winged chariot of the god, but from which he could fall without much harm, whereas Napoleon would shatter himself. In Spain especially that epic redressor of wrongs, that sublime Don Quixote failed because he mistook the impregnable forts of the adversary for windmills. He said: "When I bring back on my banner the words 'Liberty, Emancipation from Superstition, Destruction of the Nobility', etc., they will regard me as the liberator of Spain". But it was impossible to exorcise "those phantoms of the past", so living that they aroused the whole of the Peninsula against the oppressor. Murat's volley of grape-shot against the population of Madrid was but a feeble image of the bankruptcy which awaited that "regeneration" of Europe. The nations were indignant on discovering a stony-hearted mother in that Liberty which the Revolution and the Emperor offered them as a bride. In company with all those ideologists, whom he held, however, in horror, Napoleon thought, like Condorcet, the "illuminist geometrician", "that a good law must be good for all men, just as a geometrical proposition is true for everybody". It was that which made him, through conception, which was not his province, a utopist—which made him a realist through his power to carry things out, a province in which he was a master. Action personified, he was more than its genius—he was its poet, for he carried out the dictates of that genius in dreamland. The reality of his power being so inherent in that dream which he incarnated in the eyes of revolutionary France, nobody, not even Sancho Panza Talleyrand, could dispel it.

A great Polish lady, Comtesse Potocka, related that at Warsaw, at a ball given by Talleyrand in honour of the

Emperor, she saw the Prince, with a napkin under his arm and a silver-gilt tray in his hand, offer a glass of lemonade to that monarch, whom, when alone, he treated as an "upstart". To refresh that insatiable man and calm his fever, it would have been necessary for Talleyrand to have offered him peace with world-empire and universal fraternity. The greatest of diplomatists could render him only a more modest service. If Napoleon was, as M. Jacques Bainville has said, not the father but the *accoucheur* of the modern world, then Talleyrand, at that Caesarian operation, assisted him by administering the chloroform, that is to say by drawing up in legal style the decrees of force.

Talleyrand has said that Napoleon "lent his name to adventures instead of giving it to his century". In the light of contemporary events, far from correcting that judgment, he would have aggravated it, but this would in no way diminish a glory which is too highly placed to be measured on the political plane, for Napoleon's glory, like that of all heroes, is on that lofty, aesthetic level where his "adventures" appear as incomparable exploits. Talleyrand would have noted that of the monument raised by Napoleon there remains hardly anything save fragments. The Empire collapsed like a castle of cards. The central redoubt of the whole system, the French State, against which the Empire was backed up, far from being shaken by the fall, was first of all relieved. After sheltering France during several generations, behold—under the pressure of new forces—that State cracking and tottering. What was there that remained intact between electoralism, syndicalism, and the financial or industrial feudalities? Its best-tempered framework—the institutions which had so often formed the interim of a veritable government, the codes, the judicial and administrative apparatus—became dislocated and fell to pieces. Under the absolute monarchy of the Empire, France was administered, not represented. The whole of the national life depended on functionaries. Officialdom, which in Napoleon's strong hand was the weapon of the State, turned against him in the hand of the Revolution. The Napoleonic State was devoured by the monster he had nourished.

But the most complete and rapid ruin was that of the palace of ideas—the Emperor's most cherished edifice, the one he so lovingly furnished when meditating in his little house at St. Helena. It was a palace which he raised on the crumbling remains of the Empire. It will signify but little that he was conquered if his idea gains the victory. Blessed will his martyrdom be if the redemption of the world is at that price. Faintly outlined in the haze of a not-far-distant future he glimpsed the United States of Europe, a confederation of all the nations formerly assembled under his sceptre, for ever reconciled in "a great family" which would hold him in veneration and the head of which would perhaps be his own son. Had he not, in unifying Germany and Italy, laid the two principal foundation stones of that grandiose monument? And thus the cyclone of the Revolution and the Empire would have scattered more seeds than it had caused ruin and devastation.

But it was not the seed selected by Napoleon which was to fructify. In France he codified revolutionary individualism. In Europe he spread revolutionary ideology, and sought to impose it upon nations with the sword, just as the Jacobins had imposed it on France by means of the Terror. But, while ideas are propagated they undergo transformation to the point of turning against themselves. Jacobin individualism in Germany became a collective racial individualism in opposition to Europe and to the exclusion of any community of nations.

Napoleon, the gatherer of German territories together and the champion of "great agglomerations", was, with Bismarck, as Chancellor von Bülow said, the founder of German unity. Recently in Berlin, at a lecture on "Napoleon and the Nineteenth Century", Herr Hans Friedrich hailed in him "the man and superman, the heir of the Revolution, the creator of the national idea"—that is to say, the German idea—Germany armed with her unity to shatter the unity of Europe, and using her independence to threaten the unity of other nations. That is an idea which annihilates the ideal framed at St. Helena. If modern Germany personifies the malady from which Europe is suffering, then it was Napoleon who inoculated her; and what he thought to be a serum has turned out to be a virus. He dreamed of replacing the Holy Alliance of kings by a Holy Alliance of the nations. Nations are now more divided than kings were and their quarrels are otherwise tragic. Far from realizing that happy harmony of the Napoleonic dream, the world is more "out of tune and doleful" than ever. In Germany, where with sword in hand he preached the cult of reason and the enfranchisement of the individual, we find to-day the deification of brute instinct and the annihilation of the human personality.

Further away, on the confines of Europe and Asia, in Russia, where Napoleon wished to introduce, or, if not, defend, Western civilization, he was to facilitate the most redoubtable offensive that that civilization has ever encountered. Equality (which from the political domain passes to the economic domain) and individualism (which suppresses traditional groupings, the "intermediary powers") end in Communism, the natural child—like Germanic Imperialism—of the Revolution and the Empire. The results are diametrically opposed to what was intended. A spiritual Waterloo is more disastrous than the other. Napoleon has been compared to a solar myth, because he was born on an island of the Levant and was destined to die on an island of the West. His political star rose at one pole and set at the other.

The Napoleonic dream presupposes a huge Salente governed not by philosophers, for they would never be in agreement, but by wise men, or, what is still more chimerical, by nations composed of men similar to the gods, as in one of H. G. Wells's anticipations—supermen exempt from error and malice. Talleyrand, who had his reasons for believing in original sin, took that into account in his political conceptions. Because he was the personification of prevision—whereas Napoleon personified vision—and because he did not quit the earth, he went further with his crutch, without disputing with the other for the privilege of stopping the sun in its flight. He had had many "adventures" less noble than those of Napoleon, and he has still less given his name to his century, though his life was well-nigh centenarian. But in the following century, in the twentieth century, the consequences of his action still develop in the direction he wished them to take, whereas Napoleon's action—his political action only, his moral action being incalculable—is continued by reactions in a contrary direction and thus destroy his work. If Talleyrand could return among us, he would conclude that, as regards France, exposed to perish amidst the anarchy and corruption of the Directory, Napoleon was salvation, not health—a remedy, not a régime. He would see in him a constructor rather than a founder. Perhaps he would claim the latter title for himself on the ground that the essential part of his work—the English alliance and the independence of Belgium—has the advantage of durability.

There were three phases in Talleyrand's political career. In the first he was a destroyer; in the second, under the Empire, he was above all a decorator; in the third, under the monarchy, he became a constructor. A decorator under the Empire—since, as far as possible, he provided inordinate and violent enterprises with the colours of common sense and courtesy—he was not to be merely that. Doubtless at that time, when a constructor, he especially devoted himself to his own fortune in every sense of the word. However, history must not forget that, through the part he played on the 18th of Brumaire, he had an influence, more than any other person, on the choice of the architect who was to reconstruct France. More indirectly is he entitled to our gratitude for having reorganized the Ministry of Foreign Affairs, where he introduced a spirit and a staff which formed, as it were, a little isle of the old régime in the midst of the Revolution and the Empire. Thanks to him, and with the recollection of Choiseul and De Vergennes, there was perpetuated in the shade a tradition which, after defeat, was to be the principle of a resurrection. It was in the midst of defeat that he was to triumph over himself, and it was on the ruins of the Empire that he was to build. Meanwhile, while maintaining a sound doctrine and forming a staff to carry it out, when the right moment came, he formed himself. As regards pontifical diplomacy, he framed this maxim: "To make a good Secretary of State at Rome, it is well to choose a bad Cardinal". An ex-bishop, even though he be a Talleyrand, is not immediately a good Minister of Foreign Affairs. A theologian's sublety and a prelate's discretion, without a priest's scruples, do not suffice. It is only by passing through the schools and sometimes by making mistakes that one can attain mastery. As soon as events supplied him with the materials, Talleyrand was qualified to construct a home port (the Government of Louis XVIII) and also a port abroad (the Treaty of Vienna) where, after so many storms, France revived, and whence, when the wind once more became favourable, she could again set sail towards a great destiny.

## CHAPTER VIII

# TALLEYRAND AND THE RESTORATION

M. de Talleyrand is continually telling us that Constitutions are absurdities; that nations will not have
them because they possess the instinct of conservation.
PRINCESSE DE LIEVEN

ON the morning of March 31, 1814, the intimate friends
of the Prince de Bénévent were assembled as usual at his
rising from bed. He was in the hands of his faithful valet
Courtiade, who was so completely in sympathy with his
master that at the time of Talleyrand's marriage with
Mme Grant he covered his face, ejaculating: "And to
think we have had Mesdames . . ." etc., etc. He enumerated all the grand ladies who had conferred their favours
on Talleyrand. After assisting him to sit up, a task already
half completed by his position in bed, where, a straight
line being as obnoxious to him by night as it was by day—
there was a deep hollow to save him from apoplexy—the
valet proceeded to relieve him of the fourteen superposed
nightcaps which bore witness to another of his manias—
the fear of falling on his head. Whilst Courtiade was
powdering him, a visit was announced which filled him
with joy: that of Count Nesselrode, minister of the Tsar
Alexander; who, after the capitulation of Paris, had taken
up his quarters at Bondy and sent his confidential man to
Talleyrand "to concert with him the first measures to be
taken". The Prince, his hair half dressed, escaped from
Courtiade's hands to throw himself into the arms of

Nesselrode, whom he covered from head to foot with powder. The Restoration was a fact.

Since the time when Talleyrand, without waiting for the Russian disasters, was the first to announce "the beginning of the end", his ever-active mind, at the service of an insatiable ambition, had applied itself to discover in that end a way out, and even a beginning of a career still more brilliant than that which had been his under the Empire. First, preserve and consolidate the gains acquired, then increase them so as to add glory and fortune, while searching for the point where personal aims and national interests agreed; obtain advantages for himself while diminishing catastrophes for France—such was the secret programme which was to determine his public policy. With less romanticism than his friend Chateaubriand, with no intention of presenting an inspired forehead to the blasts of the tempest, but in order to justify his prevision and pocket his fee for the wreck, he also might have cried, "Hasten, O longed-for storms!" After ripe reflection and long hesitation it seemed to him that the return of the Bourbons amidst the wreck of the Empire was the best way to refloat France, while saving his own person and baggage.

In the accomplishment of this task, as in almost all the decisive moments of his life, Talleyrand felt and utilized a woman's influence. Aimée de Coigny, the young captive of André Chénier and the former Duchesse de Fleury, had been, among other sentimental experiences, the wife of the handsome Montrond, the man-of-all-work of Talleyrand. Possessing few scruples and much wit, she shared with the latter natural affinities, which, under the empire of common interests, soon developed into elective affinities. She was one of those women who seek the absolute in love, not by giving herself for all time to the same man but by yielding herself without reserve to the man of the moment. At that time she was the friend of the Marquis Bruno de Boisgelin, a royalist, whose convictions she adopted with all the ardour of a temperament which transformed those convictions in her case into passion. In fact, Bruno de Boisgelin had a warm heart but a cool head, and his politics belonged more to the head than to the heart. "I ask", said he, "that the French Constitution shall consist of two chambers and the throne, and that on this throne, instead of a turbulent soldier or a worthy man at whose feet our nation, idolater of personal qualities, would bow down, I ask, say I, that there be placed the great Monsieur,[1] then, the Comte d'Artois, then his children, and all belonging to his race in order of primogeniture, since I know of nothing which lends itself less to enthusiasm and is more akin to numerical order than the order of birth." This programme—which placed the chambers before the throne, proscribed enthusiasm and gave to empiricism that which it took away from Divine Right —possessed nothing of an elevating character, but it was all the more encouraging to Talleyrand. He recognized therein his principles of 1792, those of a constitutional monarchy—principles sacred to him, especially in 1814, because they offered protection to his interests. With such an encumbered past it was only under a liberal monarchy that he could play a part and even escape reprisals. In demanding guarantees he did not think solely of the nation.

As to the necessity of getting rid of Napoleon, the two accomplices had long been in accord. From the month of November 1812, some days after the Malet conspiracy, which, said Aimée de Coigny, "had opened a door to

[1] The title of the French King's eldest brother.—Translators' note.

hope", Talleyrand, having in her presence enumerated the Emperor's errors and the evils with which he had overwhelmed France, concluded by saying, "He must be destroyed, and no matter how". As to the régime to be substituted, he was more reserved and uncertain. A republic with three consuls, of whom he would be one, if not even the first? That combination had been considered. But the word "republic" disgusted the nation; it denoted terror, war, anarchy, ruin. The King of Rome with the regency of Marie Louise? That, at first, was Talleyrand's dream. A Queen-Regent of twenty-two years of age, lacking in will power, whose marriage with Napoleon he had advised, whose father, the Emperor of Austria, esteemed him at his value, and even at his price: that seemed to him omnipotence and permanence in the post of Prime Minister. Yes, but one of two things was certain: either Marie Louise would be influenced from Vienna by Metternich—who had not placed her on the throne of France to be agreeable to Napoleon—his government and that of Talleyrand would be denounced as the government of the foreigner, and the national feeling would revolt with even more reason than in 1792 against this new "Austrian woman"; or, so long as the "Corsican Ogre" was living and relatively free—for St. Helena was not yet thought of —he would dominate his wife and son from near or far, reign under their name and so destroy all his enemies. To Talleyrand, unable to have recourse like others to persons inferior to himself by birth, intelligence, and prestige—the Emperor's brothers and marshals—Louis XVIII was indicated at least as a makeshift but . . . First of all, the Prince de Bénévent wished to be implored and even paid to accept what at bottom he desired. Besides, he did not unconditionally accept the monarchy.

At the beginning of 1814, during the French campaign,

events followed rapidly one upon the other. Aimée de Coigny consulted the sphinx of the Rue St-Florentin; but she questioned him so imperiously as to prompt him to give a reply which was to be that of destiny. He possessed all the more authority for being less in favour. His disgrace, which he attributed to his clairvoyance and frankness, was to him a certificate of infallibility. M. de Roux has very well said: "All those who wished to belong to the victorious party held themselves ready to play the same card as he did". The reputation he had gained for being able to predict the future thus gave him the power to do so. Whether it be that his infallibility as much as his clairvoyance was due to his silence, or whether he desired to enhance the value of his final consent by a long resistance and involve Aimée de Coigny deeper than himself, he eluded her earnest entreaties, but at the same time encouraged them. Questions that were too prosaic he parried with a smile, a subterfuge, or by wilful contradictions, which were also an element of his infallibility, for the surest method of stumbling on the truth is to adopt every opinion, but afterwards explain away all those to which subsequent events have given the lie. When he was most slippery in his metamorphoses, Aimée de Coigny named this mood "his serpent's skin". However, little by little he cast it. This game of hide-and-seek necessarily had to end before the game that Napoleon was about to lose, so that the cards should be dealt for that of which his fall would be the signal. To win it, Talleyrand inspired everyone with hope, which astonished and disheartened Aimée de Coigny. "All Paris", said she, "came to see him alone and in secret. Each one who came out, meeting the other who entered, seemed to say, 'I got here before you. I am the one who can call him my chief'."

However, one day, after having examined every other

solution, including, to the great dismay of his legitimist lady friend, a "national throne" with M. le duc d'Orléans, Talleyrand rose, went towards the door of his study to assure himself that it was closed, and then, revealing his thoughts at last, said: "I certainly want a king, but—but —I don't want—I must confess to you, to risk receiving a pardon instead of thanks".

His desire was to be the Prime Minister of a sovereign who would be indebted to him. He wished, when addressing Louis XVIII, to be able to say, or insinuate, "Who made you King?" In the meantime he himself consented to be indebted to Boisgelin and his lady friend. The elder brother of Louis XVI did not know him, and, said Talleyrand, "I have no means of getting in touch with him". The next morning, Aimée de Coigny brought him a copy of a letter which M. de Boisgelin had sent to Louis XVIII to prove to him that the Prince de Bénévent alone was able to smooth his path to the throne.

Now more than a year had elapsed since Talleyrand had made tentative approaches to Louis XVIII, recalling his existence through the best of intercessors, his uncle, Alexandre Talleyrand de Périgord, the former Archbishop of Rheims, who had followed the head of the House of France into England, and who, at the little Court of Hartwell, where the tradition of Versailles was maintained, held the post of Grand Almoner. Family feeling in this excellent uncle overcoming a very natural resentment towards an apostate nephew who had never given him any sign of life since the Revolution, the Grand Almoner mentioned his nephew's overture to Louis XVIII, who welcomed it by saying: "God be praised! Bonaparte must be near his fall. For I will wager that when the Directory was near its end your nephew wrote in the same way to the Conqueror of Italy. If you answer him, tell him I accept the omen of his kind remembrance." It was a favourable omen for Talleyrand himself, who, at the time he declared he had no means of getting into touch with Louis XVIII, had received a note from his bosom friend, M. de Blacas, dated December 1, 1813, which was more than an absolution: it was a prayer, an appeal to his abilities. But the pledge of the Parisian royalists was not without its use in proving to Hartwell the sincerity of his feelings and the necessity for using those abilities. So between his worthy uncle and Aimée de Coigny, the ex-Bishop of Autun became well placed in the King's confidence.

But the confidence the King reposed in him was *not* well placed. At the back of his mind was a single fixed idea: to adopt the party which would mean for him the least effort, the least risk, and the maximum of good luck. The return of the Bourbons was still for him only one of two extremities of the alternative in which the regency of Marie Louise was the other. Whilst adopting a policy of reinsurance on the Bourbon side, he cherished the dream of a long regency in which he would be the Mazarin, more easily than the Richelieu, of Louis XVIII. Before setting out for the French campaign, the Emperor had conferred the regency on Marie Louise, putting aside his brothers, who were no less undesirable to Talleyrand than to himself. His ascendancy over the Empress was more easily exerted than over them, and all the more so as his intimacy with the Viennese Court would be his strongest claim upon her. To the attraction of this prospect was added, to make it the more preferable to him, a feeling of the obstacles which any other solution would encounter. So long as Marie Louise was in the capital, properly invested with the regency, surrounded by the Government, grand dignitaries, and great departments of State, it was

not easy to see how power could pass into other hands.
The prejudices against the Bourbons, who, it was said,
knew not France, and whom France herself no longer
knew, appeared insurmountable. On the other hand,
Napoleon's name—the most glorious in the world even
amidst defeat—would, after his abdication, rally around
the King of Rome and his mother the entire army and all
Frenchmen hostile alike to the old régime and the Revolution. Far from being a weakness, the presence of a young
woman and a child on the throne would endow the loyalty
of the nation with the strength of a chivalrous feeling.
After so many upheavals, did not wisdom demand their
limitation by enabling France to be governed by the principles and the men to whom she was accustomed—those of
the Empire—after having eliminated the despotism and
ambition of the Emperor? And since the Austrian Emperor was unable to connive at the spoliation of his
daughter and his grandson, was not their throne the surest
safeguard against the covetousness of his allies? Were
these arguments not more convincing than objections
founded on the risk of handing over the State either to
Napoleon, under the cloak of a regency, or to the Cabinet
of Vienna? Talleyrand reasoned that the firmness of the
Powers could divert the first risk and he trusted in his
skill to ward off the other. This was the time for him to
resume his "serpent's skin" with its iridescent colours;
somewhat European on the Viennese side, somewhat
nationalist on that of Paris.

Whilst the course of events demanded a decision, the
Prince de Bénévent avoided committing himself irre-
vocably to either. He took a hand at whist with the Em-
press without breaking off relations—through Aimée de
Coigny and his uncle the Archbishop—with Louis XVIII.
This double attitude, essentially due to calculation, was

also that form of sport in which he excelled, a sport which, while furthering his interests, exercised his faculties and flattered his vanity; namely, to play on two tables; commit himself to no one, so that he might be prepared for all eventualities; to astonish the world because he was never either astonished or surprised, having foreseen all contingencies and provided for them; in short, to puzzle the public by his oracular ambiguity. He gave away his secret one day in confessing to the Comtesse de Kielmansegge: "For centuries to come I should like the discussion to go as to what I have been, what I have thought, and what I intended". He was less impenetrable than he supposed, if one does not lose sight of his tendency to be a hoaxer, a dry old file—that "actor" side of him, as we may say to-day, which impelled him to pose before posterity as he did before his contemporaries, to be always in the front of the footlights, even when the play was bad, and to learn several parts provided they were leading parts in order to be sure that his name was always on the bills. He had opinions, and, just as he had mistresses, changeable schemes, so that he might never be caught napping.

It was a case of the trick known as that of "the two salmon", raised to the rank of a principle and applied to high politics. One day at a grand banquet at which he desired to display great magnificence, and at a time of the year when fish were not plentiful, Talleyrand had obtained two salmon of extraordinary size. He gave orders that both were to be prepared and in great secrecy explained to his butler how they were to be served. After the soup at that evening feast, two lordly lackeys solemnly advanced, bearing upon an immense silver dish a salmon which the guests hailed with exclamations of delight. But while the master of the house was smiling at their compliments regarding this "unique dish", one of the two lackeys, who had been coached by the butler to do so, made a false step and fell on the carpet along with the dish and its contents. Whereupon Talleyrand, supremely impassive, gave the order, "Let another be brought in". And immediately afterwards, a second salmon, no less "unique" than its predecessor, made its appearance with equal solemnity before the astonished guests.

In the same way, in 1814, Talleyrand, in the rôle of butler getting ready to receive the Allied sovereigns in Paris, considers his bill of fare. Within the ice-house of his mind he held in reserve all manner of solutions and forms of government. As circumstances might dictate, he would serve up that of Marie Louise, or Louis XVIII. He would even boast of having arranged the accident which caused the fall of the regency of Marie Louise and the restoration of the Bourbons. This accident was the departure of the Empress under circumstances which made it a desertion in face of the enemy. Napoleon, having left Paris in the hope of cutting the Allies' communications with the Rhine, the latter profited by it by marching on the capital, which was undefended, and where the most influential men, with Talleyrand at their head, impatiently awaited their arrival. On March 27 Marie Louise was sitting at her whist table with Queen Hortense, Molé, and the Prince de Bénévent: a game of whist with dummy — Napoleon, who symbolically was a dead partner in their game. She was regardless of the future and laughed heartily at Talleyrand's witticisms about the "false rumours" of an Allied attack on Paris. However, that same day Talleyrand had discussed with Pasquier, the Prefect of Police, the measures to be taken in anticipation of an imminent capitulation. Pasquier considered that the Empress ought to remain in Paris. Talleyrand strongly maintained an opposite opinion. His devotion to the Emperor rebelled at the idea of the

Empress and the King of Rome being in the hands of the enemy. The next day, the 28th, the "false rumours" being confirmed, the Council of the Regency met at the Tuileries to come to some decision on the matter. Talleyrand strongly opposed the proposal to leave, which the day before he had supported in the presence of the Prefect of Police. Boulay de la Meurthe having proposed that the Empress should be conducted to the Hôtel de Ville with the King of Rome in her arms to appeal to the people to make a desperate resistance, Talleyrand approved. Then, in a grave tone, he opposed the proposal for the departure of the Empress, which, he said, would make the defence of Paris impossible, and open its gates to the enemy by showing that the Government considered the game was lost; it would discourage and betray the Parisians for whom, in case of a misfortune, the presence of the daughter and grandson of the Austrian Emperor would appear the surest safeguard; it would be the signal for a general stampede; and finally, to abandon the capital would be to leave the field open to Napoleon's enemies, encourage their intrigues with the Coalition, and make a revolution in favour of the Bourbons inevitable. Whereupon he proceeded to set forth the scenario of that revolution with all the greater exactitude seeing that he was the author of it, and was making ready to act as its protagonist. When, his prudence being expressed in the language of conscience, M. de Talleyrand became silent, no one dared to add anything, and a considerable majority was of the same opinion. But Joseph then read the Emperor's instructions: under no circumstances to allow his wife and son to fall into the hands of the Allies—the most wretched lot in history being that of Astyanax, the prisoner of the Greeks. This command of Napoleon was dictated by his affection and the following calculation: beyond the reach of the Allies,

Marie Louise would be a source of strength to him, because she would be a pledge; under their influence she would prove a weakness because they would easily make her their instrument to dethrone him and proclaim a Regency. These unexpected but peremptory instructions put an end to the discussion. The departure of the Empress and the King of Rome was decided upon for the following morning. "I was aware that the Empress distrusted me, and that if I advised her departure, she would remain. I was in favour of her remaining in order that she might depart". This is a variant reading of the Bismarckian maxim: "I will tell the truth, and then I shall not be believed".

But is this remark, attributed to Talleyrand, sincere? Thiers affirms that, on the contrary, it was in insisting on keeping Marie Louise in Paris that the Prince de Bénévent was sincere. The essential point with him, says the historian of the Consulate and Empire, was to remain himself in Paris, where the fate of France and his own were about to be decided. Now, how could he remain in Paris after the departure of the Empress, to whom by his position as member of the Council of the Regency he was attached, without unmasking prematurely? It will be seen that this difficulty was of no account for so ingenious a mind. In fact, it was not his advice which decided the Empress to depart in order to oppose it, but the formal order of the Emperor. The most probable interpretation is that, having in thought already crossed the Rubicon in the direction of the Bourbons, he sought effectively to quit the Napoleonic shore on which he was only detained by the presence of the Empress in Paris, while her departure, liberating him and discrediting her, would be a valuable trump card in his hand. But, being a Talleyrand, and so never destroying his bridges, even over the Rubicon, he advised officially against his secret wish, so as to mislead people as to his real intentions and to protect himself, by that proof of loyalty, lest some new miracle of the god of war should make him formidable once more.

Very punctiliously, on the morning of the 29th, Talleyrand went to the Tuileries to pay his respects to Marie Louise at the moment of her departure. A pretext for not rejoining her at Blois yet remained to be found. So he made ostensible preparations for the journey and postponed it until the morrow. The essential thing was to gain time until the entrance of the Allied armies into Paris, where these would be able to shelter him from the vengeance of Napoleon. The time he had to wait was not long. Marmont and Mortier, for the sake of honour, waged a desperate combat at the gates of Paris, and, awaiting the issue of the drama, Talleyrand thought of a stratagem by means of which he might profit by it in entire security. Once again there was an opportunity to set the women to work. He sought his friend Mme de Rémusat, cousin of the Prefect of Police, Pasquier, and begged her to accompany him to the Prefecture. Though busily occupied with his duties in what might turn out to be the gravest of situations—to keep watch over the safety of the capital during the foreign occupation, the Prefect did not keep Talleyrand waiting. But no sooner had he been introduced than he let Mme de Rémusat explain matters. She explained to her cousin that M. de Talleyrand was preparing to rejoin the Empress—a great misfortune, she declared. For in that case there would be no one in Paris possessing sufficient credit to treat with the foreigner and obtain the most favourable terms. What was to be done? The advice of her dear cousin was requested. The Prefect—his visitors had scored one point—did not dispute the opinion of his fair cousin, but he did not see how he could help her. Mme de Rémusat, encouraged by this semi-acquiescence, suggested that the guarding of the gate by which the Prince intended to leave Paris be entrusted to picked men, with an order to rouse the mob against such a public calamity as his departure would be under such circumstances. It was for the sake of France! The Prefect replied that it was his business to forestall and repress riots rather than to organize them. Nevertheless, whether it was that he shared the views of his cousin or whether he was in a hurry to get rid of her to return to more pressing duties, he in his turn suggested the following procedure: that M. de Rémusat, who held a commission in the National Guard, should arrange to post his men at the gate by which M. de Talleyrand preferred to present himself for leaving the city, and the guard would be responsible for the desired riot.

This was a clever piece of work. Prince de Bénévent was deserting the Emperor and the Queen-Regent with the approval and even the support of their Prefect of Police. Returning to the rue St-Florentin, he presently emerged in travelling costume, with his secretary on horseback, to proceed towards the Barrière des Bonhommes, at Passy, upon the road to Versailles. And there it was that M. de Rémusat, punctual at the rendezvous and faithful to his instructions, requested Talleyrand to return home.

Even before the departure of the Empress, the cause of the monarchy had, in Talleyrand's opinion, progressed considerably, because it had gained considerable ground in the country. In his eyes the prestige of a party was measured in terms of its chances of attaining power. On March 12 the King was proclaimed at Bordeaux, and his authority, represented in the person of the Duc d'Angoulême,

was recognized in the Gironde and neighbouring Departments. Insurrection was brewing in the Vendée. At other
places royalist agents were recruiting an ever-increasing
number of deserters. At Paris the Municipal Council was
controlled by royalists. Its aid was all the more important
as the National Guard was placed under its authority. As
always happens in troubled times, in which the real character of human nature is brought to light, the vilest and
noblest sentiments—fear, greed, devotion, and heroism—
combined to one common result. Regicides were touched
with grace. Jacobites who had made their pile "put off the
old man" so as to remain prosperous. During the French
campaign, Baron Louis, the ex-deacon who had assisted
Talleyrand at the Federation Mass, said of Napoleon, to
whom he owed everything, "The man is a corpse, but he
doesn't stink yet. . . ." To turn away from him and inhale
the perfume of the lilies, he did not wait for decomposition
to set in. If, before its consummation, the Restoration had
its converts who, by preceding it, made its task easier, and
so created a claim on its good will, it also possessed its
martyrs, who were even more useful. Militant royalists
like the Chevalier de Gouault and de Rougeville, known as
the Chevalier de la Maison Rouge, were shot by order of
Napoleon.

Talleyrand, who had never had any vocation for martyrdom, took this into account in his forecast as a symp-
tom and a force on behalf of the monarchy. He felt that a
cause for which one dies is not a cause which dies. No one
was likely to give his life for either Marie Louise or the
King of Rome.

M. de Roux has rightly said that the Restoration was
brought about by "a conspiracy among the faithful and a
plot among the high officials"—two minorities, one devoted, the other powerful. Sentiment held priority, as it

held primacy over calculation. Devotion, sometimes the sacrifice of the faithful, preceded the schemes of the adroit and inspired them. Had Aimée de Coigny and the Chevalier de la Maison Rouge been Bonapartists, Talleyrand would probably have been an uncompromising supporter of the Regency and the fate of Europe would have been different. Able persons, priding themselves on obeying reason alone, are often, unknown to themselves, led by the affections of others.

Another example of this is found in Vitrolles' mission to the Allies in the early days of March. Talleyrand had the greatest interest in knowing their plans and, as far as possible, to direct them along the path of his own secret designs. But to reach their headquarters it was necessary to pass through the French lines; in other words, to risk one's head. Vitrolles, an ardent royalist, offered himself, because for him it was a magnificent opportunity to plead the Bourbon cause before the chief of the Coalition. Provided with false passports, he left Paris on March 6, having instructions to sound the intentions of the Allies concerning Napoleon, or any other Government to follow. He was accredited by a letter addressed to Nesselrode, and written in invisible ink: "The person that I send you is worthy of every confidence. Hear what he has to say and be grateful to me. It is time to be more explicit. You are walking with crutches: use your legs and do what you like". This message, which invited the Allies to march on Paris, and gave them to understand that they would be received there as liberators, was the work of Dalberg, then the principal confidant of Talleyrand, who, notwithstanding the entreaties of Vitrolles, gave him not a word in his own hand. "You do not know this baboon," said Dalberg to Vitrolles. "He wouldn't risk burning the end of his paw, even if the chestnuts were to be for him alone."

Vitrolles recommended Talleyrand to the kind regards of Alexander and confirmed the Emperor in his belief that nothing could be done in Paris without him. Talleyrand, on his own side, knew that nothing could be done without Alexander, the real leader of the Allied armies, the King of Prussia being merely his satellite, and the Austrian Emperor, who preferred to take a minor part in events so grievous for his son-in-law, daughter and grandson, remaining several stages behind general headquarters. The Tsar and the Prince de Bénévent were, besides, ready to collaborate once more as the result of a close intimacy sealed at Erfurt where Talleyrand had acted as Alexander's accomplice, and where, in exchange, Alexander had obtained for Talleyrand's nephew, Edmond, the hand in marriage of the richest and most fascinating heiress in his Empire.

That was the reason why Talleyrand could not contain himself for joy when, on the morning of March 31, the most important date in his life, Nesselrode, the Tsar's envoy, was announced. That was the trump card of his game.

On that historic day of March 31, Talleyrand gave proof of talents that no one suspected in him. Whereas he had reached his ends most often through nonchalance or calculation whilst loitering along tortuous and obscure paths, now we see him openly and promptly going straight to his object. Whereas, through force of habit and following Choiseul's method—that of the grand seignior who directs from above and pays no heed to mere detail—he used to confine himself to a general policy, trusting himself to his political "scullions" for its execution whilst reserving the perquisites for himself, now we see him lending a helping hand to the cook and measuring out all the ingredients for the sauce. This was because, to please his guests, who had not all the same taste, and also to suit his own, the monarchy which he had on the simmer had to be served hot and with very diverse condiments.

First of all, without losing a minute, Talleyrand bound the Tsar irrevocably, and through him the Allies to his programme. Notwithstanding Louis XVIII's proclamation at Bordeaux and Vitrolles' ardent advocacy, Alexander had another candidate for the throne of France. He was on bad terms with Louis XVIII, who had been unable to continue to be his guest at Mittau, and had been obliged to seek refuge in England; and he was under the influence of La Harpe, a Swiss trained in the school of Jean-Jacques Rousseau and imbued with the principles of the Revolution. An autocrat in Russia, Alexander was a liberal in France, the more so because, being vain and ambitious, he found that these two qualities paid there. His "liberalism" guaranteed his popularity in Paris and his authority all over France, his candidate being Bernadotte, who on the throne would be his loyal servant, after what Albert Sorel calls "an election in the Polish fashion". Prussia would say nothing provided that her mouth was stopped with a few scraps of French territory —at the least, Alsace and Lorraine. Austria would prefer the maintenance of Napoleon, wiser and more tractable through defeat, for Metternich detested the Bourbons, and in his blindness and infatuation flattered himself that he was able to dominate a fallen but not dethroned Caesar, the docile and grateful son-in-law of his sovereign. The regency of Marie Louise, thought he, would be more precarious, for it would make the hand of Austria too visible. Still, that solution was not excluded, and would be less foolish than the Bernadotte plan. If the alternative for France was between a Russian or Austrian protectorate,

Talleyrand in either case would be Resident-General, for he enjoyed as much credit at Vienna as at St. Petersburg. But he possessed too much sound political sense to deceive himself about the fragility of these plans and the mortal peril to France which would follow. Bernadotte, stained with French blood, would be vomited by the nation if he were imposed in France by the bayonets of the liberal Alexander. Whilst Louis XVIII was proclaimed at Bordeaux there would be civil war in invaded France. The regency of Marie Louise would also be the organization of chaos. That was the opinion of Napoleon, who told his marshals: "My wife, my son, would not stand firm for an hour; you would have anarchy, which in a fortnight would end in the Bourbons": unless that anarchy was prolonged and brought Napoleon back. Fontainebleau was less distant from Paris than the island of Elba, an eventuality which would make the resumption of hostilities inevitable, with no other result except to increase the Allies' demands with their distrust and their sacrifices; after, doubtless, the destruction of the capital, where the Emperor thought of waging a final battle. Besides, war would not cause the cessation of anarchy; for, even prior to the recent events which had enfeebled the Government, the Prefects had reported that, if it was intended to use force to make the conscripts march, these would resort to arms and civil war would break out. The imperial authorities—who, however, were by no means soft-handed—had been compelled (to preserve a semblance of order) to suspend the collection of taxes, so that France had only a choice between a legitimate monarchy and an abyss in which she risked destruction. It remained to convince the Allies of that, and to prove to them that, contrary to what they believed, or affected to believe in order to gain their ends, the monarchy of Louis XVIII responded

to the desire of the nation no less than to its interest. This task would have been very difficult for any other person than Talleyrand, the more so that the sole Power favourable to the Bourbons—England—was not represented in the Council of the Coalition; her army was far away from Paris, under the command of Wellington, who, coming from Spain, occupied south-western France. Moreover, the reason for this good will towards Louis XVIII was not one, on the contrary, for the allies of England: in that, as invariably after a great war, the Cabinet of London extended its hand to the vanquished foe to help him to recover, so as to re-establish on the Continent that equilibrium which is the condition of her arbitrament and supremacy.

Talleyrand could therefore count only on himself and the prestige of the Bourbons to get them accepted by the Allies who, contrary to legend, far from having imposed them, were obliged to accept them. As soon as he had Nesselrode at hand, he set to work with him and his three friends—the Abbé de Pradt, Duc de Dalberg, and Baron Louis. An admirable selection of men to play in that drama the part of the antique chorus, to express the feelings of the crowd and the will of the gods. These three persons had been loaded with favours by Napoleon. The Abbé de Pradt, after having been his Almoner, had been created a baron, a bishop, an archbishop, and ambassador in Poland; Dalberg, who was of German origin—a fact which invested him with more authority with the Allies— had been made a duke by the Emperor and received a grant of two hundred thousand livres per annum. The ex-Abbé Louis had only been created a baron, but he hated Napoleon as much as his two confederates, the archbishop and the duke. How was it possible to doubt the irresistible movement which carried all French hearts to the Bourbon cause when it involved men so closely bound to Napoleon's fortune by the bonds of gratitude?

The word of these renegades was more worthy of confidence than that of faithful royalists like Vitrolles. Therefore Nesselrode was able to come to an agreement at once with them regarding a proposed Declaration which excluded Napoleon and his family from the throne and implicitly called upon Louis XVIII to occupy it. The printing of this document raised more difficulties than its composition. The day when the Allies entered Paris, being one of joy for some and mourning for others, all workshops were closed. It was impossible to apply to the National Printing Works, whose manager, a subordinate official, was incorruptible—devotion among the Emperor's servants being in inverse ratio to their rank. However, not a moment was to be lost. But Talleyrand had foreseen everything: he had obtained a printer, an ardent royalist named Michaud, who two hours later returned with the proofs. All that remained to be done before returning them with the order to print was to obtain the approbation of the Tsar Alexander, who arrived at the Rue St-Florentin in the afternoon. He was to have stayed at the Elysée, having declined, through a feeling of delicacy which redounded to his popularity, the honour of occupying the Tuileries, but at the last moment was warned that the Elysée Palace was undermined. Was it Talleyrand who, under cover, had sent him that quite unfounded message? However that may be, it was Talleyrand who took advantage of it to offer the Tsar hospitality in his own house in the Rue St-Florentin and the invitation was accepted. Behold him secluded! He shut himself up with Talleyrand, who, after a short private talk, introduced his accomplices, who confirmed the opinion he had just expressed in favour of the Bourbons. Talleyrand summed it up in these words: "A republic is an impossibility, a Regency and Bernadotte would be an intrigue; the Bourbons alone are a principle".

Alexander, a great dandy on the foremost stage in the world, had just been acclaimed at the head of his troops by the Parisian populace. Intoxicated by this success, which he interpreted as a supreme homage, he was more than ever eager to please. He approved of the Declaration, drawn up and printed that very morning, under the illusion skilfully created by Talleyrand, that he was its author. The King of Prussia and Prince von Schwartzenburg, who had joined the Tsar during this conference and had played a silent part therein, acquiesced by a nod.

Here is the text of that Declaration:

The armies of the Allied Powers have occupied the French capital.

The Allied Sovereigns welcome the desire of the French nation.

They declare:

That if the terms of peace demanded the strongest guarantees at the time when it was necessary to curb the ambition of Bonaparte, they should be more favourable when, by reason of her return to wise government, France herself offers assurances of repose.

The Allied Sovereigns therefore proclaim:

That they will no longer treat with Bonaparte or with any member of his family.

That they respect the integrity of ancient France as she existed under her legitimate kings; *they can even do more, since they still maintain the principle that for the well-being of Europe it is necessary that France should be strong and great.*

That they will recognize and guarantee the Constitution which the French nation may adopt. Therefore they request the Senate to appoint a provisional government able to provide for administrative requirements, and to draft a Constitution suitable to the French people.

The intentions just expressed I share in common with all the Allied Powers.

ALEXANDER

For His Imperial Majesty, the Secretary of State,
COMTE DE NESSELRODE

PARIS, *March* 31, 1814. 3 P.M.

This declaration was immediately placarded on the walls of Paris. Through an oversight, which possibly was an epigram on the part of the printer, it still bore the indication of the time at which it had been printed, before it was possible to have submitted it to the allied sovereigns. However, it contained an additional phrase, that in italics, dictated by the Tsar himself. A phrase amiable but vague, like the soul of its author, and which aroused hopes that were not to be realized.

Liberty for France to choose her own Government, exclusion of Napoleon and his family, the Bourbons plainly designated "return to wise government", "her legitimate kings", but without being named, so that the national liberty of choice should not be impaired; respect for the integrity of France's historic frontiers; limitation of royal power by a Constitution; an appeal to the Senate of which he was president and of whose docility he was aware. It was Talleyrand's programme, which won all along the line. On March 31, 1814, he was the arbiter of France's destinies. The Tsar Alexander could say "that he had placed in his hands the Empire of Bonaparte or the monarchy of the Bourbons, and that it was only for him to choose". Talleyrand chose the Bourbons. It was, as Thiers was to say of the Republic after France's disasters of 1870, the Government which divided France the least. But while Thiers was to say "the republic will be conservative, or will not exist", Talleyrand thought, "the Monarchy will be liberal, or will

P

not exist". Above all, it was not to be that which suited Prince de Bénévent, who demanded from a Constitution less the guarantee of public liberties than that of his private interests. He was to mobilize the Tsar and England to limit the "right divine", or historical right of the dynasty by means of the revolutionary right of national sovereignty. Indeed, the Restoration, about to be sanctioned by the Senate—that asylum of old Jacobins—was more the handiwork of regicides than foreign sovereigns, and the latter were to intervene specially to introduce what it contained of republicanism.

Whilst the sentence of exclusion was being pronounced against Napoleon and his kin in the large drawing-room of the house in the Rue St-Florentin known as the Salon de l'Aigle, his envoy, the unfortunate Caulaincourt, armed with powers to accept all the conditions of the Allies, had been waiting in vain for nearly five hours. Light comedy losing none of its rights on that dramatic day, entrances and exits were watched to suit the requirements of intrigue. Princesse de Talleyrand, surrounded by a number of pretty women, remained in the adjoining salon, entrusted with the mission to keep troublesome people quiet. It was necessary at any cost to isolate the Tsar until he was irrevocably committed by the signing and placarding of the declaration. When at last Caulaincourt could approach him, Alexander, showing him the document, replied: "It is too late. Here is a signed engagement. Many Frenchmen, depending upon my word, have committed themselves".

After the proclamation of March 31, Talleyrand—the phase of slow and prudent preparations being over—was as prompt as he was bold in its execution. On the night of March 31 to April 1 the senators were convoked. Out of the total number of one hundred and forty-one then on the roster, sixty-three assembled. This was not because they were all disposed—in their haste to abandon Napoleon—to forget their servility towards him. A certain number had followed Marie Louise to Blois, while others, more mindful of their safety than their interests, lurked in hiding-places until events of which they could approve had happened. In the Luxembourg Palace, where, under the Directory he had cajoled Barras and then Bonaparte, it was child's play for Talleyrand to get that assembly to vote decisions which he had drawn up in the morning with his associates: the appointment of a provisional Government to take in hand the direction of the State and to lay before the Senate proposals for the Constitution; a Government consisting of five members—the Prince de Bénévent as president, Bournonville, Jaucourt, Dalberg, and the Abbé de Montesquiou. Talleyrand, to quote Chateaubriand's quip, had formed a Government from his whist partners. For all that, his collaborators were none the less well chosen. They were all valuable liaison officers with different forces, which it was to his interest to manage carefully and group together. In that Government of concentration were represented all the colours of the political rainbow. The Abbé de Montesquiou was the sole legitimist in his team—he was what Talleyrand called his white cockade. Bournonville, an old Jacobin, was his redcap. Jaucourt, a protestant gentleman and former liberal Constituant, was his tricoloured cockade. Dalberg, a good European, a friend of foreign sovereigns and diplomats, was his white ensign, the white flag of truce—a presage of peace.

In an assembly in which sat the most eminent jurists of the Revolution, no one disputed the legality of that investiture by the minority of a phantom Senate which had never possessed real power. The *Moniteur* transformed the minority into a majority by the note: "Senators absent through illness notified their acquiescence". In default of a numerical majority, the sixty-three formed a "dynamic majority" through the presence among them of numerous regicides, whose adhesion during the preliminaries for the Restoration was, in the eyes of foreign sovereigns, a title superior to divine right.

On April 2 the Senate unanimously pronounced the deposition of Napoleon, justifying it in the severest terms, by citing faults which that high assembly ought really to have prevented, but had facilitated.

When the Comte de Sémallé, the agent for the Comte d'Artois, produced his authority bearing the signature of "Monsieur", Talleyrand kissed the document, exclaiming, "Ah! I well recognize Monsieur's handwriting". And he proceeded to indulge in protestations of devotion to the Bourbons. But if he knelt at their feet, it was to tie their hands better. So he showed Sémallé out, and in forty-eight hours obliged the Senate to patch up a liberal Constitution. "Monsieur" was then able to make his entrance into Paris with the title of Lieutenant-General of the kingdom. Talleyrand, at the head of the provisional government, repaired to the boundary at Bondy to greet him in these words: "Monseigneur, the happiness we feel on this day is beyond all expression, if Monsieur will receive with that heavenly goodness which is characteristic of his august House, the homage of our religious feeling and respectful devotion". The "heavenly goodness" and "religious feeling" were, according to taste, either a formula of courtesy or a discreet allusion to the doctrine of divine right. It was "Monsieur" who appeared to sanctify the doctrine of the Revolution implicitly in his reply fabricated afterwards at Talleyrand's mansion in the Rue St-Florentin and published in the *Moniteur*: "An end to discord: Peace and France. At last I see her again! and nothing is changed in her, unless it be that there is one Frenchman more." The following morning, at the Tuileries, when presenting the Senate to the Comte d'Artois, Talleyrand in his speech enlarged on the "lights of the century" and the needs of the moment. It was no longer heaven which was bringing back the Bourbons, but the Senate. Said the president: "It has encouraged the return of your august House to the throne of France. Too well instructed by the present and the past, it desires to consolidate for all time the royal authority on a just division of powers and on public liberties. The Senate, convinced that the principles of the new constitution are in your heart, confers upon you the title of Lieutenant-Governor of the kingdom."

Thus the re-establishment of the monarchy was subordinated to the acceptance of a Constitution, and in the meanwhile Louis XVIII, not being invested with royal power, it was not he who conferred the title of Lieutenant-General on his brother, as the pure royalists would have liked—it was the Senate. In his reply, concerted with Talleyrand, the Comte d'Artois declared that he had no fear of being disavowed by his brother when he guaranteed that the latter accepted the principles laid down.

The provisional government then transferred its powers to "Monsieur", while holding its sitting by his side in a Council in which Talleyrand maintained a predominant position.

During the two weeks of his government, which was a dictatorship by persuasion, supported by the foreign armies, the Prince de Bénévent's house presented a singular spectacle. The courtyard was a bivouac, full of Cossacks stretched out on the straw. The first floor, occupied by the Tsar, was an imperial residence and a general headquarters. The mezzanine was the seat of the provisional government, which met in the room of its president, while in a neighbouring boudoir the Princesse de Bénévent, appointed under the circumstance to the Ministry of Favours, possessed as many courtiers as the Emperor of all the Russias. The favour most in request—for it was the condition of all others—was the publication without delay of adhesions coming in from men of the Revolution and the Empire. In Talleyrand's antechamber beat the pulse of the capital, France and Europe. Reinhardt compared this restless coming and going to that of a magic lantern. To-day he would have likened it to a film, a "documentary" one, showing the vicissitudes of political life and the recantations of politicians, with its simultaneous and contrasted pictures. It was a sample of all nations, all classes, all professions, all uniforms, and also all disguises—those of all parties fused into one alone, the party of success, in which only the unfaltering royalist had the right to show himself without shame. Amidst this crowd, foreign princes and former *sans-culottes*, marshals and archbishops, members of the old nobility and the new, Chouans and devotees of the guillotine rubbed shoulders. There were also *émigrés* who had awaited the fall of the Empire to return to France; and there, too, was the man who had banished them—Fouché.

Author, producer, and leading actor of this spectacle, Talleyrand amidst the tumult remained impassive, smiling at the invisible threads of the thousand intrigues he was weaving, knotting, and unknotting. He was a champion chess-player who played several games simultaneously and won them all: the game with Alexander, whose generosity he encouraged, while supporting his liberalism and opposing his inconstancy; the game with the royalists, whose unreasonableness and impatience he restrained; the game with the Church, the greatest moral force, which the ex-Bishop of Autun conciliated by giving orders on April 2 to treat with all respect during his journey back to Rome Napoleon's august prisoner, Pius VII; the game with the army, the strongest material force, to which he addressed a proclamation to set it free from its oath of fidelity to the Emperor, showing it the white cockade of its marshals; the game with the Comte d'Artois, whom he counselled to display the tricoloured cockade, who, whilst retaining the white emblem, was soon to enter Paris clad in the uniform of the National Guard, which was tri-coloured, and who was to lend himself to an analogous proceeding to reconcile the royal prerogatives and the proposed Constitution, the tricolour being considered as involved in the foundation of the proposals and the white in its reservations; the game with public opinion, which had to be converted to the Bourbons, but in moderation, for he would need it to play his cards against them; the game with the Senate, which, formerly an instrument of imperial despotism, was now exaggerating liberalism, mainly the mask for its passions, and from whom Talley-rand only asked a pledge against the wrath of the returned *émigrés*. The members of the Upper Chamber, who dis-puted the hereditary rights of Louis XVIII by claiming to declare him king by right of their unfettered choice, were not satisfied with claiming them for themselves by de-claring they were hereditary peers as Talleyrand encour-aged them to do; they also, while contesting the royal sovereignty, claimed to usurp it by restricting the number of peers to the actual number of senators, and so only allowing vacancies to be filled in the very rare cases in which heredity did not provide for them. Above all, they held out for the consolidation of their endowment in perpetuity. This called forth some obvious jibes at the

Senate, which, in the revolution it was bringing about, was merely conservative of itself; and at its proposed Constitution, which, it was said, was only a constitution of annuities.

Talleyrand made not a single mistake in this imbroglio, in which a less supple mind than his would have been lost. All these games—and we have only mentioned some—were, however, more complicated than games of chess, not only because the pawns were men—that is, passions—but also because they were entangled. They were to be the elements of a single game, that which Talleyrand had played for years against Napoleon. With the help of events—which to one appear as the face of Fortune and to another that of Fate—he had conquered the conqueror of the world.

Neither glory nor greatness is measured by success. Upon their higher plane the advantage remains with the vanquished. Napoleon relinquished the supreme power more nobly than Talleyrand acceded to it. Between the two manners there is the same distance as exists between Italian comedy and the drama of Aeschylus. Napoleon made his entry in that part of *Prometheus* in which he was to triumph at St. Helena, where he laid a greater claim to the admiration of the ages in his task of Sisyphus, condemned to roll the rock of universal domination. After a few moments' weakness, conceded to what there was of humanity in that demigod; after vainly attempting to commit suicide; after revenging himself by that epigram on the sovereigns who dethroned him, and whom, not so long before, *he* could have dethroned—"*I* did not do it. *I* behaved towards them as a sovereign. *They* behaved towards me like Jacobins,"—he took a nobler revenge, in once more becoming master of himself, than he had ever done when he was their master. He judged men and events then as if he were alien to them, so greatly did he dominate them with the clear-sightedness and serenity of the future. Too great to reign over a France reduced to her ancient boundaries, he declared that the Bourbons, finding France once more such as they had left her, could accept the terms of the Allies with dignity. He sincerely wished that, beneath their sceptre, France might be happy and respected. He exhorted his marshals to make their task easy: "Serve France under them as you have under me. And leave me, while retaining merely your recollection of me". He was incensed when Caulaincourt gave an account of his efforts to obtain for him from the Allies a suitable allowance. "Look after my family", he said. "As for me, I need nothing. Let them grant me the pension of a disabled soldier, and that will be quite sufficient." He admitted his faults and pardoned those of others. When those who owed him everything left him to throng the antechamber of Talleyrand—the majority without asking his advice—he showed no sign of bitterness. In his deserted palace the majesty of his fall and the ghosts of his victories filled the void which his unhappy lot every day spread around him. Finally, if he spoke of Talleyrand it was to express a wish that the Bourbons would govern in his spirit. "For them", he said, "he will be a valuable adviser." While his former Grand Chamberlain seized hold of power, by means of artifices which did not enhance him in the esteem of posterity, Napoleon, on descending from the throne, made his ascent in the annals of history.

Politics belong to an order other than morals and aesthetics. It renders to Prince de Bénévent the homage that the latter refuse. In default of esteem, the work he accomplished during the fifteen years of his government merits acknowledgment. He entered at that time on his career as a constructor, and in a way which, if it does not stimulate the imagination, satisfies the reason. He did not meditate, like Chateaubriand, over ruins, but set to work to rebuild them. In the perspective of History the errors of the Restoration no longer obscure its benefits and prevent us seeing in it the reconstruction of France. No doubt those who prophesy after the occurrence, who take a delight in imagining the consequences of hypothetical events, will discourse upon what might have happened in 1814 if Talleyrand had abstained from action or acted otherwise. It might be said that the Restoration would have been quite as well accomplished without him, since it was imposed by the force of circumstances. The force of circumstances is often only a flattering pseudonym for man's weakness. There is nothing to prove that it would have served instead of the prudent daring and supple energy of Talleyrand. In a contrary way, we may recall the choice offered him by Alexander between the Empire and the monarchy, and Napoleon's opinion that the Regency would let loose a state of anarchy which would bring back the Bourbons.

The Restoration would have been accomplished, but neither so well nor so quickly, and after shocks dangerous for the great invalid France then was. Talleyrand did not confine himself to ratifying the decrees of destiny—he inspired them. Thanks to him there was not a single day of anarchy, the consequences of which in the presence of the enemy would have been tragic. In proving to the Powers who, between them, had partitioned Poland, that she was worthy of independence, France deprived them of all pretext to treat her in the same way. After this first and perhaps vital service, Talleyrand rendered another: the liquidation of the Empire—that ruinous subsidiary of France—before the bankruptcy of the parent firm. Finally, he restored the business, without delay if not without control, to the heirs of those original founders who had ensured its greatness and prosperity. This substitution of a reconstituted monarchy for an exhausted empire, this replanting of an essential organ which was thought to have been for ever dissevered, was an operation of political prothesis all the more remarkable since it was performed while "hot" in the midst of the most formidable crisis perhaps of France's history, and it entailed no complications. If Talleyrand was merely, as his detractors affirm, an ignorant practitioner, he was at the least, in an emergency, an astounding bone-setter.

There was every reason to believe that the operation had not only succeeded but that it had also saved the patient. But was this not at the cost of a serious mutilation? This is a question which is asked—when it is not turned into an assertion—by those who, professing an unbounded and uncritical admiration for Napoleon, confuse—in his honour and to the detriment of his real glory—all his designs; those of genius and heroism for which he was incomparable and those of national importance which are distinguished from the others, and which, at the close of his reign, were in opposition to them. Nevertheless, history must take its stand upon this more modest plane if it is to judge Talleyrand's conduct towards the Emperor equitably. It is true that it is in the name of the national interest that certain historians condemn it. They would have us believe that Napoleon's fall decapitated and mutilated France. If, they say, the wounded and encircled lion had not been immobilized as in a net, by the Prince de Bénévent's intrigues with the Allies, he would by swift and sudden action have been able to extort from the Coalition a peace which, while sacrificing foreign conquests, would have ensured for France the preservation of her natural frontiers, the Rhine and perhaps Belgium. Indeed, at Fontainebleau, before being reduced to impotence by Talleyrand's manœuvres, the Emperor did dream of falling like a thunderbolt upon the Allied armies and of driving them from Paris with the aid of the aroused population, or else of finding a tomb amidst a cataclysm of his own stature under the smouldering ruins of the capital.

Assuming the most probable hypothesis, that of defeat, Talleyrand, by making the carrying-out of that plan impossible, saved Paris. It was the most probable hypothesis, since Napoleon had at his disposal only 70,000 men, of which total the lukewarm and indifferent, following the example of Marie Louise, outnumbered *les grognards*—the staunch old soldiers of the First Empire commanded by leaders who, save in the subordinate ranks, no longer had faith in his star and only longed for rest. Through discouragement everyone, one may say, chose lassitude as his rank, and, to quote Thiers' expression, this was great among the generals and extreme among the marshals. Let us not forget that these weak effectives could neither be increased nor maintained, for conscription had been abandoned through fear of civil war. In short, the morale of the country, which, exhausted by the terrible loss of blood, heaped curses on Napoleon—the raging monster, the ogre, the devourer of children—was unfavourable to such an enterprise, and especially in Paris, where the Tsar Alexander was idolized and where a woman of fashion could ride on horseback behind a Cossack, "finding intoxication in his fragrance", without causing the slightest scandal. Nor must we forget that the Coalition occupied Paris with 200,000 men and had as many more in the provinces.

Thiers declares that the possible gain from the struggle (the line of the Rhine) would have been worth the risk "even if all the splendours of Paris perished in one bloody day". But was such a gain possible, and, above all, would it have been lasting? To suppose that, if the Emperor's genius, compensating for the vast inferiority of his means, had enabled him to reconquer Paris and drive the Allies back beyond the Rhine—a most improbable event—the Coalition would have agreed to make peace on the basis of "natural frontiers", is to forget all the factors of the problem. It is to forget that to force France to return to her ancient limits was the object of the Allies when Napoleon was invincible, and specially that of England, who dominated the Coalition by her will as by her subsidies. It is to forget the Treaty of Chaumont, which she had signed on March 1, 1814, with Austria, Russia, and Prussia—a treaty by virtue of which the four Powers renewed their alliance, undertook to prolong it for twenty years after the peace in order to make it secure, and in the meanwhile to contribute each a contingent of 150,000 men—that is 600,000 men in all, which, with the 200,000 men of the minor Allies assured to the Coalition an army of 800,000 men, with the immense wealth of England at their disposal. How is it possible to imagine that the Coalition, animated by an implacable determination to conquer, encouraged by a first victory, and organized on such foundations, would have submitted to Napoleon's terms after a fresh success, which could only have been obtained, if obtained at all, by surprise? Such a success would have been placed to the already very heavy debit account of France and would indeed have cost her dear. It would have been an earlier Waterloo, infinitely easier for the Coalition and far more disastrous for ourselves, for it would not have been associated, as it was soon to be, thanks to Talleyrand, with a respect for our ancient boundaries. The most probable thing is that he preserved them just as he saved Paris by circumventing Napoleon's plan. The destruction of this risk of destruction already amounted to construction.

From another point of view, that of the irreconcilable royalists, the destruction of the Empire did not save Talleyrand from the bungling imputed to him in the reconstruction of the monarchy. He was alleged to have introduced into it, with the principles of '89, the seed of ruin. Whereas Napoleon had "cleansed the Revolution from its stains", Talleyrand had "soiled" the Restoration by that impure mixture. After representing under the Empire the foreign policy of the old régime, he was, under Louis XVIII, to represent the home policy of the Revolution.

This censure was based on a double confusion: that between men and principles and that between facts and theories. Talleyrand was anxious to retain under the monarchy the men of the Revolution and the Empire because he was one of them, and their presence in the Government was a guarantee for his own position. But the servants of the Revolution and the Empire had obtained too many advantages to hesitate when it came to sacrificing their principles to their interests. Talleyrand, who was about to appeal to the principle of legitimacy in foreign politics at Vienna, was unable to repudiate it in home politics in Paris. It is true that he based it, not on divine right but on historical right, which makes him a pioneer of the modern theorists of monarchy. "A legitimate government", he said, "is one whose existence, form, and mode of action are consecrated by a long succession of years, by time-honoured prescription. The legitimacy of sovereign power accrues from an ancient state of possession." Legitimacy was that which lasted, but it was also that which succeeded and succeeded while lasting, through the double virtue of the continuity and identity resulting from it between dynastic interest and national interest. It was success which lasted long enough to open a credit on which failure might draw, and permit, for instance, sovereigns conquered by Napoleon to return to their capitals amid the acclamations of their subjects, while the Caesar was deposed. To break his sword was to break his sceptre. According to the dictum of Talleyrand, the legitimacy of the Bourbons was better founded than any other, because their dynasty was the most ancient, and of which the nation was manifestly the work. Their right over France was above all a royalty.

The acceptance of the changes wrought by the Revolution and the Empire was not, any more than the employment of their partisans, a consecration of the dogmas of '89. It was a political necessity, because it was the condition of internal peace. It was the application of the principle that the monarchy was not a party, no more the Royalist party than any other, and that it could know no other law than that of the general interest. Moreover, the preamble of the Charter separated implicitly the facts from the doctrine by proclaiming the rights of Frenchmen, not, as did the great forefathers, the rights of man. The recognition of these for French subjects meant the assurance of internal peace; to forbid them to impose these rights on the nations by force meant the assurance of external peace. As for these rights—equality before the law, equal admissibility for Frenchmen to all employments, individual liberty, freedom of worship, recognition of the imperial nobility, security of the public debt, guarantee for the sale of national property, amnesty for votes given and opinions held until the Restoration— these were considered to be irrevocable by others than Talleyrand, notably by the Duc d'Angoulême, who, in his Bordeaux manifesto of March 15, had guaranteed in the name of Louis XVIII "all liberties" and the "ownership of domains termed national".

The authors of the Charter have been censured for not having "eradicated the Revolution from its text", distinguishing between the Revolution, a fact of the past, and Revolution, an idea which it was better to forget. Thus the counter-revolutionists had, then, no theory. On the other hand, the Revolution, having been a theory long before it became a fact, lived over again under that early form with sufficient vigour to remain partly a fact and was soon to become one more completely again. It had then, as its ally, what was called "intelligence"—the intellectuals, the majority of whom were attached to the dogmas of '89 and to the parliamentary system at the other side of the Channel. The royalists held a faith rather than a theory. They demanded a return to the "fundamental laws of the kingdom". The difficulty was to define these. Was the source of inspiration to be found in the absolutism introduced by Louis XIV, or was one to go back to the period when the royal power was limited first by the feudal system and then by provincial statutes? The distinction between the three orders was at once the clearest and the most thoroughly condemned law of the old régime. Was one to resurrect the "Parlements", "États-généraux", or the "Assemblée des Notables", which bore so heavy a burden of responsibility for the collapse of the old régime? The truth is, the unwritten Constitution of ancient France formed an aggregate of traditions and customs comparable, like the English Constitution, to lawns which require to be watered for several centuries. The truth is that the Constitution-builders of 1814 were working in a soil disturbed by a storm—a soil which, far from being unencumbered, had been burdened by its successive occupants with charges impossible to ignore without falling into inextricable disputations. The truth is that, as Joseph de Maistre acutely said, Louis XVIII ascended the throne of Napoleon rather than that of Louis XVI. Now, seeing that Napoleon was related less to the Capetians than to the Carlovingians, the most illustrious of whom, in his contests with the Pope, he invoked as "Charlemagne, our august predecessor", the continuity of the traditional monarchy had been broken since the Revolution. The truth is that, the great strength of that monarchy and its most fundamental law being the people's affection for the king, the essential object was to rekindle that sentiment by kindness. Lastly, the truth is that, to have had a better chance of enduring, the Restoration ought to have been the instauration of a new order equally conforming to the requirements of the future as to those of the present; a social and economic order as much as a political one; an order which could not make plans for the new age without repudiating the basic principle of the Revolution—individualism, which the inventions of the nineteenth century and the concentration of industries resulting therefrom were destined to destroy, while presenting the world with the dilemma: State Socialism or Syndicalism.

Although Talleyrand was capable of taking long views, he must not be reproached for not adapting the institutions of France to the great movements soon to change the face of the world. When France was invaded and ruined, the problems of the day were so grave and so pressing as to conceal those of the morrow. And perhaps the problems of the day would have been insoluble had Louis not given satisfaction to liberal aspirations, which, by reaction against the Emperor's despotism, were stronger in 1814 than to-day. As for diverting those parliamentary aspirations towards local and corporative liberties, that would have been a rash enterprise, because premature. During its honeymoon with "liberty" (as understood by members of the Constituent Assembly of '89, but without being able to realize it) the country failed to perceive how fallacious it was. Liberty was still for France a fiancée rather than a wife. Under the First Empire it was not the Republic—disfigured by the Terror and the Directory—it was Liberty, still of the nature of a dream, who was so beautiful! The antinomy between Napoleonic centralization which was retained, and the parliamentary system which was inaugurated, was not perceived. It was the heir of the Bourbons, the Comte de Chambord, who was to be the first to denounce her when he said, "Representation was granted to a country which was organized solely for administration". In restoring the monarchy —which, provided that it remained untroubled by revolution, discovered in its continuity compensation for its fallibility—Talleyrand restored to death-imperilled France the means of public safety as well as those of public progress.

If there be bad work in the edifice of 1814, Talleyrand is not responsible for it. The Charter had been drafted without recourse to him, Louis XVIII not having appointed him to the commission which drew up the final text. He confined himself, at the beginning, to the work of inspiring its general trend, after which he acted specially as its diplomat, applying himself to smoothing away difficulties in the division of power between the Crown and Parliament. To this task he brought a mind which was above all else diplomatic, a mind with a capacity for compromise which was exercised in finding a mean. Thus it was that, at the time when Louis XVIII entered Paris, he advised him—and the advice was followed—to accept the pro-

jected Constitution, but with certain necessary modifica-
tions. It was in the same spirit that Louis XVIII—who
attached more importance to the source of power than to
the way in which it was exercised—transformed a Constitution imposed as a Charter "conceded", whilst maintaining
all its essential provisions. Dated the nineteenth year of his
reign, contrary to the text of the senatorial project, the
Charter originated from the authority which the King
held from God and his ancestors—an authority whose
limits he himself defined, "since", it has been said,
"the infinite power of God is limited by His infinite
wisdom. . . ."

Talleyrand's true opinion concerning Constitutions was
stated by him in 1801 when Roederer, appointed to prepare one for the Cisalpine Republic,[1] submitted a project
to him consisting of a few articles and said: "A Constitution ought to be short and——" He was going to add
"clear", when Talleyrand cut him short, and finished the
sentence: "Yes, short and vague".

Talleyrand was aware that often, in home as in foreign
politics, when the problem was a delicate one, full agreement was only attained by silence. He appreciated the advantage of conciseness, and even ambiguity, for the more
powerfully armed co-contractor; indefiniteness of texts as
of frontiers being always beneficial to the stronger party.
Let the Prince govern boldly and wisely, and it will be he
who will impose his interpretation of the contract which,
the Charter even granted, continued to be in the eyes of
Parliament. The affirmation of a few undeniable principles would have been rather to Talleyrand's liking.
Time, experience, and custom would do the rest, adapting

[1] It was formed in northern Italy by Bonaparte in 1797. In 1802
it became the "Italian Republic" and had Milan as its capital.—
Translators' note.

them like living things to the evolution of ideas and events. Talleyrand would then have been able to add as a secret epigraph to the Charter the maxim he attributed to Napoleon: "Principles are excellent, they commit you to nothing". The rigidness of Constitutions is the cause of their fragility. It was perhaps because the Constituent liberals of 1814 wished to build up something definite with precision that they only succeeded in constructing what was provisional, whereas the monarchical constituents of 1875, when elaborating an ill-defined text, and believing they were engaged on a provisional work, founded a durable republic.

## CHAPTER IX

# THE LIBERATOR OF THE COUNTRY

The horror which the guillotine once inspired is felt
to-day for war.                                        THIERS

TALLEYRAND'S career was both a long-distance race and
a steeplechase over most diversified courses, and under
colours no less variegated. However, on March 31, 1814,
he triumphed in a speed trial: in twenty-four hours he
outdistanced all his competitors in the race to power and
made every solution except the return of the Bourbons
impossible. In April and in May he accomplished two
similar performances on the racecourse of foreign politics: the armistice of April 23 and the treaty of May 30. He
congratulated himself on that, for it meant peace; others
censured him, for it meant the abandonment of the conquests of the Revolution and the Empire.

By the armistice of April 23, Talleyrand agreed to the
evacuation of all fortresses and territories outside the
French frontiers of 1792. Therefore it contained in em-
bryo the treaty of peace on the basis of the old boundaries.
Thus, with a stroke of his pen, Talleyrand sacrificed the
left bank of the Rhine, Nice, Savoy, fifty fortresses still
occupied by French troops and provided with immense
stores. Why, it was asked, so much haste on the part of a
man who, usually, was never in a hurry? Why relinquish
pledges so valuable in peace negotiations?

These criticisms were based upon a complete misunder-
standing of the situation. We must, on the contrary,

praise Talleyrand for not having lost a moment in signing the convention of April 23. From the military point of view the occupation of those fifty forts impossible to re-victual was precarious. On the 16th, Prince Eugène had signed the capitulation of Mantua; on the 18th, Carnot abandoned Antwerp. From the political point of view, this pledge, even had France been able to retain it for some time, was not negotiable, the victorious Coalition being determined to bring her back to her former boundaries. This was, indeed, the sole point on which the Allies were unanimous, for Prussia, intoxicated with rage and the spirit of revenge, wished to treat France as Napoleon had treated her after Jena. Not to have renounced, immediately and unreservedly, the conquests of the Revolution and the Empire would have been to rekindle all kinds of sus-picions and expose the country to all sorts of perils. It would have been to forget that the capital and more than half of France, invaded on every frontier, were occupied by the enemy, and that on March 1 the Allies, by the Treaty of Chaumont, had renewed their alliance for *twenty years* after the forthcoming peace in order to consolidate the fruits of their victory. It would have been to forget that France was at their mercy, and that the slightest error would have compromised her independence and even her existence. Talleyrand rightly says in his memoirs: "A single day's hesitation might have given rise to ideas for partition and subjection". And he adds: "In Spain, gen-erals who were jealous of King Joseph asked Napoleon to divide it into fiefs and give each a part. France might per-haps have had as many emperors as armies, and, torn to pieces by her own hands, she would have perished in the convulsions of civil war."

Talleyrand had no inclination to minimize the danger he had averted. The danger was none the less real and even of a double character: the postponement of the armistice would have meant the certainty of foreign war and the probability of civil war. The capitulation of Paris was merely a local armistice which did not involve cessation of hostilities throughout the country. A few days later, on April 10, Marshal Soult lost the battle of Toulouse against the army of Wellington, who had crossed the Pyrenees. The Convention of April 23 was therefore indispensable for putting an end to sacrifices worse than useless; their only result being to exasperate the victorious enemy and increase his demands. Now, Talleyrand would never have obtained it without the evacuation of fortresses out-side the ancient boundaries of France. This ebb of the tide of conquest could alone refloat France in her sinking condition.

The armistice was as much a necessity at home as abroad. The abandonment of fortified places occupied by France had as its equivalent the evacuation of French territory by the Allies, and that meant the end of exactions which were exhausting the last resources of the country, and of atro-cities which, reducing the population to despair, enclosed it within an infernal circle of vengeance and reprisals. If, in Paris, thanks to the presence of the sovereigns and the ascendancy Talleyrand exercised over them, the con-duct of the Allied troops was correct, in the provinces the worst excesses were suffered, especially from the Prussians. Thiers, who has refought Napoleon's battles, has still more easily remade Talleyrand's treaties. He criticizes the Convention of April 23 by means of argu-ments which take no account of realities. But he justifies it by describing the horrors of the foreign occupa-tion: outraged women, harvests plundered, villages in ashes, populations in flight, communications interrupted, bridges broken down, roads broken up and infested with unburied corpses, murderous vendettas between peasants and soldiers of the enemy. As a liberator of his country Talleyrand gains by comparison; he had against him, not, like Thiers in 1871, a single Power, but a Coalition; the foreign occupation was far more extensive; the wrath of the victors, whose countries, France, under Napoleon, had devastated from Cadiz to Moscow, was more justifiable. Nevertheless, Talleyrand liberated the country far more quickly and at a lower price—without a war indemnity and without the Commune. Not a drop of blood was on his hands, not a crown piece in those of the enemy. From crucified France—crucified but still living—he had painlessly removed the nails.

Talleyrand brought back the King, and obtained his acceptance, only because Louis XVIII returned with liberty in one hand and peace in the other. But if liberty was useful to gain the adherence of leaders, the majority of whom had been either accomplices of the Terror or of Napoleonic despotism, when they had not been both, peace was indispensable to reassure the masses who had suffered so much from the war. If Talleyrand had not given satisfaction at once to this deep and insistent aspiration of the country, civil war, already threatening at the close of the Empire under the iron hand of Napoleon, would soon have added its horrors to those of invasion. The anarchy would have been all the more terrible inasmuch as the regular Government—if there had been one—to combat it would only have had at its disposal the fragments of armies exhausted by the French campaign. The choice would have been between the triumph of anarchy or its suppression by foreign arms. On the other hand, the armistice, which suppressed the main cause of disorder, supplied at the same time the means of re-establishing order in case of need; not only did it liberate the country, it also set free the garrisons of evacuated fortresses—an army of some three hundred thousand men, who, once reorganized, were able to assure royal authority at home and national independence abroad. That army which was soon to enable Louis XVIII to speak more firmly face to face with the Coalition, and even to break it up, was more useful to France than the possession of forts it was impossible to hold.

If it were not that nations are less grateful for catastrophes from which they are spared than for the illusions, baneful even, with which they are imbued, Talleyrand should be given the first place in the pantheon of revolutionists. The revolution which he effected on March 31, 1814, by substituting the Bourbons for Napoleon, was not merely pacific; it was pacifying and restorative. It brought an end to war without inaugurating civil war; it ensured the salvation of France—conquered, invaded, and ruined; it opened up a prospect of rest, recovery, prosperity, and glory. Yet it had never been so popular as the revolution of the Fourth of September, also the daughter of defeat. This perhaps was because it had been accomplished without the help of the people. It was a revolution from above. It was entirely, if not in its origin, in which sentiment played a part, at least in its accomplishment by Talleyrand, the result of political intelligence. It was the work of a Cabinet in which neither the street nor the forum played any part. Its originality consisted in asking nothing from the people, in serving but not making use of them, in owing them nothing but costing them nothing. Talleyrand neither consulted nor flattered them beforehand; neither did he shoot them afterwards.

The armistice was only the promise and outline of peace. This was completed by the Treaty of Paris on May 30, 1814. With the object of drawing a distinction between matters appertaining only to France and those relating to Europe, the Allies wished to treat the former in Paris and reserve the others for the Congress of Vienna, where they planned to settle them without reference to France. The Austrian capital was chosen because it was at one and the same time the most central city and the residence of the sovereign who deserved the highest esteem, as much because of the antiquity of his family and the splendour of his crown as because of the proof he had given of his solidarity with Europe by joining the Coalition to dethrone his son-in-law and daughter.

As presaged by the armistice, the treaty of May 30 confirmed for France the restoration of the ancient frontiers of the monarchy. However, the Emperor Alexander, having in his declaration of March 31 promised some extension, the interpretation of this promise gave rise to a lively discussion. Louis XVIII knew that if this extension was to be practicable it would have to be very moderate. At the time of the Treaty of Lunéville in 1801 he had studied the conditions for a lasting peace with Europe and had arrived at the conclusion that such a peace would only be possible if France, out of the revolutionary annexations, retained an ample rectification of her frontiers. In a handwritten note, then made at Mittau, he specified this rectification, which in the north strengthened the belt of France's fortresses by those of Belgium and ensured her a better strategic frontier in the Vosges and on the Rhine, the whole area representing a population of one million. This document, which was used as a basis for French demands in 1814, showed in Louis XVIII an old-standing care for the true interests of France, and refutes the hypothesis that his moderation was the result of engagements accepted in London at the time of his return to France.

To the Allies this moderation appeared to be presumptuous. They protested against France's claims as scandalous. Alexander's declaration, they asserted, was binding only to himself. Talleyrand made a great effort to overcome their opposition, but in vain. Metternich compared the pretensions of Louis XVIII to those of Napoleon. France was again informed that the promised extension ought to be "the sequel and not the object of the line drawn". If this formula was obscure in meaning, the intention was clear: the extension was not to have any strategic object, but merely a symbolic value, a premium in the face of public opinion, conceded to the Bourbons in consideration of the guarantees they offered for the repose of Europe.

England, haunted by the recollection of the Continental blockade, had waged that implacable war to hold France at a distance from the estuaries of the main rivers. This objective could only be attained by raising an impassable barrier between the shores of the North Sea and France, a barrier which could be nothing else than the kingdom of Holland increased by Belgium. To ask England to weaken this by leaving France the Belgian fortresses was simply to ask her to renounce her principal object in the war. The London Cabinet was all the less disposed to do this because it wished to be generous towards Holland on the Continent in order to compensate her for the colonies England had reserved for herself, and particularly the Cape of Good Hope. Had Alexander pleaded France's cause by invoking his declaration of March 31, he would have been obliged to bow before the *non possumus* of London.

Notwithstanding his preference for advantages on the vulnerable frontiers of the north and east, and despite his repugnance to despoil his brother-in-law, the King of Sardinia, Louis XVIII accepted the half of Savoy, with

Annecy and Chambéry. In the north he only obtained Philippeville and Marienburg, and between Maubeuge and Givet, a frontier which, ceasing to be concave, became convex. In the Sarre France retained Sarrelouis and the line of the Queich, which connected the enclave of Landau to French territory. With the enclaves of Montbeliard and Avignon, detached, one from the German empire and the other from Rome, and restored to France by the Revolution, these fragments of France's conquests only left her with 636,000 population instead of the million demanded. The Allies informed France that if the latter figure was a question of self-respect and the impression to be produced on public opinion in France, she had only to declare it in her official publications and they would not issue a contradiction.

France recovered her colonies, except Tobago and St. Lucia in the Antilles, and, what was a more serious loss, Mauritius, the "Ile de France". The "Malta of the Indian Ocean" was too useful to England to preclude its very utility conferring upon her a right to it.

As to questions of a general character reserved for the Congress of Vienna, the Treaty of Paris specified some of them and indicated the main outlines of the solutions on which the Allies were in agreement. The scruples of Louis XVIII in annexing a portion of Savoy were appeased by the agreement to compensate the King of Sardinia with Genoa. Belgium was to be annexed by Holland. The German states were to be independent, but connected by a federal bond. Bavaria was to receive a portion of the ancient ecclesiastical electorates in exchange for Tyrol returned to Austria, which was also to regain its former possessions in Italy and annex the republic of Venice. Doubtless these adjustments, already agreed to in principle by the Allies, appeared in the Treaty of Paris, not so much to associate France with it, as to notify her and bind her to it. However, a man like Talleyrand could not fail to obtain authority from it to intervene in the final settlement, and especially in the grave problems not mentioned in the treaty, such as the fate of Poland and Saxony. This silence was evidence of disagreement. Talleyrand's experienced eye had no difficulty in discovering this first fissure in the allied *bloc*. At Vienna he was to be able to widen it and insert the explosive which was to blow up the Coalition. The Treaty of Paris procured to France the means of re-entering at Vienna the European concert, to resume there her rôle as a regulating State and establish in her own and the general interest the bases of a new equilibrium.

Above all, in not stipulating that a war indemnity be paid, and in allowing France to keep the artistic treasures gained by the Empire, the Treaty of Paris avoided the appearance of one dictated by the victor. To tell the truth, if French museums were not emptied, that was owing less to generosity than to absence of mind and egoism. During their sojourn in Paris the sovereigns paid frequent visits to the galleries without perceiving that their admiration hallowed them. Besides, the four Great Powers which constituted the European tribunal could not exercise any right of resumption in the case of collections made at the expense of Spain and the smaller Italian states.

The desire for peace being general and sincere, the Allies, in Article 16 of the treaty, made an agreement which they respected, not to trouble anyone under any pretext, within the territories restored by France. This precedent, when compared with the scenes of savagery recently enacted in the Ruhr and the Rhineland after the departure of the French troops, enables us to measure the regression of the international spirit in this progressive century of ours!

Conquered France then protected her dependents more effectively than victorious France did to-day.

Like the armistice of April 23, which liberated old France, the treaty of May 30, which maintained its integrity, has been keenly criticized, and with the same argument. In both cases Talleyrand has been reproached for a precipitation to which his reputation for nonchalance has given a harder name. Why, it is asked, did he ignore his favourite collaborator, time, which was working on France's behalf, as it always does for the vanquished, since coalitions do not usually survive their victory? Why did he not postpone the completion of France's special treaty until the Congress, where divisions among the Allies would have afforded her facilities for manœuvring and allowed her to obtain better conditions? Why accept in advance the general views of the Allies concerning the reorganization of Europe? Would it not have been better to have retained freedom regarding the line of French frontiers and the division of the spoil, peace being an indivisible whole like the equilibrium which was its object, and France's situation requiring to be considered less in itself than in its relations to the situation it would have created for other Powers?

This argument would not have been without value if France had had the choice. But she did not have it. The sovereigns and statesmen of the Allies, her guests, were charming, but that was because they felt themselves strong enough to dispense with harshness. Their airs and graces were the coquetry of their force—homage paid to the wisdom and majesty of the Bourbons. If Louis XVIII had strayed from the path of wisdom, his majesty would not for long have restrained the still-boiling hatred; Blücher would not have waited for Waterloo to want to blow up the bridge of Jena, and not one of his Allies would have lifted a little finger to prevent him. If France was not treated as a conquered country, that was because Louis XVIII and Talleyrand had not forgotten, like their detractors, that she was a country defeated and occupied by the enemy. This enemy, it is true, was soon to be divided against itself, and the Coalition dislocated. Yes, but that was because it had first of all been fully tranquillized from France's side, Louis XVIII and Talleyrand having succeeded in convincing it that her repudiation of the conquests of the Revolution and the Empire was sincere and lasting.

This repudiation was the preliminary condition of the disagreement which they anticipated in order to avoid it. Once let the Allies conceive the slightest distrust as touching that matter, and their common front, established at Chaumont to last for twenty years after the peace, would be automatically reconstituted. That was what France saw when Napoleon disembarked in France, in spite of his haste to accept the Treaty of Paris. What would France have been to-day, after Waterloo, if Louis XVIII and Talleyrand had not bound the Allies to respect her historical frontiers? It would have been the end of the quarry after the sounding of the huntsman's horn. If the Hundred Days justified only too well what has been called their "precipitancy", France did not need that episode to prove the necessity of their policy. The situation, which required the conclusion of an immediate armistice, also demanded that peace should be signed without delay. The armistice had liberated the territory. It remained to reconstruct France on the ruins of the Empire and to establish all the departments of State—army, diplomacy, finance, administration, commerce, and industry. That enterprise, impossible to postpone without exposing the country to the risk of entire decomposition, demanded, within and without, a security and a credit that peace alone could procure.

Lastly, even if the internal situation had permitted the postponement of peace, it was not the Congress which would have given France the means of improving it, for the signing of peace was the preliminary condition of her admission to the Congress. After the exclusion first pronounced against France by the Allies with full knowledge of the case, how can it be supposed that they would not have maintained it when France's refusal to treat before the Congress had revived the cupidity of some and the distrust of all?

Certainly the return of France to her frontiers of 1792 did not suffice to make that peace a fruitless one, and the twenty-two years' war which it closed a drawn game. In spite of her meagre gains her account showed a heavy territorial deficit, owing to the enormous increases in territory obtained since that year by other Powers, and the changes to her detriment which followed in the equilibrium of forces in Europe. While Russia, Prussia, and Austria helped themselves freely in Poland, Germany, and Italy, and England extended her colonial empire, France kept only a few colonial conquests.

Even if France had not aroused the wrath of Europe by overthrowing it, it would have been vain for her to seek, by peaceful means, compensations for those aggrandizements, mostly old (like the partition of Poland) and already digested. It is particularly in the case of territories that a swallowed morsel has no more taste, and that, to have one's share of the feast, one must sit down with the other guests. To claim their leavings, Louis XVIII could have appealed neither to force—for lack of an army—nor to justice, those aggrandizements being so many iniquities. Neither, above all, could he have pleaded his principle, that of legitimacy—the negation of conquest—nor the expression of a public opinion which denounced the treaty of 1814 only after the fact, and principally through a spirit of opposition. During the campaign in France in December 1813, when Napoleon was not completely vanquished and in spite of the terror which he inspired in servile assemblies, the legislative body, by 243 votes against 41, had demanded the abandonment of those conquests. On March 30, in Paris, Caulaincourt, the Emperor's confidential adviser, took the responsibility of accepting all the Allies' conditions. The Tsar Alexander had been received in Paris as a liberator, frantically cheered at the Opera by a crowded house, and the owners of the most sumptuous mansions in the capital had vied with each other for the honour, which fell to Talleyrand, of offering him hospitality. In a diplomatic struggle—the only one within France's means—to wring from the Allies better terms than those of the treaty of May 30, 1814, the civilians, including those who later on were to curse it, would not have held their ground. None the less France remained, with her twenty-nine millions of inhabitants (double those of England), the most populated, homogeneous, and most united nation in Europe. As Talleyrand said, she could again become great by ceasing to be gigantic.

After having overthrown Europe and provoked a formidable Coalition, conquered France was far better treated than she was to be after Sedan, without quitting her own soil, when she had only a single enemy, and when Napoleon III had been an ally of England and Italy. The authority of Louis XVIII and the ability of Talleyrand, who had re-established that authority, must have counted for something in that.

After the reconstruction of France through the return

of the Bourbons and the conclusion of peace, Talleyrand undertook the reconstruction of Europe. In his plan it was the same edifice of which France was the keystone, and of which all the parts rested on the same principle. "The Bourbons alone are a principle", he said to Alexander, in order to set aside all other candidates for the throne of France. This principle, legitimacy, valid for internal use, because even for those who do not profess it it is an undeniable fact, was no less valid for external use. If a Government, said Talleyrand again, wishes to last, it must remain faithful to its principle. That of Bonaparte, based on conquest, was obliged to maintain itself by conquest and collapsed with it. That of Louis XVIII ought to remain faithful, within and without, to its principle, legitimacy. Napoleon was aware of this when, affecting (in order to gain time) to accept the Allies' conditions, he spoke of "that kind of peace which the Bourbons alone can make", and added: "If no one wishes to fight, I cannot make war alone; if the nation wants peace on the basis of its old frontiers, I shall say to it: 'Look for someone to govern you, I am too great for you'".

Europe was soon to discover that Louis XVIII was too great for her, because, better than all the other sovereigns, he represented that principle, in all its strength and purity, which she hypocritically invoked to oppose Napoleon, but which she was prepared to violate when she believed it to be to her interest. By forcing her to respect it, Talleyrand consolidated both the throne of Louis XVIII and the security of France. After having liberated French territory, he guaranteed it at Vienna by placing its integrity under the aegis of legitimacy and providing France with allies among the sovereigns who also invoked it. Europe had been convulsed by the conquests of the Revolution and the Empire. France, after overflowing her bed for twenty-two years, returned to it. The nations she had submerged did not ask themselves whether they had been fertilized by her alluvium, whether they were indebted to the cataclysm for more seeds than ruins, and whether France would not discover the seeds of ruin therein. Nations are only mindful of the present, and the present signified the immense disasters of the conquest, the "usurpation" as the sovereigns called it, when they paid the bill for the benefit of Napoleon. Talleyrand noted a piece of evidence when he said, "Europe's first need, its greatest interest, was to banish the doctrine of the usurpation". It was to the greatest interest of France to set that example and proclaim that evidence which became her talisman. By opposing legitimacy to conquest and Louis XVIII to Napoleon, Talleyrand ensured for France an eminent and even dominant position. In his view, legitimacy was *the ancient state of possession.*[1] It was the laicization of divine right, but almost a deification of the King of France. Whereas Napoleon was considered as the "scourge of humanity" and called "Antichrist", because he incarnated the conquest, Louis XVIII, by the greater antiquity of his throne, the origin of his kingdom, formed of free unions and not from violent conquests, incarnated more than any other sovereign the opposing principle, the safeguard of kings, but also of nations, legitimacy for them signifying stability. If Napoleon was the Antichrist and scourge of the world, Louis XVIII, after the calvary of exile and his resurrection, was a Christ, the saviour of the world, and Talleyrand was his prophet.

A certain lady thus expressed her feelings about the Prince de Bénévent: "It would be difficult to refuse him

---

[1] Macaulay's definition may be recalled : " The doctrine of divine right which has now come back to us, like a thief from transportation, under the *alias* of legitimacy."—Translators' note.

one's favour, but impossible to give him one's confidence". At Vienna, as in Paris, he specially addressed himself to the task of gaining the confidence of Europe in order to obtain from her, not favours, but justice. With this in view, the surest method, he thought, was to bring justice to her. The representative of Louis XVIII—who had inherited the full patrimony of his fathers in the name of legitimacy—he was to be the unwavering champion of that principle, if need be against the entire Coalition and, because the latter could not openly disavow it by sacrificing it to its greed, he was to triumph. It was a sacred principle in his eyes, because it was then the perfect expression of French interests. Talleyrand found in it, with Louis XVIII's claim to the inviolability of France's old frontiers, the best argument to force Europe, as far as possible after so many upheavals, to return to an equilibrium more precious to France than to her. This doctrine, a condemnation of conquests, forbade her to lay claim to those which she was in fact powerless to preserve, but it forbade the Allies, by law, to make use of their victory to deprive France of ancient provinces, or to dispose of unoccupied territories in contempt of a public right which coincided wonderfully with her private interests. It was a doctrine with a double object, useful for both defence and attack. Talleyrand's shield against dismemberment in Paris, it was in the Vienna tournament to be his lance against the ambitions of France's rivals.

This doctrine which was so well adapted to circumstances, was, however, neither in the eyes of Louis XVIII nor in those of Talleyrand, a doctrine for the occasion. It was one which doubled their authority. Imposed on the King through his principle, through the position of defeated France, through the logic of the Treaty of Paris, it was a necessity. But out of this necessity, which in others might have been a weakness, Louis XVIII and Talleyrand drew energy, because for them it was also a tradition.

Louis XVIII, a great reader of the Latin poets, whom he quoted in his political correspondence, had a classical mind and a sense of proportion. Having since the age of twenty-two travelled about Europe in every direction, from Italy to Russia and thence to England, he was much better acquainted with it than with France. His reason and experience united to prove to him the advantages of that moderation which characterized in its entirety the policy of the Capets, and which in his youth, during the ministry of Vergennes, had shed a last ray of glory on the decline of the old régime. Seeking for peace in an equilibrium, for the greatness of France in her justice, her ascendancy, especially a moral one, in the protection of the weak against the greed of the strong, he was naturally the enemy of conquests. He was notoriously so. In 1795, at Verona, he condemned the revolutionary annexations in his conversations with foreign diplomats, who notified their courts accordingly, and he instructed his agents to say likewise. The same attitude after the Treaty of Lunéville in 1801 inspired him with the note which, in 1814, was to serve as the basis of his proposals to the Allies.

But in the case of Talleyrand—the old favourite of the Constituent Assembly, the renegade bishop, the accomplice of all the gigantic spoliations which had extended the French Empire from the furthermost end of Spain to the Baltic—was it not the height of callousness or cynicism to pose at Vienna as the champion of public law, the redresser of all wrongs, and to show that he was more conservative than Metternich? An excellent sporting dog under Napoleon, provided he was allowed to eat a portion of the game, he now posed as the Newfoundland of that wretched Europe torn to pieces through his attentions.

Such he was indeed and sincerely so. None among those who knew him well was either shocked or astonished. The fact is, Talleyrand—a classical thinker, like Louis XVIII —had always, at bottom, held the same views as regards the conditions of French greatness and European order. During the Revolution, without a word passing between them—for they did not know each other—they expressed those conditions almost in the same terms. We have already quoted his report from London in 1792,  advising the Constituent Assembly to renounce ideas about *primacy* and *preponderance* because "real wealth did not consist in invading the dominions of others, but rather in enhancing the value of one's own". In 1814, as in 1792, he considered that France ought to remain within the circle of her own limits, that she "owed this to her glory, justice, reason, interest and to that of other nations who will be set free through her". A minister in the Directory in 1797, he professed the same opinion and denounced the treaties made by the republic, treaties which, he said, were only "military capitulations", ephemeral truces, contrary to the requirements of European order and to France's permanent interests which were solidary with them. At Vienna he was to apply those principles just as, a supporter of the constitutional monarchy in 1792, he re-established it in Paris in 1814. In home and foreign politics he returned to his starting-point. With the ease of a great acrobat in the matter of diplomacy and constitutions, he looped the loop. In the continuity of his thought and of France's destiny, the Revolution and the Empire were two bars for nothing—after which he returned to the same air. Better still, the fact that he had played his part of the score in that cacophony qualified him as conductor of the concert restored by the Powers. It was because he had followed another policy that he was in a position to re-

store that of the old régime. Had he remained outside
affairs since 1792, he would not, in 1814, have possessed
the experience and authority which fitted him to apply the
principles he had laid down. He was to boast of having
violated them so as to remain their defender. And what
was more, having worked on the construction of that formidable and fragile machine the Empire, he was to know
how to take it to pieces without causing disaster.

If, in politics also, infidelities are the test of constancy,
that of Talleyrand was brilliant. Besides, he had never,
even in action, been quite unfaithful to his creed of 1792.
In so far as compatible with events, he was inspired by it
when counselling Napoleon, and to an even greater degree when he vilified him before the Powers. In a caricature entitled "The Six-headed Man", the *Nain Jaune* depicted Talleyrand holding in his right hand an episcopal
crosier and in his left a weathercock. From his six mouths
there proceeded as many streamers with the inscriptions,
"Long live the King", "Long live the Emperor", etc. The
sixth streamer was blank; it was awaiting the unknown
god, who was to be Louis Philippe. Like the weathercock,
he revolved at the mercy of the winds around his axis, but
was never detached from it. This symbol is only correct
inasmuch as it expresses fixity in mobility. As for the six
heads, one only was alive, that which drew up the report
in 1792, the others being merely masks which Talleyrand
assumed in order to figure in the political carnival. The
Allies, in whose presence outside official life he unmasked,
were not in ignorance of this, and in Vienna they recognized his real countenance. In order to remain on the
scene during the Revolution and the Empire, he had accepted rôles in which he was no dupe. Behold him now
that he is on the stage of the Congress in his old part. No
one, therefore, was more apt than he to inspire Europe

with confidence, particularly the Tsar Alexander and Metternich, whose accomplice he had been at Erfurt. He was accredited to them in virtue of his treason. He was all the better armed to represent France in a situation which compelled him to repudiate what were styled "the horrible principles of Bonaparte", and to identify her cause with that of a general peace. The Allies could only reproach Talleyrand for being a better European than themselves.

Sinuous, but never broken, the political graph of Talleyrand tallied with that of Louis XVIII. They were therefore in complete agreement when drafting his instructions in preparation for the most important congress which had ever been called together prior to the Congress of Versailles. The Treaty of Westphalia had settled only the problems of Germany. At Vienna the Powers were assembled to decide the fate of the whole civilized world, including the colonies, from the double point of view of the distribution of territories and political organization. At one and the same time it was a liquidation and a reconstruction.

Amidst the ruins of the Revolution and the Empire, Louis XVIII and Talleyrand laid bare the foundations of the past to construct those of the future. The instructions of September 10 would have earned the approbation of Richelieu, Mazarin, and Vergennes. They set forth France's traditional policy while adapting it to fresh contingencies; a policy which, after having realized the unity of France and sheltered her from invasions from the time of the treaties of Westphalia until the Revolution, was to re-establish her authority after defeat, and might have assured her greatness amidst peace for a long period. Unfortunately the lessons of experience did not prevent the repetition of those mistakes from which France in 1814 very nearly expired. That policy was summed up in the organization of peace by equilibrium; this equilibrium being realized under the aegis of France by opposing all attempts at supremacy, and by the protection of the smaller against the covetousness of the greater Powers. Hence a programme whose four principal points were connected with a single objective:

1st. That Austria be allowed no opportunity to get the states of the King of Sardinia into the hands of one of the princes of her house, that is to say, into her own hands. (The old King of Sardinia, having no direct heir, the succession of his throne had to be so arranged that Austria should be prevented from obtaining it through marriage.)

2nd. That the Kingdom of Naples be restored to Ferdinand IV.

3rd. That the whole of Poland should under no circumstances pass under the control of Russia.

4th. That Prussia should acquire neither the kingdom of Saxony, at least entirely, nor Mayence.

This was taking up a position along the whole line against imperialism: in the first two clauses against Austrian imperialism which operated in Italy, where in the early days of 1814 it had confirmed Murat in the kingdom of Naples in order to detach him from Napoleon; in the third clause against Russian imperialism; and in the fourth against that of Prussia. These three "imperialisms" were all the more formidable since they were Allies.

In these instructions Louis XVIII was partly influenced by family considerations; Ferdinand IV, the deposed King of Naples, being a Bourbon, and the King of Saxony, dethroned by the allies as a punishment for his alliance with Napoleon, being a relative. But these family feelings of Louis XVIII were in harmony with his principle, legitimacy, and with the higher interest of France and Europe, equilibrium.

With a foresight which the course of events was to demonstrate only too clearly, the instructions therefore justified this programme: "In Italy, it is Austria who must be prevented from dominating by opposing contrary influences to her own; in Germany it is Prussia. The physical constitution of the monarchy turns ambition into a sort of necessity. Any pretext is good enough. Scruples do not stop her. Expediency is her right. Her emissaries and partisans throw Germany into agitation; they represent France as prepared to invade her again; Prussia is alone ready to defend her, and they demand that Germany be delivered up to her for preservation. A brake must therefore be applied to her ambition."

The instructions pointed out that "in almost the entire range of matters to be settled by the Congress, equity follows from one and the same principle, and to abandon it on one point would be to abandon it in all". The document ended with a maxim which raised the special interest of France to the dignity of a universal law: "France is a State so powerful that other nations can only be freed from fear through the idea of her moderation, which they will accept all the more readily as she will have given them a still greater idea of her justice".

## CHAPTER X

## THE COACHMAN OF EUROPE

I argue in a political meeting, not because I hope to
convince anyone, but because I desire to make my
opinions known to the world.          TALLEYRAND

IN diplomacy as in all the arts, execution is often more
important than conception. At Vienna, each was worthy
of the other. Talleyrand surpassed himself there, because
for the first time he was himself. After having, under the
Empire, collaborated in schemes which were not his own,
and the fatal consequences of which he was the first to
foresee, he at last applied the doctrine he had formulated in
1792, a doctrine which the experience of his political way-
wardness made still more dear to him. He regained his
strength by returning to his own path. Thanks to him,
France, vanquished by Europe, was to become its arbiter.
In Paris, while hastening the return of the Bourbons, the
evacuation of the territory, and the conclusion of peace,
this pleasure-lover, who seemed made to steer the ship of
state only in fine weather and through calm waters, was
able to pass through the tempest and amidst the rapids of
History without a mishap. In Vienna he displayed qualities
which often mutually exclude and enhance each other—
patience and decision, energy and suppleness, charm and
authority. Alternately caressing and menacing, ironical
and solemn, expansive and impenetrable, insinuating and
peremptory; knowing how to justify confidence and only
place his own when he considered it was justifiable to do

so; knowing also how to run up and down the subtle gamut of implication and half-truths while excelling when necessary in a plain and even tone, he was always to make his language and his attitude appropriate to circumstances.

Like all real leaders, who must preserve their liberty of mind and never appear busy or too absorbed, Talleyrand knew how to make his subordinates work. Tasks impossible to delegate to others he reserved for himself, one of which, however, was of a practical nature: he recopied in his own handwriting personal letters which had been composed on his behalf for Louis XVIII. Like all true leaders, he also knew how to choose his collaborators, to control them, inspire them with devotion to himself, and with that team-spirit which is not less necessary in diplomatic matches than in others. With him he brought Dalberg, who was highly useful through his close relations with all the German courts. "He will spread abroad", he said, "the secrets that I wish everybody to know." As Dalberg's colleague he added Noailles, La Tour du Pin, and, for the "laborious work", a head clerk, La Besnardière, who had been chief draftsman of the instructions of September 10.

Talleyrand considered that, for a great ambassador, saucepans were more important than secretaries. He was therefore assisted by a chef whose reputation was as European as his own, but less dubious.[1] Appointed to the

---

[1] Talleyrand's chef was the celebrated Carême (Marie Antoine), who was born in Paris in 1784 and who died there in 1833. A pupil of La Guipière, the cook of Napoleon, Carême had been the chef of the Prince Regent of England (George IV) and the Emperors of Russia and Austria before he provided culinary masterpieces for Talleyrand's sumptuous table. He was the author of a number of important works on the art of cookery, including *Le Patissier pittoresque* (1815) and *Le Patissier royal Parisien* (1825); and from a double point of view—culinary and literary—his name has become proverbial for that of a perfect cook.—Translators' note.

propaganda service, but without official standing, his niece, the delicious Dorothée, Comtesse de Périgord, and soon to be Duchesse de Dino, who, for some time had presided over the honours of his house, was soon to reign there over the Congress. At the age of twenty-one she was a more thorough diplomat than the majority of the professionals who have grown grey in harness. Through the combined gifts of youth, intelligence, and beauty, enhanced by a superior culture and perfect tact, she exercised an irresistible seduction over all the men and even over all the women who approached her. Her portrait by Prudhon inspires the thought that her rarest charm was the blending of the Latin lucidity of her intelligence and the Slav mystery of her glance and smile. Through her radiance she was in some degree for Talleyrand a minister, an incomparable private Minister of Foreign Affairs; which did not prevent her being, at home, an intellectual and moral support at all times. And what perhaps still further enhanced her ascendancy over the Prince was the fact that she seemed to him to be the living phantom of her youthful mother, the Duchess of Courland, one of his most enduring passions.

But, for the reconstruction of Europe, Talleyrand found the principal source of his strength in a sovereign who, by origin and age, was the king of kings, while remaining through his principle, his misfortunes, and the circumstances of his accession, the symbol and the guarantee of necessary reparations. Thus, making the attainment of his own equilibrium the prelude to that of the world, the Prince de Bénévent set forth with firm tread on the tight-rope of principles, armed with a balancing-pole bearing at one end the crown of Louis XVIII, at the other Dorothée's fan and Carême's spit. Thus he performed an affecting solo. For him alone principles were something

257

more than words. As for the "big four" of the Coalition, principles had never been anything more than an excuse for their appetites. As regards principles, the Coalition, after having beflagged itself with them during its struggle against Napoleon, no longer looked upon them as anything more than embarrassing encumbrances, now that the "monster" was in chains. England, by far the least pharisaical of the Powers, because in all sincerity she identified her own cause with that of civilization, thought above all else of retaining, for their own good, the largest number of colonies possible, even at the expense of her ally Holland, with the reserve that she would compensate the latter with Belgium, in order to have a Continental sentinel against France. With a similar object in view, her desire was to fortify Prussia. She also contemplated preventing her rival in the East, Russia, from following her example in taking whatever suited her, namely the whole of Poland. But the Tsar Alexander, chivalrous and crafty, adapted his "principles" to his ambitions and generosity, while preparing to "grab" with the gesture of one who gives. He claimed the whole of Poland, but for its regeneration, to endow it with a constitution and liberal institutions after the fashion of London, whom, he flattered himself, he was thus gaining over to his own ends. Better still, his abnegation knowing no limits, he was prepared to renounce willingly his share of the former partition of Poland, and to include it in the new State of which he would be pleased to be king, thus distinguishing it from the Empire of all the Russias. As for Prussia, her disappointed hunger in France was to be temporarily appeased by the annexation of the kingdom of Saxony, a land certainly German and more advantageous than her former Polish territory, which she ceded to Russia. Austria, on her side, was not content with recovering

Marie Louise. Neither did she content herself with the annexation of the whole territory of Venice—a republic, and therefore, from the point of view of dynastic law, a *res nullius*; she also contemplated laying her hands, through a marriage, according to her motto, *felix Austria nube*, on the inheritance of the King of Sardinia. Meanwhile she exercised her protectorate over the kingdom of Naples through Murat, who had become her client. Metternich, the most doctrinaire of all the allied statesmen, assigned as a task for the Congress *the reconstruction of the moral order, the regeneration of the European political situation, an enduring peace founded on a just distribution of power*, the whole in the name of *eternal law*. But his private secretary, Friedrich von Gentz, wrote in his memoirs that these pompous words "were uttered to pacify the nations and to impart to this solemn assemblage an air of dignity and greatness". And he added: "The real object of the Congress was the division among the victors of the spoils taken from the vanquished". Metternich, champion of eternal law, considered himself qualified to preside over the allotment, the best bits being assigned to Austria, whose lasting interest was, in his eyes, the terrestrial form of that "eternal law". Had Austria not given a proof of her respect for principles and their adaptation to existing institutions by taking part in the dismemberment of Poland? And, still more recently, by handing over, through the offices of Metternich himself, an archduchess to the "Corsican Ogre"? The most thorough application of principles had been, more recently still, the collusion of Metternich, Chancellor to His Apostolic Majesty, with the usurper Murat, not only at the expense of the Bourbons of Naples, but also at that of the most august of all sovereigns, the Pope. On that particular occasion fidelity to principles was replaced, in the interest of Austria, by fidelity to a voluptuous memento, Metternich having for a long time worn a bracelet made from the hair of the beautiful and accessible Catherine Murat. Under the signboard of "eternal rights" Metternich had always kept a shop for territories, populations, and *souls*. At Vienna it was the liquidation of that exceptional stock, the Napoleonic Empire. Whereas Talleyrand's desire was to make the Congress an imposing law court, the Allies wished it to be nothing more nor less than a huge *foire d'Ampoigne* [1]—an occasion for thievery.

Certain contemporaries and a few historians have regretted that Talleyrand excluded France from that massacre of principles and the distribution authorized by it by settling her fate and renouncing every claim in the peace treaty of May 30. Now, it was precisely that which enabled Talleyrand to lead the game at Vienna. Without that sacrifice, forced moreover by defeat, there would have been neither peace nor Congress, nor, above all, any possibility for France's representative to hold the Coalition in check, and then to break it, marking the triumph of the first of her interests—equilibrium. It was by the exploitation of the idea of disinterestedness that he succeeded. War had been made on the Revolution and the Empire in the name of principles that Louis XVIII was the first to recognize, not only by proclaiming them like the Allies, but in submitting to them without any mental reservation. What answer could be given him when he demanded their application to everyone, beginning with those who had inscribed them on their banner? The Coalition had overthrown Napoleon to vindicate the

---

[1] *Foire d'Ampoigne*. To purchase an article "à la foire d'Ampoigne" is synonymous in French slang with "to steal". *Foire d'Ampoigne* is a pun on the word Ampoigne, a town in the Department of Mayenne, and *empoigner*, to take.—Translators' note.

right of dynasties to their patrimony and the right of nations to independence. It transgressed both those rights: that of the dynasties by maintaining Murat on the throne of Naples, and dethroning the King of Saxony, and the right of nations by taking no account of their feelings. Victorious, the Coalition turned against equilibrium—that is, against France—the "horrible principles" of Bonaparte, whom it imitated, but with less greatness and more hypocrisy.

On the contrary, Talleyrand turned against the Coalition its own principles which it derided but could not publicly disown without looking ashamed and losing credit everywhere, for European opinion, mobilized against Napoleon, had not yet demobilized, and was not so prompt to veer round as diplomacy. To frustrate the scheme of the Coalition it sufficed to unmask it with authority, the first condition of which was not to be associated with the plan in any way whatsoever. In Talleyrand's opinion the principle of legitimacy was of greater value by reason of its rigidity than because of its sanctity. Its inviolability was the reason for its fecundity. It might suffer damage, there being nothing absolute in politics; but, Talleyrand himself having to suffer the same, he would exert himself to *restrict* it to matters of secondary importance, and particularly to avoid anything likely to cause France to be suspected of desiring to profit by it in order to retain part of her conquests. The sovereigns and statesmen of the Allied States, judging Louis XVIII and Talleyrand by themselves, expected greed and duplicity. They were determined to cede nothing to France beyond her ancient limits, confirmed in the Treaty of Paris. But they would have considered themselves authorized by her claims, or merely by the mental reservations they ascribed to her—had she not denied them so plainly—to reinforce their union and perhaps impose fresh sacrifices upon her. Why trouble about an impenitent France, inspiring as much distrust and less fear than that of Napoleon? In any case, if France were disarmed in the Vienna negotiations, while discovering another ambition than that of the general interest, that imprudence would have enabled all private interests to organize Europe without her and against her. The Coalition, accustomed to be "kept collected", as the riding-master says of a horse, through the resistance of France, and to find in it a rallying-point in its race for conquest, went all to pieces when that circumstance ceased to act, like a galloping charger to whom his rider suddenly gives rein. Talleyrand's triumph consisted in perfecting this training of the Allies with their own horsewhip, mercilessly lashing them with the grand phrases which they had hissed so vigorously into the ears of France and the world. He affected the belief that these phrases were in their hearts, as they were on their lips. It was by taking the adversary seriously that he laughed at him, an attitude which rejoiced the heart of that satirical cynic who was ever uppermost in Talleyrand even under the most serious circumstances, but it exalted the statesman in him. Thanks to him, vanquished France, after being the scourge of Europe, became its conscience.

Talleyrand had not long to wait for the opportunity of being the voice of the conscience of France. On arriving in Vienna the representatives of England, Prussia, and Russia came to an agreement with Austria to form a board of four directors, the other Powers, including France, being invited merely to ratify decisions taken wholly without their consent. Talleyrand at once put himself at the head of the dissentient States, those of secondary and of still less importance, thus forming a majority which, grouped together, represented an imposing force. This was restoring to France her traditional rôle of protector of the weak and the guardian of a balance of power. It was placing in opposition what is called to-day the vertical or hierarchical system, founded on superior strength, to the horizontal or juridical system, founded on equality of rights. Talleyrand declared that no decision would be valid unless reached by a plenary meeting of the Congress. The current of opinion which he created against the "Big Four" was strong enough to force Metternich to transform it into six, by adding France and Spain. But he summoned them by means of confidential letters, in order to give the meeting a private character. Talleyrand kept them waiting, arrived the last of all, but played the leading rôle. To the insolence of the conqueror he opposed the chastity of justice. He set to work to put the Allies in the wrong, this wrong being for him an additional weapon. First of all, he denounced the word "Allies", which they had used in an official statement. "Allies against whom? Not against Napoleon, for he is on the island of Elba. Not against France, for peace is concluded. Not against the King of France, for he is the guarantor of the duration of peace. Let us speak frankly. If there are still allied Powers, I am in the way here. Nevertheless, if I were not here you would need me. I am the only one who does not ask for anything, save fair treatment—that is all. I bring you something of vast importance." He brought the Allies, or rather brought back to them and in spite of them, the principle upon which, according to them, the entire social order rested, and which, after being their bond of union, was about to divide them. In the name of that principle he made himself the champion of the smaller states. "We cannot, however," replied Hardenburg, the Prussian representative, "have European

affairs decided by the Princes of Lippe and Lichtenstein."
To which Talleyrand rejoined, "Neither can we have
them decided by the representatives of Prussia and
Russia". Friedrich von Gentz, the secretary to the Conference, summed up his impression by saying that the
plenipotentiaries were "well lectured for two hours".

The "Four" appealed to the Tsar, the sovereign who,
having rendered Talleyrand the greatest services, was in a
position, it was supposed, to obtain the most concessions.
Alexander, sulky with him since his first disappointments
in Paris, showed no alacrity to see him; it was only on the
morning after Talleyrand's first collision with the "Four"
that he granted him an audience. Alexander employed all
his artifices to move Talleyrand, but without success. At
last the Emperor of all the Russias, losing his composure
before the stubborn representative of a higher sovereignty,
that of Law, exclaimed, "The convenience of Europe is
Law". "This language, Sire," replied Talleyrand, "is not
yours; it is alien to you and your heart disowns it."—"No,
I repeat it, the convenience of Europe is Law." "I then
turned round", says Talleyrand, "towards the wainscot,
near which I was standing, and resting my head against it,
struck the panelling, exclaiming, 'Europe, Europe, unhappy Europe!' Then, turning round to the Emperor, I
asked him: 'Is it to be said that you have been its ruin?'
He answered me, 'War rather than relinquish what I
possess'. With the gesture of a sorely tried but determined man, I dropped my arms as though to say, 'the
fault will not be ours'—and then I remained silent."

It was at the same interview that Talleyrand, on Alexander referring to the King of Saxony, who had been boy-
cotted by the sovereigns because he had been Napoleon's
last ally, as "he who betrayed the European cause", when
he himself had been an ally at Tilsit, replied with a sen-

tence which, in his eyes, excused his own betrayal: "Sire, that is a matter of dates".

Never having been intimidated by the greatest potentates in the world, Talleyrand was even less so by their representatives. At another conference he "lectured" them again for two hours. He insisted and obtained that the expression "public law" should be introduced in the following phrase concerning the proposals to be laid before the Congress "which should conform to *public law* and the expectation of Europe". These words *public law*, after having been the flag of the Allies, produced upon them the effect of the red rag waved in front of a bull at a bull-fight. The Prussian plenipotentiary, Humboldt, being deaf, had them repeated to him. Whereupon, in a fit of anger, he exclaimed brutally: "What is public law doing here?"—"It is *obliging* you to be here," replied Talleyrand.

There is no more contentious idea than that of law, especially of public law, where there exists neither legislator to define it, nor tribunal to apply it, nor policeman to carry it out, the sole penalty being war, which is not always just, and, when it is just, not always victorious. Even if public law is only a word, Talleyrand was not wrong to arm himself with it. Nations are restless, but they are led by words, and every assembly, be it only one of diplomats, consists of people. Introduced, in spite of the Allies, into an official declaration of the Congress, that phrase, which signified legitimacy, sacrificed "convenience", as the Tsar Alexander called it, to propriety. But the Allies were unable, without incurring general reprobation, publicly to repudiate it, after having thrown it in reproach against Napoleon. Nevertheless that phrase bound them to the re-establishment of the King of Saxony and the Bourbons of Naples, a double obstacle to the hegemony of Prussia in Germany and Austria in Italy.

That phrase, expressed by Talleyrand with such solemnity, who was the only man to laugh at it *in petto*, created a favourable atmosphere for him and crystallized around him the resistance to the dictatorship of the "Four". But, above all, it passed beyond the circle of the Conference to be spread abroad in the outside world and awaken there a profound echo. Talleyrand was far too acute, and possessed too great an experience of diplomatic controversies, to be unaware that one is wrong to be too much in the right, that it is necessary to negotiate, not to plead, that nothing is so dangerous as apparent success, always placed to the debit of him who obtains it by the antagonist who strives to get it paid to him. He possessed, also, too much of the mentality of "dear colleagues" to be unaware that to humiliate them is not the way to obtain their support or to neutralize them. He did not forget but did not trust too much in his charm or that of his niece to heal wounded vanity. But he was also aware that the game was not being played at Vienna between diplomats only; he knew that the nations took the promises of the Coalition seriously, that after so much suffering they expected a new era of peace, rest, and order; that the phrase "public law" borrowed a magic power from its obscurity and meant for them the promised land. He knew that this messianic frame of mind was particularly potent in London, expressed itself there freely both on platform and in the press, and that the English plenipotentiaries were obliged to take great account of it. His notes, attitudes, and theatrical words were calculated to captivate that tremendous force, English opinion. He addressed himself to the sentimental ideology of clergymen and spinsters, whom, according to Paul Cambon—one of France's ambassadors who remained the longest time in London—France must always have on her side if she is to collaborate with

England. It was because he was able to gain those allies, who often lead the power which leads the world, that France was about to quit her isolation and possess allies. It was by that method of indirect fire that he hit his target.

It was, indeed, the English plenipotentiary, Castlereagh, personally quite indifferent to "public law", who supported the French demand to insert that mystic phrase in the declaration. Talleyrand had had no difficulty in proving to him that public law was demanded by the British conscience, since it was required in the British interest, for it excluded the attribution of all Poland to Russia, whose power the London Government aimed at confining within such limits that it would not threaten her system of Continental arbitration. However, Alexander irritated became menacing: "Poland is ours", he said. "I will never renounce it. I occupy it with 200,000 men. It remains to be seen who will drive me out." Castlereagh, who was more willing to leave Saxony to Prussia than Poland to Russia, made useless efforts to isolate him by detaching Prussia from him. But the secondary states of Germany, with Bavaria at their head, talked of making war to prevent a spoliation which would have been a presage of their own. Talleyrand, after having stirred them up secretly, sent them to Metternich, better qualified to defend them against Prussian ambitions. They found him already much disturbed by the Austrian General Staff, which feared the domination of Prussia over Saxony, whose strategic importance had been demonstrated in the recent wars, particularly at the battle of Leipzig. England flattered herself that she was conciliating all interests by offering the Rhineland to Prussia, the restitution of Saxony to her king, safeguarding the Legitimacy so dear to Talleyrand, and, what was of more importance to

London, the ancient partitions of Poland. But the Tsar Alexander and King Frederic William, whose union was impregnable, declared that they would never renounce, one his claims to all Poland, and the other to Saxony. They adopted so high a tone that Talleyrand, who meantime had warned Louis XVIII to look after the army, having seized the psychological moment to offer the alliance of France to Metternich and Castlereagh, signed with them on January 3, 1815, a secret treaty.

In his letter of January 4 to the King, Talleyrand triumphantly wrote: "The Coalition is dissolved. France is no longer isolated in Europe". After having broken the diplomatic blockade of the Coalition, he broke the Coalition itself. When he first reached Vienna he had been received with great respect for himself personally, but officially he had been relegated to a side table, one might say even to the servants' room. But now he was more the master of the house than the sovereigns themselves, and all Europe was in his waiting-room. "Talleyrand", said the Tsar, "plays the part of the minister of Louis XIV."

This was the blunder that, according to certain historians, he made. Thiers blames him for having, through his habit of playing the leading rôle under the Empire and being identified with success, lost sight of France's real situation and missed the opportunity of repairing defeat instead of taking the front of the stage, playing the star part and eclipsing the entire company. Why did he not remain in the background and await his opportunity? Above all, instead of proclaiming so loudly a disinterestedness, deceptive when not reciprocated, why did he not try to profit by inter-allied rivalries by discreetly putting the French alliance up to the highest bidder and so obtain the best price? Instead of following in the wake of England and Austria, powers surfeited and "static", why did he not take a seat at the board with Prussia and Russia, young, insatiable, "dynamic" powers? France's aid, being indispensable for the satisfaction of their ambitions, to make sure of it, they would have helped her to satisfy her own, had she desired, for instance, to revise the Treaty of Paris while recovering the Rhineland and even Belgium. Talleyrand has sacrificed the substance for the shadow, the national interest to puerile personal satisfaction. In short, at Vienna, he was merely a great but unsuspected "incompetent", made worse by a venality and vanity only too notorious.

Putting the question of venality aside, let us remember that Talleyrand possessed too much pride to be accessible to vanity. Far from yielding to a habit in thus apparently taking a leading part and indulging in brilliant bursts of eloquence, this classic comedian did violence to his nature. His preferences had ever been for the inward drama, permitting him to attain the maximum of meaning with the minimum of demonstration. Far from contenting himself with hypocritical pretexts, this realist only interested himself in appearances if they gave rise to realities. If, when he reached Vienna, he affected to wield an authority which he had not then attained, it was to create it by asserting it, and to conquer it at the Congress by first establishing it in public opinion. If he raised the tone of his voice it was because he appealed to the world, in the name of law, against the action of triumphant force. Being unable to displace armies, he made up for that by the displacement of imponderables, one of those psychological phenomena which sometimes paralyse armies and alter the course of events. That was precisely the case.

Sir Henry Lytton Bulwer, the English biographer of Talleyrand, says that the idea of Prussia or even Russia ever consenting to reinstall France in the Rhineland is "extravagant". Prussia had made war on France to expel her. Why should she face the risks of another war to bring her back there? For—Sir Henry Lytton Bulwer contents himself with the supposition—this result could only have been attained at the cost of a new war in which France should have had to contend against England and Austria; a disastrous war indeed, the superiority of these Powers being overwhelming. The Prusso-Russians had at their disposal 350,000 men; England, Austria, and the secondary German states (which would have gathered around Vienna if, as would have been highly unlikely, Berlin, sacrificing everything to the annexation of Saxony, had abdicated its rôle of champion of Germanic independence against France) were able to put into line 600,000 men, or almost double. After the treaty of January 3, 1815, which obliged France to add 150,000 men, the disproportion of forces excluded all risks of war, even when taking no account of the armies of Spain, Sardinia, and the Netherlands, which, after the secondary German states, adhered to the treaty. Talleyrand therefore did not, as he has been accused of doing, expose France to the risk of a fresh conflict for the pleasure of depriving Prussia of Saxony and placing the former on the Rhine. On the contrary, by accepting the other system of alliance and raising, by France's quota of 150,000 men, its effectives up to 500,000 against 600,000, he would have made war more probable, without making it, on any hypothesis, profitable to us. When Alexander, who, however, was easy at making promises, especially at the cost of his allies, solicited our alliance, he abstained from making the slightest allusion to the Rhineland. In exchange for France's support on the question of Poland and Saxony, he only offered his good offices against Murat. But Talleyrand was not in the habit of paying for what he could get for nothing and he counted on the force of circumstances to rid himself of Murat. To those who desired to make that an object of barter, and who said to him, "That is essentially your own business", he replied: "The Naples affair is no more mine than it is everybody's; as far as I am concerned, it is purely a matter of principle. Europe owes it to her dignity and tranquillity to tolerate such a scandal no longer."

The spirit of illusion which animated the advocates of the alliance with Prussia and Russia was destined to be again refuted, without being entirely dissipated, in 1830 when Polignac, dreaming of acquiring the Rhineland by abandoning Saxony to Prussia and encouraging the ambitions of Russia in the East, was shown the door at Berlin and St. Petersburg. In 1830 that policy was dangerous; in 1815 it would have been fatal. When France could only regain prosperity amidst peace, and recover her rank in the council of the nations by showing great prudence and moderation, to join herself with the "dynamic" against the conservative Powers would have been to court certain and perhaps irretrievable disaster. After having passed through so many storms and sustained so many injuries, her first care on entering the port of the monarchy had to be, not to enter upon new adventures with the pirates of Europe, but to "let go the anchors", to use the words of Napoleon, who, however, never succeeded in doing so, save in internal politics.

The alliance with England and Austria did not only safeguard the security of France. That combination, which, in addition to its military and moral superiority, rested on the financial and naval power of England, was also strong enough to impose its will on the Congress. Although the treaty was a secret one, the attitude of Metternich and Castlereagh caused the Tsar and King of Prussia to recognize the necessity for making concessions.

One relinquished the whole of Poland, the other relinquished the whole of Saxony.

The treaties of Vienna embodied, in their totality, the programme outlined for Talleyrand by his instructions. Austria laid no hands on the states of the King of Sardinia nor, under the cloak of Murat, upon the kingdom of Naples, restored to the Bourbons. Metternich, after having treated with Murat, was not content to depose him: he shot him. Parma was also to be restored to the Bourbons after the death of Marie Louise. Metternich restored the Legations to the Pope, who reigned once more in Rome. The King of Sardinia recovered Piedmont, increased by Genoa. Austria, who ruled in Lombardy, Venetia, and Tuscany, did not dominate the whole of Italy. England's disinterestedness being only Continental, she retained Malta and the Ionian Islands.

Germany was now organized in a confederation of which the Emperor of Austria was made permanent president, this being a counterpoise to Prussia. She remained divided, not as after the treaties of Westphalia, but so far as allowed the agglomerations created by Napoleon I. Mayence was ceded to Hesse as a federal fortress. Bavaria annexed the Rhenish Palatinate. Hanover, which belonged to the King of England, was enlarged and separated the old Prussia of the Rhenish province. Prussia, indeed, which recovered her former Polish province, annexed one-third of Saxony, and, as a compensation for the remainder, the Rhenish provinces.

Prussia, installed at France's very doors—that, in the opinion of certain people, was Talleyrand's great blunder, if not his crime. Nevertheless, on that point as on others, his work at Vienna is praised by such eminent historians as Albert Sorel, the Duc de Broglie, and G. Pallain. More recently, Charles Dupuis and Albert Pingaud have endorsed their conclusions and have strongly reinforced them by new arguments.

To judge that result with equity it ought not to be isolated from the whole to which it belongs, nor must one lose sight of the principle inspiring Talleyrand's entire system. Faced with the alternative of installing Prussia on the Rhine or allowing her to annex the kingdom of Saxony, that principle—legitimacy—dictated his choice. It was impossible to violate it in Saxony and at the same time to invoke it for the benefit of France, whose integrity it guaranteed; nor for that of Europe, whose equilibrium it assured—that equilibrium which, in its turn, assured the independence of France and her rank in the world. It was that principle which prevented or limited Austrian domination in Italy, for it covered the other Italian states. It also prevented Russian domination in the East, for it covered Turkey and imposed respect for existing treaties, including those which partitioned Poland. Finally and above all, it prevented Prussian domination in Germany, for it protected the other states against her. If it presented some disadvantages in such a case, that was more than outweighed by its immense advantage, its absolute necessity, in another.

But, in the case of Saxony, was the disadvantage as serious as has been asserted? Do all France's misfortunes arise from Prussia's proximity on the Rhine? To-day, after the calamities of 1870 and 1914, and face to face with Germany unified by "fire and steel", under the aegis of Berlin, France no longer sees there only Prussia: that which, on the historical plane, distorts perspectives, proportions, and judgments. In 1815 the German Empire did not exist; the states which since that time it has absorbed, preserved, thanks to Talleyrand's system, their sovereignty. And they made use of it by allying themselves with France, as they had just done by adhering to the treaty of January 3, 1815. Their princes were indignant over the spoliation with which the King of Saxony was threatened and were prepared to take up arms to save him and themselves, their cause being one with his. If, indeed, Saxony had been reunited with Prussia they would speedily have shared the same fate. On the Rhine she was much less formidable to them and, in her own opinion, too, for it was against her will that she was transferred there. By rounding off her estates with a Saxony having 1,700,000 protestants easily assimilated, Prussia would have acquired, in the heart of Germany, a cohesion which would have strengthened her attraction to the point of making it irresistible, and all the more as this extension would have been attained in contempt of the principle which constituted the title of the other sovereigns. In the Rhineland she received only vacant territories, those of the former ecclesiastical electors who had been dispossessed by Napoleon and remained so definitely, the principle of legitimacy being applicable only to dynasties. Those regions were peopled by Gallicized Catholics, who were in despair on becoming Prussian subjects, and who were to become so at heart only after several generations. Finally, that province, cut off from Prussia by Hanover, was "in the air", at the mercy of a sudden attack. Instead of being, through the annexation of Saxony, the most populous, homogeneous, and concentrated state of Germany, Prussia was the most dissimilar, most dispersed, and most amorphous one. "It is an indefinable State", said the Abbé Dominique de Pradt. "It sees enemies everywhere and frontiers nowhere . . . it is like those houses in Berlin which are only built to face the street; a State which has still only a frontage in Europe". For Austria also, Prussia was less to be feared on the Rhine than in Saxony. At Dresden she would

have commanded the road to Vienna, and the Hohenzollerns, reigning thenceforward over a *bloc* of German
subjects larger in number than those remaining, without
the same cohesion, under the sceptre of the Habsburgs,
would not have been long before expelling the latter from
the confederation and seizing the Empire. But—and this
is yet another grievance against Talleyrand—was it wise
for France to avert the risk of conflicts between Prussia
and Austria instead of fanning the flame of their discord in
order to neutralize one through the other? But to neutralize them one through the other, it was necessary to organize between them not a conflict, but, as Talleyrand did, an
equilibrium. Conflict would have destroyed equilibrium,
and in all probability to the advantage of Prussia, whose
hegemony was more dangerous to France than that of
Austria.

Less to be feared on the Rhine than at Dresden by
Austria and the other German states, was not Prussia less
formidable to France also—the natural ally of those states
against the machinations of Berlin? The fact that this
alliance has been neglected, and even reversed—for Napoleon III, like his uncle, preferred "great agglomerations"
on France's frontiers—is not to be imputed to Talleyrand.
That was not his policy; it is the abandonment of his
policy which has been the cause of all France's misfortunes
and those of Europe. So long as the confederation existed
and the kingdom of the Hohenzollerns remained divided,
Prussian Rhineland was more easily, in the case of conflict,
the hostage of France than the advance guard of Prussia.
Its annexation was also easier against Prussia than against
the King of Saxony, if the latter had received it as compensation for his former states. If France was content, as
under the old régime, with a policy of extending her prestige in the Rhineland, this policy was also easier to apply

among populations stirred up to revolt by Prussian brutality, and therefore wholly opposed to Berlin, than it would have been under the paternal authority of the King of Saxony. Would this sovereign, at least, have been France's friend, and would his kingdom have served as a buffer for her against Prussia? That is not certain. Perhaps he would not have been very grateful to France for transferring him from Dresden to Bonn—that was the capital chosen for him—where he would have reigned over 700,000 new subjects, for he was only offered a portion of the Rhineland instead of the 1,700,000 bequeathed to him by his ancestors. Above all, he would have been in a position to find out where, between Paris and Berlin, strength of will and power were to be discovered. Besides, at that point, hypotheses lend importance to facts. In 1870 Bavaria was France's neighbour in the Palatinate and an ally of Prussia against her; at Dresden the King of Saxony was the same. And he would have been the same on the Rhine, like the King of Bavaria. The great peril for France was not the proximity of Prussia, but the domination of Prussia over Germany. At that time she was everywhere at home there, and everywhere a menace—on the Rhine as on the Danube. The safety of France consisted, not in the attribution of the Rhineland to the King of Saxony, nor in a special status for that province, but in the equilibrium of the German "corpus", and in her fidelity to the policy which, inaugurated by the treaties of Westphalia, had, so far as was possible, been maintained in the treaties of Vienna.

Those who attach greater authority to M. Thiers than to the lessons taught by events will be convinced of the inanity of his criticisms by M. Thiers himself. He wrote: "If I had been allowed to have my way in 1850, I would in a single summer and without difficulty have ensured the greatness of France. I would have extended her territory as far as Mayence—the key to Germany." It is true that Mayence—still thanks to Talleyrand, and in virtue of his instructions—belonged not to Prussia, but to Hesse. It was none the less, according to Thiers, "the key to Germany", and therefore to Prussia, beginning with the neighbouring Rhineland. Seeing that that magnificent result could have been obtained without difficulty, it must therefore have been because Talleyrand's work was faultless. Later still, in 1866, Thiers denounced the policy of Napoleon III, who was fascinated by the mirage of compensations with which that tempter Bismarck deluded him, while planning Sadowa and Sedan. "There is too much common sense in France", he said, "to permit such a policy to be welcomed; and allow me to add that, even should it bring you an increase of territory, such a policy would only be the more shameful, for it would amount to consenting to receive a salary for the greatness of France, unworthily compromised in the near future." In the same speech he thus epitomized his thought: "The greatest principle of European policy is that Germany should be composed of independent States". It would not be possible to define Talleyrand's policy better, nor to condemn that which was just the reverse, and with which Thiers, in his *History of the Consulate and the Empire*, has reproached Talleyrand for not having followed. These words were spoken on May 3, 1866, on the eve of Sadowa, a fact which, after the event, lends a prophetic quality to them. Talleyrand had the advantage over Thiers of not having changed his ideas nor waited until it was too late to denounce the danger. It was in 1814 at Vienna, where, in agreement with the King, he devoted himself to prevent Russia from dominating Germany, that he warned Louis XVIII against "those who desire to replace all the governments of this country (Germany) by a single one". "With them", he wrote, "university men and youths, infected by their theories, conspire. 'Unity of the German fatherland' is their cry, their dogma, and their religion, exalted to the point of fanaticism." That fanaticism would not have been extinguished by transferring the King of Saxony to the Rhineland. It could only be withstood by dynastic particularism, of which the principle of legitimacy, proclaimed by Talleyrand, was the guarantee. On the other hand, that fanaticism would have been nourished by a repetition of Napoleonic ambitions in Germany. France's encroachments in that direction, under the old régime, had been pacific, because they were accompanied by a policy of dividing the "Germanys", and because they were characterized by great moderation and were the fruits of patience rather than of violence. It was an ingenious puzzle which French kings bequeathed to each other, but which none flattered himself that he had solved. But because Napoleon, working for the present, not for the future, had devoured Germany without assimilating her, France was obliged to wait before nibbling at her again up to the natural frontiers, forgetfulness of that excess and favour of the course of events aiding France's efforts.

It was first of all necessary to save France and inspire confidence. Talleyrand succeeded in that by opposing "legitimacy" to appetite, disinterestedness to suspicion. Notwithstanding his detractors, those were no empty formulas with which his mind elegantly concealed the weaknesses of his character, after the fashion of Cleopatra who out of a swoon could create an additional charm. Legitimacy and disinterestedness at that time constituted the sole doctrine of national salvation. Napoleon undertook to offer a new proof of that more startling than all others, when, during the Hundred Days, the "invasion by a single man" placed everything in jeopardy.

In vain did Napoleon protest that his intentions were pacific, write to the sovereigns to reassure them, accept the Treaty of Paris, send Alexander an authentic copy (forgotten by Louis XVIII in a drawer at the Tuileries) of the secret treaty of January 3, 1815, which bound the King of France to Austria and England against Russia. Nothing was to be done. The "Four" did not even await his arrival in Paris to become reconciled and renew the Coalition, anathematize him, outlaw him, deliver him up to "public vengeance", declaring him the "enemy and disturber of the world's peace". Talleyrand did not lose his composure. He separated the cause of France from that of Napoleon, in order to spare the nation the conqueror's vengeance and preserve the conditions of the Treaty of Paris after the Emperor's inevitable defeat. He joined the Allies, who were not therefore the enemies of Louis XVIII and France, although they were fighting against the French army. "The display of such a fine discrimination", said Talleyrand, "had never before occurred in politics."

Despite that precaution, the Allies, after Waterloo, talked of despoiling France and of driving her back beyond her ancient frontiers. The fact that she had welcomed Napoleon after his return from the island of Elba was a proof of her incorrigibility. The world would only be at peace when she had been for ever reduced to impotence. Lord Liverpool advised that the conquests of Louis XIV should be taken from her. Others were inclined to allow France what they derisively styled her natural frontiers, namely the Jura, the Vosges, and the Ardennes. The second Treaty of Paris, dated November 20, 1815, enforced upon France by ultimatum, deprived her of

500,000 inhabitants, condemned her to an occupation for five years, and an indemnity of seven hundred millions. "This is the spite of a pygmy, not the anger of a giant", said Talleyrand. France, nevertheless, preserved her ancient boundaries, and her position as the leading Continental power. The damages were restricted through the wisdom of Louis XVIII and the ability of Talleyrand. The Vienna treaties, having maintained the independence of the German states, none of them was sufficiently strong to dismember France at the expense of the others. They did not succeed in coming to an agreement as to the attribution of Alsace and Lorraine. The pan-Germanists proposed to allot them to an Archduke. Prussia opposed that. Talleyrand had acted judiciously when he stirred up jealousy between Vienna and Berlin. He was also right in asserting and proving that disinterested attitude from which France was to benefit, particularly after Waterloo. The immediate re-establishment of the Allied front after the Emperor's return refutes the criticisms against Talleyrand for having neglected to obtain an advantage from their disagreement, as though France's disinterestedness was not the primary condition of their dissensions. Finally, Talleyrand was well advised when he erected legitimacy into a dogma and incarnated it in the person of Louis XVIII. His realism is shown even in the mystical atmosphere with which, for his protection, he surrounded the King of France. Thus, on January 21, 1815, the former member of the Constituent Assembly, the ex-Bishop of Autun, ex-minister of the Directory, who in 1797 had commemorated that date in the revolutionary ranks, caused a solemn service of expiation to be celebrated in Vienna. "On this day of horror and eternal mourning", he wrote to Louis XVIII, "I have not followed the desire of my heart only; I have also thought that Your Majesty's ambassadors, making themselves the interpreters of the grief of France, should blazon it forth on foreign soil before the eyes of assembled Europe." He devoted himself heart and soul to the organization of that ceremony at which all the sovereigns in bounden duty had to be present. Though he wrote to Louis XVIII, "I do not know what this will cost", he could say what it would bring them in. "This is one of the most effective methods of sanctifying the principle we are attempting to establish." The panegyric on the Martyr-King, delivered from St. Stephen's pulpit by a priest of French origin, had been composed by Talleyrand's collaborator, Comte Alexis de Noailles, but under the great diplomatist's inspiration. It was a hymn to the glory of legitimacy, the Bourbons and France, whose love for her king was presented as not the least of her virtues. It was an immense success. Talleyrand was so pleased that, in the very detailed account which he sent to the King after the 21st, he entreated His Majesty to bestow the Legion of Honour upon the architect who had decorated the cathedral, the composer who had written the music for the Mass, the choir-master, and several members of the French Embassy. When, during the Hundred Days, Louis XVIII, despoiled of all temporal power, became a refugee at Mons, he was none the less recognized by the Powers as the sovereign of France. That was because Talleyrand had made him a spiritual chief of all kings. Having canonized Louis XVI as the Saint of Legitimacy, the ex-Bishop of Autun appointed Louis XVIII as its Pope.

Through the timeliness of the principle which he advocated, Talleyrand maintained the *absolute* power of France while safeguarding her ancient boundaries and her *relative* power, at the same time establishing at Vienna a tutelary equilibrium for herself and her associates.

That service—negative, as some may judge, but all the same, vital—is not the only one that France owes to Talleyrand. Having ensured her safety, he then assured her future by directing her course towards the English alliance. That was, indeed, the event which gives the most emphatic denial to Chateaubriand's words: "He signed his name to events; he did not bring them about". It was that event which he most plainly brought to pass, without anyone's assistance. For it was not provided for in his instructions. Talleyrand, who, within the bounds of those instructions, had full powers at Vienna, where the slowness of communications with Paris forced him to make decisions without referring to headquarters, possessed full initiative and bore all the responsibility. Amidst darkness and even storms, Anglo-French collaboration, initiated by Talleyrand, has yielded advantages for both countries, as well as for the cause of peace and civilization. What would France, Europe, the world have been to-day if, at the moment when he had to choose between England and Russia, who solicited him, he had done what certain historians reproach him for failing to do—chosen Russia?

Even admitting, against all probability, that that would not have meant war, and a war which could only have been disastrous for France, England would have harboured a resentment the effects of which would have been felt by the France of Louis XVIII after Waterloo. It was, on the contrary, the support of London which—notwithstanding the cupidity of Berlin—helped her to preserve the integrity of her territory. After the second Treaty of Paris it was the English banks which permitted her to pay the war indemnity and thus to shorten the occupation. It was Wellington, commander-in-chief of the army of occupation, who concluded the anticipated evacuation. When the conference of the four ambassadors (England, Austria, Prussia, and Russia) turned itself into a directory of France's politics—even her home affairs—and the opposition stirred up national sentiment against Louis XVIII, whom it accused of governing with foreign bayonets, the occupation could not have been prolonged without recommencing in France the era of revolutions and the foreign perils which follow in their train. Some years later Anglo-French collaboration was to accomplish or facilitate great things: the resurrection of Greece, the conquest of Algeria, and the independence of Belgium. If, instead of inspiring confidence in the English and allying France with them, Talleyrand's attitude at Vienna had imbued them with invincible mistrust, will anyone believe that, after becoming Louis Philippe's ambassador in London, he could have overcome the opposition there against France's establishment in Africa and the difficulties of the Belgian crisis?

It was especially in that connection that the succession of events magnified his work beyond his own anticipations. The Anglo-French alliance, sealed on the battlefields where it preserved the liberties of the world, originates from the conquest of Algeria through the Anglo-French agreement of 1904 concerning Morocco and Egypt, which is its logical result, and from Belgian neutrality, guaranteed by the two Powers. If these two great events, both of which tested the relations of France and England to the point of exposing them to grave conflict, were, on the contrary, the origin of their brotherhood of arms, it is doubtless because their alliance in 1815 induced them to settle their disputes in a friendly spirit and because the author of that alliance was better equipped than anyone else to preserve it in 1830.

Napoleon once said: "England and France have held in

their hands the fate of the world, and particularly of European civilization. What harm we have done each other! How much good we could do each other!" It was Talleyrand who made the wish expressed in that regret a reality.

Talleyrand was more faithful to the Emperor's thought than to his policy. If in 1915, a century after Waterloo, Wellington fought with France against Blücher on the plains of the Marne, the wisdom of Talleyrand had something to do with it.

The man who, when he had re-established France on the ruins of the Empire through the Restoration, afterwards built the edifice of our security at Vienna, and added in London the buttress of Belgian independence to it, deserves the name of constructor, and even the more glorious name of founder. The important thing is not merely to construct, but to build something lasting. That edifice, in two of its essential parts—the English alliance and Belgian independence—still stands. The other essential part, the Germanic confederation, indispensable to the equilibrium and independence of Europe, has collapsed, or rather, it has been destroyed by the folly of the nations, including the French, for whom it was a shelter. If the diplomatic wing of the building raised by Talleyrand is the best preserved, the foundations of the other wing (the constitutional) partly subsist in spite of the fall of the Restoration. It is true that these foundations are chargeable with certain ruins. It is to Talleyrand, the principal author of the Charter of 1814, that France owes "parliamentarism" and the institutions which spring from it. The Restoration was, indeed, the true instaurator of the liberties proclaimed by the Revolution, but immediately destroyed by it. "Liberty or Death" meant the death of liberty and liberties. After being moderated by the guillotine of the Terror, then by deportation during the Directory, they were suppressed, in principle as in fact, by the dictatorship of Napoleon. It needed the return of "tyrants" to make them a reality. It is that which has created for Talleyrand more animosity on one side than gratitude on the other. The ultra-royalists reproached him more seriously for having given liberal institutions to France than for not conserving a part of the military conquests of the Revolution. A conservative of the Revolution in home politics and a revolutionist among conservatives in foreign policy—for it was a revolution to substitute legitimacy for conquest in public law—Talleyrand solved that apparent contradiction in the unity of a higher synthesis: peace within and without. Indeed, if he yielded to the spirit of the age when imposing conditions on Louis XVIII, it was principally to make himself indispensable to the King by surrounding him with his friends and setting aside the *émigrés* who execrated him. That realist made no fetish of immortal principles. If they were errors, errors are facts of which politics must take account, either to fight against them or compound with them. Now, like poisons, which in minute doses act as remedies, those errors, if not pushed to excess, were necessary to get the monarchy accepted by the body of opinion still devoted to the dogmas of '89. During their eclipse under the Empire, France remained quiet because Napoleon had put her into the double irons of the dictatorship and conscription, while intoxicating her with glory, which is less the ornament than the glittering funereal attire of liberty, for military glory demands such a rigorous discipline that it becomes the negation of liberty. After Napoleon's fall, war was no longer the guarantee of the sacred union—as though the nation were a powder which required its blood to form it into a block. The problem was how to maintain it as a block without that cement. It was necessary to ensure concord and neutralize the trouble-makers, even at the cost of making allowance for their prejudices. Similarly, the principle of legitimacy, even if it had no absolute value, was then the best guarantee for peace abroad. Under that aegis of peace, notwithstanding their apparent opposition, the home and foreign policies of Talleyrand were united.

It has been said that Talleyrand, prince of diplomatists, was not a statesman. If the word means a "man of state" (*un homme d'état*) the "of" is possessive, and the phrase is not applicable to him. Talleyrand belonged less to the State than it belonged to him. He never entirely gave himself up except to himself. He was one of the most autonomous persons in history.

If the diplomat differs from a statesman as a tactician differs from a strategist, if he is only the executant in a determinate sector of a plan which is larger than his own sphere of action and is the concept of the statesman, then Talleyrand was both, for he carried out his own plan, only a part of which had Louis XVIII for joint-author.

If a statesman is the contrary of a specialist, and must possess an intelligence wide enough to embrace the universality of great political problems, and elevated enough to dominate them, Talleyrand fulfilled that condition. He had not specialized in diplomacy, which, unless it is everything is nothing, for it is the synthesis of all national activities in their relations with those of other nations. But, in a grave crisis at home or abroad, Talleyrand conceived and applied a programme of home policy as though it were a programme of foreign policy, and strengthened his mastery in the harmony of those two programmes which supported each other and interlocked.

If a statesman is a man who has "a mind conscious of

the future", as Choiseul had, according to Talleyrand himself, then our hero did not come short of the title. His views were often prophetic. As for his work, we have seen that it has been fruitful where it still continues and that elsewhere its abandonment has been fraught with disaster.

If a statesman is a man who rises above the immediate or apparent interests of his country to discover the point of convergence between its permanent interests and those of other nations, this definition also applies to Talleyrand. That convergence being profounder in the case of France than for any other nation, and Talleyrand having had the leisure during his travels to meditate on the unity of the world and the interdependence of its parts, he was, at Vienna, the most European and the most human of all diplomats. It was owing to him that the treaties of 1815 guaranteed through equilibrium a general peace until the time when Napoleon III reversed his policy. It was by a return to an equilibrium, it was by taking his inspiration from the past that he assured the future, not by integrating, as has been said, but by reintegrating France in Europe and Europe in a general peace.

If a statesman is a man who exercises, when in power, the faculties peculiar to Man—judgment, will, and conscience—and who exercises them in the name of humanity, then the ex-Bishop of Autun realized at Vienna the paradox of that ideal. His work, in fact, gives the lie to the determinist, materialistic, democratic (these words are perhaps synonymous) conception of history. His judgment discerned the conditions of an equilibrium and his will imposed them; his conscience, or his consciousness of the necessities of peace, built those conditions as much upon moral as upon material forces; and, finally, he conceived and applied his system without taking into account the rights of nations and while neglecting the opinion of the people. But the interests of the nations were only to be the better served. If he had invoked the rights of nations his voice would have found no echo, and his efforts would have been fruitless. It was by fighting the Coalition with its own principle, legitimacy, that he dissolved it.

Doubtless legitimacy excluded the republics—those of Genoa and Venice were sacrificed at Vienna—and postulated the identity of dynastic rights and national interests. Talleyrand's policy ought to be judged, not by the absolute value of that postulate, but by its practical value in 1815. At that time it was not only a necessary expedient for the salvation of France; it was also an immense step in advance in comparison with the right of conquest which previously had been the entire law of Europe, avowed by Napoleon, more or less unavowed by the other sovereigns. The evils ascribed to legitimacy are insignificant when compared with the scourge of conquest which it exercised.

A smile is permissible when Talleyrand talks morality, particularly at Vienna, where the Congress suppressed black slavery but sanctified white slavery, "Legitimacy" being opposed to the rights of nations. In certain cases this antinomy was not purely theoretical. The "brewing" of the nations, practised by Napoleon, far from having mixed them, aroused national feelings through reactions against foreign domination, and all the more so as the sovereigns cultivated and exploited those feelings against the usurper. But more often dynastic rights were in accordance with the interests of the nations.

The modern conscience resents a principle in virtue of which sovereignty is exercised over territories and populations, like the principle of proprietorship over a farm and live-stock. As a matter of fact, the choice lying between that principle and conquest, the live-stock found in the former is the best of guarantees; logically, indeed, it was led out to the pastures by its traditional masters, who, if only for the sake of their own interest, took care of it, and to the slaughter-house by some temporal master without any other claim or title save that of conquest. Besides, the carnage among the nations was to beat all the records of history when humanity, with the proclamation of its rights, launched forth into that war "in totality" of which Napoleon had given us a foretaste and whose seed was implanted in the principle of nationality, a war thus described by Napoleon's collaborator, Jomini: "Armies are no longer composed of troops recruited voluntarily from the superfluity of a too numerous population; they are entire nations, called to arms by law, who no longer fight for the demarcation of frontiers, but to some extent for their own existence. This state of things takes us back to the third and fourth centuries, recalling the collisions between immense hordes in their contests for the European continent. It is impossible to foresee where this devastation will stop. War will become a more terrible scourge than ever, for the populations of the civilized nations will be mown down. . . ."

Whilst awaiting that progress which blossomed in 1914, Talleyrand's system was one less precarious. Opposed to conquest, legitimacy was a moral force. Its equilibrium was another. It was not entirely materialistic; its duration presupposed moderation and a volition towards peace of a group of Powers strong enough to hold the others in check and wise enough not to provoke them.

Talleyrand is therefore worthy of praise for having imposed on the Congress of Vienna those undesirable entities, the moral forces, for having insisted that law should prevail over brutal conquest, and for having, so far as the minds of men then permitted, reconciled that law with justice.

## CHAPTER XI

## THE REVOLUTION OF 1830 AND THE INDEPENDENCE OF BELGIUM

Talleyrand is a philosopher, but one who knows
when to bring his philosophy to an end opportunely.

NAPOLEON

BEFORE the signing of the decrees of July 1830, which
were to be the signal for the raising of barricades and
occasion the fall of Charles X, Talleyrand gave orders for
speculation on a fall in State funds. The champion for the
rights of the legitimate princes of the Bourbon family
staked his money on the Revolution. His "tip" was better
than that of M. de Rothschild, who at the same time speculated on a rise. Talleyrand had his reasons for being well
informed; as on the 18th of Brumaire and March 31, 1814,
the old trainer, first of Bonaparte and then of Louis XVIII,
collaborated with luck. After having scratched Charles X,
he prepared "to dope" his favourite, the Duc d'Orléans.

On all sides the majority of contemporaries saw in the
Treaty of Vienna only the sacrifice of France's natural
frontiers and her humiliation. The party of the Right, being unable to lay the blame on the King, attacked the
"devil on two sticks",[1] whom it regarded as the evil
genius of the monarchy, all the more violently. Gratitude
in politics being less strong than rancour, the Left forgot

[1] *Le Diable boiteux.* A reference to Asmodeus, the companion
of Don Cléofas in Le Sage's satirical novel, *The Devil on Two Sticks.*
—Translators' note.

Talleyrand's services quicker than the Right forgot what it called his crimes. It accused him of having entered into a compact with the enemy of the nation, and withdrew its sympathy from him, to the loss of that influence over part of public opinion on which the Court ought to have been able to count. The recriminations of the Left—then ultra-nationalist and even bellicose—against the treaties of Vienna were more furious than those of the Right, but less dangerous to Talleyrand, because they were specially directed against the King. The Press, less free than in our days, but more independent, did not undertake to re-establish the truth by pointing out a success where badly informed public opinion saw a failure. The Government of the Restoration, dominated by its great concern for public welfare, did not demand such zeal; it knew that its work at Vienna, being conceived in view of the future, not the present—a future to be attained by secret methods —would only have been compromised by lauding, or even explaining, it.

Talleyrand felt that too keenly to permit him to score a personal success at the expense of national interests. But he made the mistake of not triumphing, in private circles, as modestly as his sovereign lord. By dint of saying he was indispensable, he made himself undesirable. Looking upon himself as sacred, on account of his services, he saw in their necessity at Paris as at Vienna a no-less-favourable title than the legitimate right of Louis XVIII. After Water-loo he arrived, on June 23, at Mons, where the King was. He made pretence of not calling upon him to present his respects, and waited for advances. Having waited for them in vain until far into the evening, his "humour", as Chateaubriand said, "was that of a King who comes to the conclusion that his authority is no longer recognized". His whole attitude appeared to say to the real King: "Who made thee king . . . before Vienna? Who will make thee king . . . afterwards?" When it was announced to him that Louis XVIII was continuing his journey towards Paris, he replied: "He will never dare to do it". However, when at three o'clock in the morning he was awakened by cries of "The King is on the point of setting off!" he dressed himself in a mighty hurry—an almost unprecedented thing for him to do—and rushed on foot to the King's residence, where he arrived at the very moment His Majesty's coach issued through the gateway. Talleyrand, who in the case of other sovereigns had the advantage of coolness and dignity, did not display it with Louis XVIII, who notified his dismissal by the words: "Prince, you are leaving us. The waters will do you good. You can let us hear from you later on." If Chateaubriand is to be believed, "M. de Talleyrand foamed with anger". Nevertheless he was summoned by the King, rejoined him at Cambrai, and got him to approve of a proclamation which he countersigned promising "ministerial unity" as the strongest of guarantees. At the time of the first Restoration, Louis XVIII had preferred a Cabinet of which he would have been the sole chief; a Cabinet which was not, therefore, a ministry in the parliamentary sense of the word, and which was still less so since it lacked homogeneity—a feature which, in the King's eyes, increased security; "the horses, which are always kicking each other, having less chance of injuring the carriage".

The coachman of Europe was to find that that carriage and pair was more difficult to drive. First of all, he found on the box-seat his old accomplice and rival, Fouché, who wrangled with him over the reins, so as to pull them more to the Left. Since Napoleon's departure the Duc d'Otrante had become the master of Paris and the favourite of the *faubourgs*, including the St-Germain quarter. Talleyrand, with his aptitude for accepting the inevitable, in order to turn it to account, offered him the post of Minister of Police. It was at that price only, he thought, that the King would return to his capital without hindrance. As regards this he had no difficulty in persuading Louis XVIII, to whom Fouché had already been recommended by "Monsieur", whose speech, read at the time of his first entrance into Paris, in the presence of the senators who had conferred upon him the post of Lieutenant-General of the Kingdom, Talleyrand had written for him. Talleyrand, accompanied by Wellington, introduced Fouché to the King, whereupon Fouché immediately handed him a memorandum demanding important concessions, such as his approval for everything that had been done during the interregnum—dismissal of the military household, etc. Chateaubriand, who was keeping visitors waiting at the King's residence, gave vent to his indignation in the following celebrated lines: "Suddenly a door opened, and silently there entered Vice leaning on the arm of Crime— M. de Talleyrand supported by M. Fouché. The infernal vision passed slowly before me, entered the King's closet and disappeared. Fouché swore fidelity and homage to his Sovereign Lord; on bended knee the trusty regicide placed the hands which caused the head of Louis XVI to fall between those of the brother of the Martyr-King; and the apostate bishop was surety for his oath."

On July 9 Talleyrand was appointed President of the Council and Minister of Foreign Affairs. In home politics he showed himself more liberal than Fouché as regards persons, but more conservative as far as institutions were concerned. Fouché, either because he wished to pay court to the Ultraists or through the old habit of a proscriber, had drawn up a list of people who were compromised during the Hundred Days. Talleyrand forced him to strike out half of the names. On the other hand, it was he who obtained from the King the privilege of heredity for the peers.

In foreign politics his task was limited to platonic protests to the Allies, who, as a punishment for the Hundred Days, excluded France from their deliberations and imposed their conditions upon her by means of an ultimatum. In his memoirs Talleyrand explains his resignation, handed in on September 24, by the impossibility for him to countersign a treaty which injured the one he had obtained on May 30, 1814. As a matter of fact, he resigned— and Louis XVIII accepted his resignation with a feeling of relief—especially because his position was equally difficult from the parliamentary point of view; the undiscoverable Chamber holding him in horror and, from the diplomatic standpoint, the Tsar Alexander not being able to pardon him for his "treason" at Vienna. It was to please him that Louis XVIII made an appeal to his best French friend, the Duc de Richelieu, an *émigré* during the Revolution in Russia, where he had been Governor of Odessa. That was the reason for Talleyrand saying that the principal title of his succesor to the presidency of the Council was his admirable knowledge of the Crimea.

Talleyrand's Government had lasted only two months and a half. We cannot regret it either on his account or on that of France. He did not inspire the King with that confidence which is the condition of a fruitful collaboration. Nor did he inspire confidence with the Assemblies. Although the parliamentary régime was only in its early days, frequent incompatability was already appearing under that régime—the expression of private interests, amidst the vices necessary to attain or preserve authority, and the virtues necessary for exercising it to the sole benefit of the State, the instrument of general interest. Notwithstanding his bad reputation—still almost intact, Talleyrand did not possess all the vices, even in politics, where they sometimes are current for virtues. Against ideology he was rendered immune by his scepticism, and his pride stood in the way of demagogy. Now, in order to direct a parliamentary government which relies on public opinion, one must not be a stranger to the passions which dominate it. Talleyrand, too intelligent to experience those passions, was not sufficiently hypocritical to feign them. Nor did he possess all the virtues. In particular he lacked the only passion which may be a virtue in the case of a President of the Council, a passion for the public welfare in itself. National interests were hardly sacred to him unless they coincided with his own personal interests. They could not ask him to be, as Richelieu was, a saint of the State, a saint who would have become a martyr if it had been necessary to choose between the State and himself. By his character and intellect Talleyrand was rather a leader of the State than a statesman, and especially than a President of the Council. For a leader of the State, when he is hereditary, the identity of national and personal interests may do duty for conscience. In addition, Talleyrand's intellect being wider in its scope than in its precision, and more penetrative than tenacious, looked down on affairs from on high and left detail work to mere subordinates. Though, intermittently, he possessed in critical times the creative strength of a statesman, he did not possess that faculty for co-ordination which is more currently exercised by a President of the Council, or else he did not deign to use it. With that touch of dilettantism which was ever raising its head in his manner, even in the midst of the most serious circumstances, he complied badly to the obscure and daily slavery of the profession. Destined for those leading rôles in those plays on the world's political stage which prove to be "hits", he did not care to play the part of a mere utility actor, nor become an understudy, even though it might be that of an Emperor or a King. Authority was for him a sport, or a means to pleasure, rather than a ministry. Consequently, in political cookery, this chef was magnificent in the preparation of "extras", but paid little heed to ordinary fare, as a President of the Council ought to do; for though "extras", when they are successful, may save nations, it is thanks to good solid food that they thrive.

Talleyrand found in his "extras" the wherewithal to assure his ordinary everyday existence. Louis XVIII added to it a salary of 100,000 francs, attached to the post of Grand Chamberlain, which he filled in the King's household just as he had done in the case of the Emperor's, and with equal fidelity. But that was not enough either to satisfy or disarm him. Circumstances still permitted him only a minor war of epigrams. His quips against the régime were bandied about, notably the reply he made to a lady afflicted with squinting when she asked: "And how is business, Prince?"—"Just as you see, Madame." Against his successors he gave voice to a torrent of insults, even in foreign embassies, and to such an extent that the King ordered him to appear no more at the Tuileries. On January 21, 1817, on an expiatory service being celebrated at St-Denis, Talleyrand appeared in the choir of the basilica to carry out his duties as Grand Chamberlain, the Tuileries *alone* being forbidden ground. M. de Dreux-Brézé, the Grand Master of the Ceremonies, requested him, on behalf of the King, to leave the choir and take his place among the peers. Without turning a hair he continued to assist at the ceremony. So many other ceremonies had he seen! After a time, the fear of emphasizing him as the leader of the opposition and also the intervention of Wellington brought about his recall to the Court. Apropos of this incident, Mme de Staël writes: "Our excellent Maurice bears a resemblance to those little mannikins with cork heads and limbs of lead they give children. Throw them about as you like, turn them head over heels, they always find their feet."

This return to favour emboldened Talleyrand in his opposition to such an extent that Louis XVIII advised him to leave Paris.

"Are you not thinking," he said to him one day, "of returning to the country?"

"No, Sire; unless Your Majesty goes to Fontainebleau. In which case I shall have the honour to carry out my duties."

"No, no; I don't mean that. I am asking whether you are not going to set off again to your estates."

"No, Sire."

"Ah! But tell me now, how far is it from Paris to Valençay?"

"Sire, I can't say off-hand, but it must be about the same distance as it is from Paris to Ghent."

This bantering tone sometimes assumed a patronizing air.

"I admire your influence," said Louis XVIII to him, "as regards all that has happened in France. How did you manage to shatter first of all the Directory and later Bonaparte's colossal power?"

"Bless me, Sire! Really I didn't do anything in those matters; it was something inexplicable in me which brought misfortune to the governments which neglected me."

Talleyrand was no more respectful towards Charles X. When he was still only Monsieur the Prince de Bénévent did not hesitate to summon him to the Council and charge him with the responsibility for all the errors committed during the first Restoration. He persuaded Louis XVIII even to exclude his brother from the Council. To the Comte d'Artois' recriminations he replied: "Monsieur will thank me for this when he is King".

When Monsieur became King he did not on that account bear Talleyrand a grudge, but retained him in his post as Grand Chamberlain; and it was in that capacity that he was present at the coronation of Charles X. Half a century after the coronation of Louis XVI, where, as the Abbé of Périgord, he ogled the pretty women—eighteen years after Napoleon's coronation, when, already Grand Chamberlain, he was in the front row, standing at the foot of the altar, that was his third coronation. The ceremonial of the ancient Court imposed upon him a more active and a more humble duty, for, despite his bad leg, he was kneeling when he repeated the formula, "Monsignor the Grand Chamberlain has shod His Majesty with the violet velvet boots, ornamented with golden fleurs-de-lys, which he received from Monsieur le Marquis de Rochemaure, Master of the Ceremonies". But this genuflexion was not repeated in his attitude towards the King. When, on the opposition becoming anti-dynastic, Charles X said to him that a threatened king had only a choice between mounting a horse or a cart, his Grand Chamberlain replied, "Your Majesty forgets the post-chaise".

That prediction was soon to be fulfilled. Talleyrand contributed to the event by announcing it and also by accustoming public opinion to the idea. He also contributed to it by his influence on the two leaders of the opposition: Royer-Collard, President of the Chamber and leader of the constitutional opposition; and Thiers, who was to become the head of the revolutionary party.

Royer-Collard, chief of the "doctrinaires", said: "There

are two beings upon whom I have never set eyes without my whole soul rising in revolt—a regicide and a married priest". That was theory. Practice consisted in making advances to Talleyrand and dining frequently at his house. His whole being might well suffer a revolution, for he met many regicides there.

When Talleyrand and Adolphe Thiers met for the first time, the former was sixty-nine years of age and the latter twenty-five. The little man from Marseilles immediately gave the illustrious old man a lesson: he interrupted and contradicted him; he even taught him something about politics. His natural audacity was strengthened by that of his comparative youth and by the enthusiasm he felt over his early success in the newspaper world. He had just published a number of noteworthy articles in the *Constitutionnel*. Far from taking offence and holding him at a distance, Talleyrand listened with interest and even consulted him. If he wished him well and smilingly accepted what he would not have tolerated from the most important of statesmen, it was not merely because his own resentment against the régime was in accordance with the impatience of this "boy who was filled with the sacred fire". It was above all because Thiers had ingratiated himself into the Prince's favour by a secret pathway. In the *Constitutionnel*, where he displayed his universality and even laid down the law in that section of the journal which was devoted to the Fine Arts, he had published an enthusiastic article on the first picture sent to the Salon by Eugène Delacroix, Talleyrand's natural son.

It was at the Prince's house in the Rue St-Florentin and at Rochecotte,[1] the country house of Mme de Dino,

---

[1] The Château de Rochecotte in Touraine. Talleyrand frequently came over from his Château de Valençay to spend the summer with his niece, the Duchesse de Dino. Talleyrand made her his heiress

that the creation of a new journal, *Le National*, under the management of Thiers, Miguet, and A. Carrel, was decided upon, and the violent campaigns of which prepared the Revolution of 1830. Talleyrand launched the firebrand but did not light it; it was not he who was going to pay the expenses. If Chateaubriand is to be believed, "he merely soiled the spirit of the journal by contributing to the common fund his contingent of treason and gangrene". But above all he brought a contingent of wisdom, so as to reconcile revolution and order as far as possible. For he it was who directed the journal's campaigns towards the advent of the younger branch of the royal family. That was one of his old ideas, set aside in 1814 under the influence of Aimée de Coigny. He returned to it owing to his grievance against the ultra-royalists and his intimate relations with the Duc and Duchesse d'Orléans, as well as with the sister of Louis Philippe, Mme Adélaïde.

Talleyrand, said Napoleon, was a philosopher, but one who knew when to bring his philosophy to an end opportunely. However, his philosophy did not *come* to an end; for its principles were ever being renewed, so as to adapt them to circumstances, and this gave a remarkable continuity to his philosophy. "From the moment when legitimacy itself betrayed its own principles by breaking its vows, it became necessary to seek for the salvation of France haphazard, and at least save, if that were possible, monarchical principles, independently of legitimacy,

and thus she came into possession of his papers, including his memoirs, which she did not see published, since she died on September 29, 1862, six years before the date fixed for their publication. However, the Duchesse de Dino had the satisfaction of raising another monument to her uncle's memory, a pretty chapel adjoining her château, and built on the site of the bedroom Talleyrand usually occupied. See *A Summer in Touraine*, by Frederic Lees (Methuen & Co., 1909), pp. 150-68.—Translators' note.

amidst the great tempest raised by the latter". In this passage from his memoirs, Talleyrand formulates his theory of a conservative revolution. He lent his hand in overthrowing Charles X, but in order to consolidate the throne. He did not even change his principles; it was only a prince he changed. But what was his principle? At Vienna it was legitimacy, the only principle which could be opposed to the ambitions of Europe. In Paris he laid stress on the Charter, which he made the principle of legitimacy, the Restoration having been subordinated by him to the granting of constitutional guarantees. Forgetfulness of those guarantees was therefore equivalent to abdication. The King reigned only by virtue of a contract with the nation. He could not break that pact without liberating the nation. Just as Bonaparte had broken his contract, since his reign knew no other law than the will of the sovereign, so Charles X had broken his by the decrees. By substituting the King of the French for the King of France, Talleyrand flattered himself that he was balancing authority and liberty, thus putting a close to the era of revolution, and stabilizing the Crown by converting it on a basis of parity with the nation.

Casuists of constitutional law are not yet in agreement on the subject of the foundation of authority, nor on that of the nature of the contract invoked by Talleyrand, nor as regards the existence of that contract, nor as to the import of Article 14 of the Charter by virtue of which Charles X had issued his decrees, the legality of which did not appear to him to be doubtful. Moreover, those decrees in no way interested the nation; they were aimed at only the most militant fraction of the "legal country", which consisted of barely 90,000 electors. What interested the nation was peace and prosperity. The Restoration had re-established and maintained them. What interested the future of the nation (and it was in blissful ignorance of it) was the conquest of Algeria, that lure of the African empire which is to-day the token of its grandeur; also the independence of Belgium, which in 1914 was to be its shield. On July 5, a few days before his fall, Charles X gave us Algiers. Our best troops were in Africa or in the north, in view of events in Belgium. The insurrection had a free field in Paris and it triumphed without difficulty. The treaties of Vienna were the principal grievance of the so-called liberal and national opposition, which dreamed of tearing them up—and that meant war. The legal country, which was not making it, readily accepted the idea. The contradiction between its programme and the deep aspirations as well as the permanent interests of France was complete. The chief error of the Restoration was in not relying upon her to resist the politicians. Like Louis XVI, the victim of his greatest boon—the independence of the United States—Charles X was the victim of its immense benefits more than of the imprudence he committed on signing the decrees.

Talleyrand, the philosopher of legitimacy at Vienna and of liberalism in Paris, employed practical philosophy in both cases. At Vienna it was practical for France; in Paris it was practical for himself, since it brought him back into power.

After the rioting, if he had not possessed a sense of the ridiculous he would willingly have cried out to the people, after the fashion of a demagogue of comedy, "Citizens, cease firing! I am the Minister!" Let us render him the justice of recognizing that he had never encouraged them to fire. His liberalism, forming part of his philosophy, he knew when to bring to an end opportunely; not so strong as Thiers' liberalism, it did not go as far as rifle-shots. In 1830 his rôle consisted less in preparing the Revolution than in keeping it within limits and making it profitable for the younger branch of the royal family. As on the 18th of Brumaire and on March 30, 1814, he was less the grave-digger of the régime than the *accoucheur* of the new one. A constructor rather than a destructor, he made use of ruins rather than caused them. He prevented the Revolution from degenerating into upheavals by submitting it to the law of continuity. In 1814 he introduced, with parlia-mentarism, revolution into the monarchy; in 1830 he introduced the monarchy into the Revolution. This revolutionary was so conservative that, to attack a régime, he waited until that régime was condemned through its own errors, as in the case of the Directory or the Empire, or, as in the case of the Restoration, by its imprudences and the blindness of what was called public opinion. In the last instance, he contributed to the blinding of opinion because he was himself blinded through his disappointed ambition. But the Restoration, like the Directory and the Empire, would have succumbed without him. This emi-nent servant of successive governments served them first of all loyally; then, when they had disserved themselves, or were disserved by events, he served them in the sense of the word used in cynegetics: he despatched them; gave them their quietus with a whoop! It was not he who brought them to bay; but he was not the last to be in at the death.

Talleyrand suggested to *Le National* his campaign in favour of the younger branch of the royal family. The editor of the journal, his protégé Thiers, who was the most active leader of the opposition under Charles X, and the future President of the Third Republic, was soon to cry from the rostrum: "France holds a republic in horror. When it is mentioned to her she starts back in terror, for she knows that that form of government leads to blood, or imbecility." In 1830 a republic meant anarchy and war. Nevertheless it was for that the insurgents fought; and it was owing to Talleyrand that France was spared such a fate. He prepared the accession of Louis Philippe through the campaigns of *Le National*, through the orders which the Liberal party received at the Rue St-Florentin, and through the pressing advice he gave the Duc d'Orléans. On the day of July 29, when the victory of the insurgents was a certainty, he sent a messenger to Mme Adélaïde (he was too prudent to write) with instructions to tell her that the Duc d'Orléans had not a moment to lose, and that he ought to come to Paris immediately to place himself at the head of the movement. The Duc d'Orléans, who then lived at Neuilly, followed that advice, took up his residence at the Palais Royal, and accepted the title of Lieutenant-General. When invited to proceed to the Hôtel de Ville, he hesitated and consulted Talleyrand, who replied, "Let him accept!" And he returned from the city hall King of the French.

When, on July 28, Talleyrand, whose rôle in the ending of the crisis was to be decisive, heard the tocsin which announced the victorious entry of the people at the Hôtel de Ville, he gave orders that the inscription in golden letters—"Hôtel Talleyrand"—above the entrance to his house in the Rue St-Florentin be removed. He considered it wise not to attract to his mansion the attention of that crowd which politicians call "the people" when it cheers them and "the riff-raff" when it sets to work to pillage them. On order being re-established Talleyrand had the inscription replaced.

He saw also to the setting to rights of something more important—his policy. The Revolution of 1830 had been accomplished against the treaties of 1815 as much as against the decrees. The liberals were doubly bellicose:

through a spirit of opposition and because war was to them the instrument of liberation—the liberation of France enclosed within her ancient boundaries, and the liberation of nations oppressed by the Holy Alliance. However, in order to disarm the opposition, the Polignac Ministry conceived a rearrangement of the map of Europe, founded on an alliance with Russia and the liquidation of Turkey, which was then at war with the Tsar. This chimerical plan, which its authors expected would lead to the recovery of France's natural frontiers, would have drawn her, if Russia had not refused to become a party to it, into war against England and Austria. It was a complete reversal of Talleyrand's policy at Vienna.

Louis Philippe was raised to power through the efforts of the party of the "movement", and he donned the three colours which had made the tour of Europe. Was he not condemned by the fatality of his origin to wars of conquest and enfranchisement? Edgar Quinet was to write: "The Revolution surrendered its sword in 1815; it was thought that she was about to seize it again in 1830." When France is feverish, the temperature of Europe rises. An immense hope stirred the martyred countries— Belgium, Poland, Italy, and Greece. The Revolution— that "article de Paris", a strange Parisian novelty indeed! —became the rage there, and was renewed in the country of its origin when re-exported. The call of the nations responded to the volleys of musketry from our barricades and, in its turn, awoke a profound echo in France. But the absolutist powers—Russia, Austria, and Prussia— strengthened their alliances and resolved to oppose by arms any attempt which France might make against the existing order of things. Hence, for Louis Philippe, a tragic dilemma: either to follow the party of the "movement" and collide, at the risk of being shattered, against the resistance of Europe; or else resist the "movement" and disappoint the expectations of his most ardent partisans, who, because there had been a bad deal in 1830, wanted to reshuffle the cards, that is to say, the Revolution, in 1848. Nevertheless the "King of the Barricades" received from the hands of four marshals of France the crown, the sceptre, the sword, and the hand of justice, a symbol of the initial contradiction which weighed on his reign and was to put the final stop to it. The "movement" which raised him to the throne was revolutionary and bellicose. His policy was to be conservative and pacific. The crisis which was to sweep him away was a recrudescence of the checked fever of 1830. Between the foreign danger, which was above all serious for France, and the home danger, serious above all for France and his dynasty, he chose the latter. Like Louis XVI and Charles X, he was to be the victim of his own benevolence. He was to be dethroned for having been—as people have called him derisively—"the Napoleon of Peace."

Of that Napoleon, Talleyrand was Chief of the Staff. Appointed Ambassador to London, where the pulse of the world was beating more strongly than anywhere else, and where the fate of peace and the monarchy of July was to be decided, he considered that post more important than the portfolio of the Ministry of Foreign Affairs, the direction of which was practically under his control. He was to carry out there that policy for an understanding which he had extolled from 1792 and achieved at Vienna. Recalling his landing at Dover on September 24, he wrote in his memoirs: "On hearing the guns of the fort announce the arrival of the Ambassador of France, I could not resist the recollection that, thirty-six years before, I had left those very shores of England, exiled from my native country and driven from British soil through the

intrigues of the Emigration. I returned there now animated by a hope, and above all a desire to establish that
Alliance between France and England which I have ever
regarded as the most solid guarantee of the happiness of
the two nations and the peace of the world."

At Vienna Talleyrand had chosen an alliance with
England, and this qualified him more than any other person for the task of renewing it. Henceforth the force of
circumstances imposed it. A suspect in the eyes of the
sovereigns of the Holy Alliance, which treated him as
a usurper, Louis Philippe could find support only in
London. The Revolution of 1830 was a reproduction of
the English Revolution of 1688: it replaced the elder by
the younger branch and, theoretically, divine right by the
sovereignty of the people. Louis Philippe was the first
French king to speak English. The sympathy he inspired
was increased by the resentment felt against Charles X,
who had disquieted England by his attempt at a *rapproche-
ment* with Russia and by the Algerian expedition. All the
King's skill and that of his representative was necessary to
prevent the Cabinet in London from taking advantage of
France's isolation and burdening her with a tyrannical protection. Talleyrand alone, thanks to his gifts and his authority and the part he had played at Vienna, was capable of conciliating the putting into practice of that indispensable but
exacting friendship with the interests and dignity of France.

Louis Philippe's ambassador received a most flattering
welcome in London. His friend and collaborator of 1815,
the Duke of Wellington, who had become Premier, left
the country—a meritorious step to take in the month of
September—to offer a banquet in his honour. Crowds
cheered him in the streets. He delighted people in high
society by his magnificence and charming manners, and
to these he added the charm of the Duchesse de Dino, who

did the honours of his house. Thirty-three years of age at that time, she possessed all the splendour of her beauty and already all the strength of her fine intellect. On the subject of the prestige and prerogatives of Talleyrand in London, Mérimée, who visited him there in 1832, supplies a curious piece of information.

"The English", he writes, "who have great pretensions to elegance and good breeding, do not approach him. Wherever he goes he forms a court and lays down the law. Nothing is more amusing than to see the most influential members of the House of Lords near him, all of them obsequious and almost servile. The Prince, however, has a curious habit. After dinner, instead of rinsing his mouth, as is the custom in London and in Paris, it is his nose he rinses, and in the following manner. They hold under his chin a sort of napkin made of oil-cloth, and then he absorbs through his nose two glasses of water, which he ejects by way of his mouth, This operation, which is not carried out without making a great noise, is performed at a sideboard a few feet away from the table. Now, yesterday, in the course of this singular ablution, the whole of the Diplomatic Corps, with lowered eyes and standing, silently awaited the end of the operation, and behind the Prince, Lady Jersey, napkin in hand, followed the succession of glasses of water with respectful interest. Had she dared she would have held the oil-cloth basin. This Lady Jersey is the most haughty and impertinent woman in the whole of England. She is very beautiful, witty, well educated, and of the bluest blood in addition. The Prince must indeed be a most seductive man to be the object of such condescension on her part. 'This is a most excellent habit, Prince', said Lady Jersey to him. 'Oh, very dirty, very dirty!' replied Talleyrand, and he took her arm, after keeping her waiting five minutes."

At the conference which was about to open to decide the fate of Belgium, Talleyrand also took England's arm, but without keeping her waiting and without pushing nonconformity as far around the green table as he did at the dinner-table. In that redoubtable crisis, which put Anglo-French relations to the test, he came to an agreement with the Cabinet in London because his experience enabled him to see unhesitatingly the limit of the concessions to be obtained and the best solution to be arrived at to conciliate the interests of the two countries.

The insurrection which smouldered at Brussels before the Revolution of July, and which contributed to it while part of the garrison of Paris was retained in the north, received from it, in its turn, a decided encouragement. The Belgians, who in everything—ideas, feelings, interests, religion, and language—were opposed to the Dutch, had risen against their domination. They threw themselves into the arms of France; some in order to be united with her, others to ask her to assure their independence. At Paris, the entire party of the "movement" could conceive of no other solution than the reannexation of Belgium. That would have opened a first breach in the treaties of 1815 and have repaired one in the French frontier. But the kingdom of the Netherlands had been formed especially at the instigation of England, in order to oppose a barrier to the ambitions of France, to hold her at a distance from Antwerp, and, while keeping her from the Rhineland, weaken her in the face of Germany. Reunion with France would have meant a rupture with England. On the other hand, the independence of Belgium was a challenge to the Holy Alliance, founded to guarantee the authority of legitimate sovereigns over nations; in their eyes the Belgians were merely rebels, whose example would be dangerous for them unless they were punished and brought back by force under the yoke of Holland. In France, public opinion, in the name of Liberty and the Revolution, fired up in favour of the Belgians. Liberty was, in that case, a magic word which covered many different things. The Belgian Revolution, a daughter of France's, bore no resemblance to it; for in Paris the Revolution was political and anti-clerical, whereas at Brussels it was national and directed against the priests. The two movements were none the less solidary. If Louis Philippe had been overthrown, France, given over to anarchy, would have been powerless to protect the Belgians against the rancour of the Holy Alliance; on the other hand, if the Belgian insurrection had been stifled, indignation in Paris would have been so violent that the badly constructed throne could not have resisted it. The King was exposed to war if he intervened, and to an immediate revolution if he abstained. The national and dynastic interest bound him to profit by the event to modify the *status quo* to the advantage of France; his political sense and deep knowledge of Europe cautioned him against the temptation to recede France's northern frontier, when it was not even recognized by Europe and the attitude of certain Powers was hostile. A circumspect landowner, like all the kings of France, he knew that one could not start a lawsuit regarding boundaries when the very ownership of the field was contested.

Thanks to Louis Philippe and Talleyrand, France came out from this most difficult situation with honour and profit. Its key was in London, where, despite the difference of the times and the contradiction of principles, the problem was the same as it had been in Vienna fifteen years before. The goal was still to guarantee peace and the independence of France; the means consisted in dissolving a coalition declared in 1815 and

latent in 1830. Talleyrand, with whom variety of resources often veiled the unity of his objective, succeeded
by invoking legitimacy under Louis XVIII and national
sovereignty under Louis Philippe. To the league of absolute monarchies on the Continent he opposed the union of
the two great liberal monarchies. He wrote to Paris as
follows: "It is the progress of civilization which will
henceforth form our bond of relationship. We ought to
seek to draw closer to those governments where civilization is the most advanced. There are our real family embassies". The English monarchy and, more recently, the
French monarchy were the issue of the national will.
Should a monarchy rise in Brussels on the same foundation, it would be a third sister in the family which, if it
remained united, would be sufficiently strong to maintain
peace. Coalitions were indeed impossible without the
assistance of England—the very soul of them because
she was their banker.

In the carrying-out of that programme Talleyrand encountered more difficulties with his Embassy and Government than he did with the British Cabinet. Leaving for
London when the revolutionary fever had not yet de-
creased in Paris, he sported in his hat a huge tricolour
cockade, and his staff was composed of "three young
*sans-culottes*"[1] of July whom he had taken with him to give
himself an air of Republicanism". One of these official
"patriots" attended a Radical banquet given in honour
of Poland and proposed a revolutionary toast; another
declared that he would not drink to the health of King
Louis Philippe until he descended from the throne. As the

---

[1] The term *sans-culottes* (without breeches) was applied to the
Republicans of 1793, and was then synonymous with "good
patriot". It fell into disuse towards the close of the Convention.—
Translators' note.

situation in France was becoming stabilized, Talleyrand dismissed his collaborators and removed the tricolour cockade from his hat. But he remained in conflict with Molé, his Minister of Foreign Affairs, to whom he was sending merely insignificant despatches; as, for example, one relating to the importation of port wine into England. He showed a predilection for giving an account of his negotiations to the King himself, either directly or through a personal correspondence with his sister, Mme Adélaïde. Louis Philippe was wholly in agreement with his ambassador as regards this rule of conduct, which was the expression of the whole of his foreign policy, namely not to interfere with the affairs of other states, but on the condition that everybody followed his example; France to be considered as inviolable on her own territory and the neighbouring regions which protected her. This was opposing the principle of non-intervention to that of intervention, which had the support of the Holy Alliance. But to countenance non-intervention meant counter-intervention as a reply to the imitation of others. For instance, should Prussia send troops into Belgium to re-establish the sovereignty of William of Orange, French troops would immediately follow suit. The same in Savoy, where Austrian intervention would quickly have resulted in the occupation of Ancona by French troops. That was why, in Talleyrand's opinion, intervention and non-intervention were two metaphysical expressions which at bottom meant the same thing.

Molé—furious at being set aside—sent Talleyrand instructions asking him to insist that the Conference on the Belgian question be held in Paris, in order to show that that question was a Franco-English and not an Anglo-French one. That was absurd. Though, in fact, the question was Franco-English because it was particularly vital to us, and Anglo-French because a favourable solution depended above all on English goodwill, it was legally a European matter. Then, very skilfully, Talleyrand, by flattering Wellington, who in London was to be president of the Conference, managed to suggest to him the proposal which fitted in exactly with France's desires; for, excluding recourse to force against the Belgians, it implied recognition of the accomplished fact. On the other hand, the ambassadors in London had already authority to sanction immediately that result, which ran the risk of being compromised by some incident or other that might happen during the time necessary to enable the Conference to deliberate in Paris validly. Finally, if it met there, when the capital was still the scene of agitation—and sometimes even the scene of riots, which showed the fragility of the régime—the voice of France would have much less authority there than in London, where, in addition, that voice was the voice of Talleyrand. Relations between the ambassador and the minister became so strained that Molé offered his resignation.

Supported by Louis Philippe, the ambassador won the day. The Conference opened in London on November 4 under the chairmanship of Wellington, and on the same day imposed an armistice on the Belgians and the Dutch. To treat them on a footing of equality was to sanction the disjunction of the kingdom of the Netherlands and the independence of the Belgians. It was also, through the cessation of hostilities, a pledge of peace imposed on the Holy Alliance by an agreement between France and England. It was, thanks to Talleyrand, and under Wellington's presidency, a pacific revenge for Waterloo. A revenge more complete than people were then able to foresee, since Belgian independence contained the germ of the Franco-British Alliance of 1914.

A parliamentary crisis having set Wellington aside, he was replaced by a Whig Cabinet whose liberal tendencies appeared as though they ought to have facilitated Talleyrand's task. But the contrary was the case. The Foreign Office was entrusted to Palmerston, one of those intractable liberals whose character belies theory. In order to bring him round to his own view, Talleyrand displayed as much suppleness and patience as energy and perseverance. So that on December 20 the independence of Belgium was recognized. On January 20 the Conference declared its perpetual neutrality and inviolability, which put an end to the hopes—dangerous for peace—of the annexationist parties of Brussels and Paris, while protecting the new State against a return attack on the part of Holland, with the support of the Holy Alliance. Henceforth the barrier raised against France in 1815 protected her now against invasion. That memorable result was obtained after an interminable discussion of eight hours and a half.

"Talleyrand", wrote Palmerston, "fought like a lion to extend the neutrality of Belgium to Luxembourg. As an objection, it was pointed out to him that this Duchy belonged to an independent sovereign and to the Germanic Confederation. Finally, we ended by making him come to an arrangement by the means which induces juries to be unanimous, namely hunger." After making, in vain, the most strenuous efforts to extend the guarantee of neutrality to our most vulnerable frontier, at least he obtained the destruction of thirteen forts raised against us on Belgian soil. Then came the delicate problem of the choice of a sovereign for the new kingdom. The Duc de Nemours was the nominee in Brussels, but his acceptance of the crown would have been considered as a disguised annexation by France and would have brought about a general war. Louis Philippe, says Talleyrand, was obliged, in refusing, to use all the will power and all the art which others employed to attain the result in question. When Prince Leopold of Saxe-Coburg, a German by birth but English by adoption—he was the widower of Princess Charlotte of England—was appointed, Talleyrand sought to attach him as much as possible to France. "He might", he said, "marry one of the King's daughters."

The determining of the frontiers of Belgium was a no-less-thorny question than the appointment of the King. In Brussels they claimed the left bank of the Scheldt, Limburg, and Luxembourg. On that point, Palmerston's non-acceptance was ratified by Talleyrand, who bore the whole of the responsibility for it in the eyes of the Belgians. They adopted, however, the project for a treaty with Holland which the London Conference had drawn up. So everything appeared to be settled. But as a matter of fact everything was brought up again by the King of Holland, who, disappointed as regards his hope that a disagreement among the Powers and with Belgium would result in the maintenance of his authority there, suddenly denounced the armistice, and reopened hostilities. Encouraged by Berlin, he flattered himself on being able to bring about a general war, under cover of which his kingdom of the Netherlands would be re-established. War was averted through the wisdom and decision of Louis Philippe, as well as by the trustful collaboration with England which Talleyrand had inaugurated. Applying the doctrine which he had formulated regarding intervention on coming to the throne, the King, with the unanimous approval of his ministers, immediately sent a French army under the command of Marshal Gérard across the Belgian frontier. The appearance of the French flag in Belgium aroused profound emotion throughout the whole of

Europe, which was stirred at that time by a warlike feeling. But every precaution had been taken to keep within the limits of a fortunate incident that which, in other hands, might have been a terrible catastrophe. The King, in sending the French army into Belgium, consequent on the intervention of Holland, acted in conformity with a maxim he had made known to the Powers, without their raising any objection to it; his decision was taken after it had been solicited by King Leopold, a sovereign recognized by Europe and very popular in England. In London the Conference, dominated by Talleyrand, even under the presidency of the imperious Palmerston, severely blamed the Dutch for breaking the armistice, gave its approval for the employment of the French army for a limited time, and decided on the sending of an English squadron to defend the Belgian coasts—the first armed collaboration, fifteen years after Waterloo, between France and England, so as to defend that Belgian neutrality which, eighty-five years later, was once more to bring them into association —too late to avert war, but at any rate to win the war and thus save Europe.

All these stages of Belgian independence and neutrality were so many dangerous defiles in which, but for the admirable diplomacy of Louis Philippe and Talleyrand, the peace of Europe and the fortunes of France were exposed to the danger of being lost. This masterpiece bears the double mark of the veritable masterpieces of diplomacy; namely, the unanimous approval of posterity and the unanimous criticism of contemporaries.

In London Talleyrand's predominant rôle exposed him, despite his endeavours to veil it, to Palmerston's animosity, and especially after the success of a caricature, entitled "The Lame leading the Blind", which depicted him following in the footsteps of the French Ambassador.

In Brussels Talleyrand was keenly criticized. He was made responsible for the attribution of Limburg to Holland, a step imposed by Palmerston, and was accused of plans for a partition which never had any great consistency, but to which he rallied momentarily, perhaps as a tactical move, either in order to break down the sometimes rash die-hard policy of Belgian patriots over the question of the frontiers, or in order to put people on the wrong track in Paris, where the party of the "movement" demanded annexation, and whence Sebastiani, who had become Minister of Foreign Affairs, sent to London to speak in favour of partition the Comte de Flahaut, one of the natural sons of Talleyrand, who was exceedingly irritated on receiving this collaborator, which leads one to suppose that he had little enthusiasm for the object of his mission.

In politics only results count. Despite a few transient and maybe necessary contradictions, Talleyrand remains, after the Belgian nation itself, the chief artisan of the independence of Belgium; and that is his imperishable title to glory. Yet the Order of Leopold, established in 1832 by the first King of the Belgians, is the only one which does not appear in the show-case containing his decorations, a show-case which, even with that omission, is the most complete of all known collections. For in addition to being the holder of the Grand Cross of every other foreign order, he was a Knight of the Holy Spirit, Grand Cross of the Legion of Honour, and Knight of the Golden Fleece —having, it was remarked, shorn a sufficient number of lambs to merit it. In Paris, though the King and men of understanding appreciated the great importance of the work accomplished by Talleyrand, public opinion on the whole was not more grateful to him than it was in Brussels. While in London Talleyrand was leading the ball—and, as the English said, even making Palmerston waltz—he was reproached in Paris with humiliating France at the feet of England. Leopold's election, to which he had lent his name—Leopold, the founder of the foreign dynasty which is the most venerated in France to-day—exasperated the spirit of chauvinism. "They see in him", wrote Mme Adélaïde to Talleyrand, "merely a British agent, and, one must confess, he is most unpopular. If he should ascend the throne and marry one of our little ones"—in accordance with the wish which was happily realized by France's ambassador—"people will regard that as a sale concluded between his country and England."

However, Talleyrand, approached by Sebastiani with a plan for a partition which gave Antwerp to England, opposed it energetically. "That would be giving her", he wrote, "another Gibraltar in the north and . . . not until ten battles had been lost could consent be obtained for it. If France needs expansion, it is towards the line of the Rhine she ought to look. But to-day peace is worth much more than all that. Belgium would bring us more trouble than advantages, and as regards the latter neutrality assures us of almost all of them." In another letter he wrote: "If France makes war against Germany, without England taking a part in it, it will be England who will defend the neutrality of Belgium". And there we have the reason why, in 1914, England came into the Great War.

The future substantiated the wisdom of that policy. By maintaining peace Talleyrand obtained from Louis Philippe, who at first was a suspect, what he called the right of the middle-classes in Europe. "The throne of Louis Philippe", he wrote, "is to-day as old as that of Saint Louis. But with war its birth would be as though it had been only yesterday." And he welcomed criticism with the greatest serenity. "We are reproached with being Dutch, and the Dutch reproach us with being Belgians. When everybody complains we are very near being equitable." He had not only maintained peace; he had guaranteed it as far as it could be by revising those clauses of the treaties of Vienna which were the most redoubtable to us, by transforming, through Belgian neutrality, the outpost of the Coalition into the rampart of our independence, and especially by taking advantage of a crisis which exposed France and England to a bloody conflict to lay the most solid foundations of their alliance.

To be able to rule events in that manner, intellect, experience, and technique do not suffice. The more we study those negotiations—a mere sketch of which I have been able to give in these pages—the more we admire the virtuosity with which Talleyrand fingered, as on a keyboard, the map of Europe, and struck there an accord the resonance of which has not yet died away. The more, too, we admire a method which embraced the whole of a vast and complex problem without neglecting any means of solving it. It was, as is right and proper in diplomacy, a piece of work broadly conceived, but carried out with the aid of a magnifying glass. However, to make it a success, moral qualities were necessary; it was above all through them that he shone in London, and that this specialist in the "sweetness of life" attained a sort of professional asceticism. It is indeed a touching spectacle, that of an old man, loaded with honours and riches, who sacrificed his health in a daily struggle of more than two years, and who engaged himself in discussions which were often continued far into the night and from which he returned home thoroughly worn out.

"I am, perhaps, killing myself", he wrote to the Princesse de Vaudémont, "but I shall succeed." Still more rare than that energy and perseverance was his disdain of popularity, his indifference to the criticism of his own country, though sometimes he may have congratulated himself on it as it served as a sort of fulcrum against the foreigner. After attaining success he gave himself in private life the credit he merited, but he did not compromise that success by spreading his glory right and left. He triumphed with modesty, knowing full well that the diplomatist who sings of his victory is comparable to a treasure-loaded mule which, making a great clatter with its bells, merely attracts the attention of brigands.

Consequently his diplomatic constructions are superior to others. The independence of Belgium and the Franco-British alliance which ensued have resisted all attacks; the Charter of 1814, the plan of which he outlined, was overthrown at the first shock. One day in London Talleyrand said to Lamartine: "Mirabeau was a great man, but he lacked the courage to be popular. In that respect, you see, I am more a man than he was. I surrender my name to all interpretations and to all the insults of the crowd. They believe me to be immoral and Machiavellian, but I am merely impassible and disdainful." He was, indeed, capable of braving unpopularity, but only as regards foreign politics, where it is less dangerous, if the danger even exists at all there, for the people are not interested in foreign politics and do not understand them. In home politics, he looked not only straight in front of him, but at the same time to right and left; he squinted, and that is perhaps why he did not always aim straight. In foreign politics, his eyes, both in Vienna and in London, were fixed on the objective indicated by national interests—and he hit the mark. In Vienna he made the King the arbiter of nations; in Paris he did not succeed in making him the arbiter of parties. In foreign politics he organized equilibrium; in home politics he organized, with the aid of parliamentarism, only a see-saw, which is the very opposite of an equilibrium, for the ups-and-downs of parties puts the machine out of order and precipitates the driver. He realized greater stability in diplomacy, which he withdrew from the party of the "movement", than he did in the Constitution, which was the work of that party and which was to be its victim.

But stability is not immobility—on the contrary; it is, in politics as in physics or in architecture, a condition of every useful movement. The stability of a policy is no less necessary to its progress than the stability of the ground to the security of any movement or to the solidity of a building. Had the party of the "movement" dominated foreign politics as it did home politics, the result would have been a backward movement, towards a war in which all the chances would have been against France. The stability which Talleyrand gave Europe through the treaties of Vienna, and which he strengthened through the alliance with England, brought us peace and enabled us to accomplish, under shelter of that peace, immense progress. For instance, to mention only the two most important advances in the sphere of foreign politics, apart from Belgian independence—namely, the conquest of Algeria and the independence of Greece. It was during Talleyrand's embassy in London and thanks to his authority and the confidence he inspired as well as to the wise advice he sent to Paris, that the London Cabinet resigned itself to France's establishment in North Africa. "As to Algiers", he wrote, "I have avoided speaking of it; and I should much like our newspapers to do the same. It will be a good thing if they become accustomed to our occupation; and silence is golden." He recommended an advance into Algeria—"as though on tiptoe". But already there burst forth in Paris the contradiction (more violent since those days) between the necessities of foreign policy—in which, according to Richelieu, secrecy is the very soul—and the parliamentary debates which compromise it, no matter whether these are glorifying or attacking it.

Likewise, it was during Talleyrand's embassy in London and thanks to his care that the independence of Greece was consolidated and her frontiers established. There was some credit in that, inasmuch as France alone, without any ulterior motive, took an interest in the lot of Greece. Russia, since she had concluded peace with Turkey by the Treaty of Adrianopolis, did not wish to compromise her by showing solicitude towards rebellious subjects. As to England, in her eyes Greece possessed three great faults: she did not pay the interest on the loan concluded in London during the War of Independence and she refused to guarantee it; the proximity of that independence was a bad example for the Ionian Islands which England had occupied since the treaties of 1815; and the merchant service of the Greeks was already competing with the British mercantile service. It was Talleyrand who proposed the most favourable frontiers for Greece: from the Gulf of Volo to the Gulf of Arta.

After the restoration of France and the re-establishment of European equilibrium, Talleyrand's constructions stretched, on the foundation of a general peace, from Belgium to Greece *via* northern Africa. Yet "he was born a destroyer and not a constructor", wrote his rival Metternich, to whom this judgment of his applies better. Above all, compared with the celebrated Austrian Chancellor, was Talleyrand the Prince of Diplomatists. Metternich was one of the greatest destroyers in modern history, because he incarnated in Austria two destructive forces: Germanism and absolutism. He did not realize that the

French Revolution, transported to Germany, became there a national revolution, that the danger to the Habsburg dynasty was there, and that its salvation lay in a policy independent of Germany and paternal as regards all its nations. By placing them, on the contrary, under the domination of Germanism and by aggravating the situation through absolutism, he prepared the enslavement of Vienna to Berlin, and revolt on the part of the oppressed nationalities. Hence the catastrophe of 1914 and the downfall of an Empire which was an abridgment of Europe and would have been its guarantee had it been the model, instead of being the negation and plague of that through the hegemony of one nationality over the others.

Save that the Magyars have since been associated with that hegemony which has bound Vienna to Berlin still more closely, Metternich's policy survived him until the downfall (of which it was the cause) of Austria. The reputation for infallibility which he usurped was fatal to his successors, to the Habsburgs, and to Europe. The legend attached to his name has been more powerful than he was, but for destruction.

In the waiting-room of the Ministry of Foreign Affairs at Vienna, and above one of those majestic lounges which, at the Court of the Habsburgs, were the altars of etiquette, there used to hang a huge portrait of Metternich by Lawrence. This portrait indeed depicted one of the great culprits of War. In its turn it played indeed the part of the "Coachman of Europe", but in a race to the abyss. It kept alive, in that temple of Austrian diplomacy, the worship of the false god, even in the case of foreign diplomatists who entered there. Waiting interminably, they contemplated the portrait and came, as it were, under its magnetism. It reminded them of the splendour of the House of Habsburg, the summit of its power, the time when it was the arbiter of Europe, and, inspiring them with reverential awe, put them, for their audience, in a state of grace; that is to say, of least resistance, so that when they were received, after that intimidating sitting, by the pale successors of Metternich, the Aerenthals and the Berchtolds, they were prepared to listen to oracles and receive remonstrances rather than to ask questions or to give advice. Never would advice, however, have been better placed. Mention is made of generals whose very shadows have won battles. As regards Metternich, *his* shadow caused the loss of an Empire and heaped ruins everywhere. These would be more easily reparable and peace would be less precarious if the image of Talleyrand had the same power over his successors and over their interlocutors.

Another of Talleyrand's rivals, Chateaubriand, was no less blinded by his pride. In 1837, when France had enfranchised Greece and Belgium, when daily she was setting the seal of her genius more deeply on African soil, Chateaubriand wrote: "If, perchance, there still moves something great in this nether world, our country would do well to remain lying down". That recumbent one was to become so very much alive that it resuscitated the dead. In 1914, when the virtualities of the Franco-English Alliance, prepared by Talleyrand, developed, other sister-nations rose in answer to their call; and they are to-day standing upright on the tomb of the empires which Metternich and Chateaubriand thought were immortal.

## CHAPTER XII

## RÉ QUÉ DIOU ("NAUGHT SAVE GOD"): THE TALLEYRAND MOTTO

> For statesmen there are many ways of being up-
> right. TALLEYRAND

AT Talleyrand's obsequies the catafalque displayed the family motto ("Ré qué Diou") in the dialect of Périgord. The most pious among the congregation considered it either a mockery or an act of faith; the better informed saw in it an explanation and even a justification.

"Naught save God"—an admirable motto for the ex-Bishop of Autun who had transgressed every divine law! Would it not have been more appropriate, so as to adapt it to the deceased, to accept the variant reading imagined by a gentleman from Périgord—"*Ré qué yo*" ("Naught save myself")? Nevertheless, were not those words really in their place above the relics of one of the mighty of this world, perhaps the mightiest of his century, since he made and unmade kings and emperors? What better opportunity to proclaim the nothingness of human greatness? Never, either, was the Church to have a better symbol of mortality for recalling the vanity of all those earthly possessions with which the Prince de Bénévent had been gratified without ever being satiated, nor a more signal scandal for imploring heavenly mercy on behalf of the one who had been the object of it.

According to the family interpretation, and particularly as regards its most illustrious member's application of the words, "Naught save God", the motto of the ancient Comtes de Périgord has no religious signification. Therefore, inscribed on the catafalque, it was neither a blasphemy nor a prayer. It had a political meaning: its aim was not salvation in another world, but fortune in this one. It meant that this illustrious race recognized no other sovereign on earth save God. Thus interpreted, it throws light on Talleyrand's character and gives the answer to the riddle—already partly solved when it was put to us. The confession to the Comtesse de Kielmansegge has often been quoted: "For centuries to come I should like the discussion to go on as to what I have been, what I have thought, and what I intended". Already he is telling us. Whilst confiding his secret to us he lays bare the mystery: his fixed resolve to astonish posterity, which, as soon as it was enlightened, must not be astonished at anything. His motto completing his confession, he was less impenetrable than he supposed. It shows us in his actions, which elude ordinary standards, the behaviour of a prince. And that is so in a double sense. Was he not twice a prince, intellectually and by right of birth? He did not wait for Nietzsche to lay down the law of anarchy by saying that the superman himself creates his own scale of moral values. To that prerogative, valid for his private and public life, he added another, that of a quasi-royal blood, valid particularly for his public life, and governing his relations with heads of states. From that double prerogative he derived his morality, if it had any connection with morals.

Morality? . . . That was not Napoleon's opinion, who said, when at St. Helena: "Talleyrand's triumph was the triumph of immorality. He was a priest married to the wife of another, a woman who gave a large sum of money to her husband for his permission to allow her to marry Talleyrand!—a man who betrayed in all ways, deceived everyone, and every party!" That is a condemnation without light and shade and therefore baseless in the case of an accused person who was nothing but lights and shades. It is a condemnation without attenuating circumstances, therefore not according to equity, and when circumstances never demanded greater impartiality. In his memoirs Talleyrand is not content with pleading "not guilty"; he actually glories in the "crimes" with which he has been reproached. He was not unaware that a politician must try to win, not a good conduct prize, but historical laurels. In adopting that attitude he put into action a professional morality which was less striking in the choice of means than in their conformity with the object of all politics worthy of the name; that is, the welfare of human communities. Talleyrand did not sacrifice his private interests to that greater object, but he claimed that he never sacrificed the latter to the former. It was above all for the purpose of proving it that he became a professor of morals. Above that morality—as retrospective as it was justificatory—which he introduced into his life, and in which severe critics will see merely the technique of recantation, a less dubious morality was to be deduced from his work. There, this "immoralist" was really moral, and this sphinx pronounced his oracles so plainly that they are seen to be primary truths. And above all are they the more salutary for an age which has reversed them to the point of turning them into paradoxes, which thus confers upon them an anachronic actuality.

Talleyrand's work was superior to his life, which in its turn was better than his education and particularly the time in which he lived.

The worst way of spoiling children is, perhaps, to neglect them. Left to the care of hirelings, the young Charles Maurice did not profit by his lessons and the example of his parents, who were virtuous, but after the fashion of the old régime, which, as far as children were concerned, consisted in having a great many, and in troubling little about them. Their authority went no further than to inflict upon him an ecclesiastical status, whence arose a spirit of revolt more favourable to evil than to good instincts. Some of his faults were qualities which went astray through lack of guidance.

The time in which he lived was worse than his education. "Laws", said Rivarol, "are made to restrain the passions." The contrary was the case during the Revolution, which let loose passions by establishing its laws on individualism, the essence of its doctrine, and at the same time destroying the restraints of tradition and religion. After the Terror, which was not only an orgy of blood, sanctifying the lowest vices—envy, hatred, and secret accusation—the Directory gained in corruption what it lost in fanaticism. Example came from those in high positions. "The political science of a Director consisted in being able to deceive a colleague; his moral science was—to dine with Barras." Talleyrand, Minister of Foreign Affairs under the Directory, improved on that—he deceived all the Directors. And he did better than dine with Barras; he supped privately with his favourite, Mademoiselle Lange, on the night of the 18th of Brumaire, after thanking him (he was indebted to Barras for his post) while he extorted his resignation to make room for Bonaparte. Having committed a thousand follies after reaching years of discretion, his years of ingratitude were destined to be long in the land.

"This malaria-stricken Republic has done more harm to France than the Republic of the Terror: to corrupt the blood is worse than spilling it." During the Saturnalia of the Terror and Directory, a moratorium for morals was the sole law scrupulously observed by the masters of France.

The Consulate and Empire set bounds to that moratorium, but did not suppress it. At that time France was a country in which there was more heroism than virtue. On the steps of the throne and even in the Imperial family every excess of liberty was permissible, save against the Emperor. Furthermore, Napoleon did not act with rigour when his brothers and grand dignitaries plotted against him! They were too highly placed, too near him, to run the risk of being molested. Treasonable audacity and impunity were measured by their benefits. At Court and among high functionaries, private virtue was held in no more esteem than civic virtue. Corruption, or at any rate, the stock-jobbing which is the first phase of it, were encouraged as methods of government. Before Guizot's day, Napoleon said to those around him: "Get rich; and as to how—close your eyes." The tamer fed his wild beasts so that they might assist him to tame the nations, until the time when, completely satiated, they longed only to devour and digest him. Meanwhile they served him only the better for it. In a certain comedy, the heroine, condescending to accept the liberalities of her adorers, observes: "It is not that I love money, but it is a means of attracting men". Napoleon thought: "It is not that I love corruption, but it is a means of attracting high officials". Napoleon, who will always receive the homage of humanity because he incarnated its highest possibilities in action, and the homage of France because he had faith in her and obtained miracles from his faith, himself glorified humanity and France in the mass, but as single units he despised men and the Frenchmen he employed. Apart from his genius, it was perhaps this double and contradictory feeling which gave him the empire of the

world. He discovered therein two mighty levers: a chimerical, but all the more fascinating ideal, and a policy so realist that it almost realized the ideal. It was the alliance of myth and practicality.

Talleyrand's ideal, being more accessible, and his practical sense not being less, he did not sacrifice it to the dream of Napoleon. When this epic Don Quixote bestrode the chimera, Sancho Panza, not without having attempted to bring him back into touch with reality, parted company with him. He considered that duty ceased where the impossible began. This was the source of all that has been called his treasons, where he saw only adjustments profitable to himself, but also for France. In an appendix to his memoirs the ex-Bishop of Autun justifies these considerations, which, coming from his pen, resemble a catechism on opportunism. These considerations "concerning the duties of men in office during those disastrous periods when it pleases Providence to separate violently the personal fate of kings from that of their peoples", begin with a *distinguo*: "Does the government to which obedience is given command you to commit a crime? Unquestionably, and without the least hesitation, it must be disobeyed. Whatever the risk of incurring disgrace, one must be prepared to suffer all the consequences. But does this government, without your participation, make itself criminal?"

Here follows a new *distinguo*: "If the crime endangers public order, if it involves, or may involve the country in great dangers, if it tends to social disorganization, to the contempt of law, to the ruin of the State, there is no doubt that one must not only resist, but shake off the yoke and arm against a power which has become thenceforward an enemy of the country which it has lost all right to govern."

In the first hypothesis, Talleyrand is at one with St. Thomas whose maxim he paraphrases: "The subversion of a tyrannical régime does not partake of a seditious character unless, as may happen, the operation gives rise to more grievous disorder than the tyranny itself".

Like a good theologian, the author of these considerations distinguishes the essential from the accidental by formulating a second hypothesis: "But, if the crime be, in its character, isolated, circumscribed in its object, and in its effects, if it has no general result except to brand the name of its author and hold up to public execration the names of those who made themselves its tools, its executioners, and its allies, then one must abandon oneself to bitter and inconsolable suffering, one must", . . . and so on. But, above all, "if the safety of the state and public order are not impaired, one must continue to serve". The entire passage, drafted under the Restoration and destined for Louis XVIII, is, in Talleyrand's intention, a defence of his conduct in the trial of the Duc d'Enghien.

In his participation in the events which brought about the fall of Napoleon in 1814, Talleyrand has St. Thomas for his surety. In his ephemeral loyalty to the Directory, Consulate, and Empire he has on his side the consciousness of duty accomplished. He exclaims: "Let us imagine a government suddenly deprived of all the capable, generous, enlightened, and conscientious men in the country, and all its machinery of government suddenly invaded by the scum and the dregs of the population!" Talleyrand was far too good a citizen to expose his fatherland to such a calamity. He remained at his post and was rewarded for his devotion by the glory of having planned, while appearing to abjure it, the triumph of the monarchy. For it was with the Restoration in view (let us not forget that he writes in the reign of Louis XVIII) that he had served every government which had followed the end of the old régime. He observes: "To pass from the condition in which France was then to the royal régime was impossible. Intermediate régimes were necessary, and several of them." These were the models—more and more perfect—of that masterpiece, the Restoration. First of all, the clay or the shapeless mud of the Directory which disgusted the nation with anarchy. Next, the Consulate, already presenting an outline of the monarchy. Then the Empire to complete the re-education of France by disgusting her with dictatorship. She was thus ready for a government which, avoiding both extremes, could only be the paternal kingship of the Bourbons. Yet a few more touches, and the statue rises on the threshold of a radiant future. For, as Talleyrand again observes, it was "for the benefit of the future" that he had resigned himself to continue in office during the eclipse of the monarchy. But for such a long and delicate piece of work it was necessary to avoid changing sides. This continuity witnesses to his fidelity, concealed amidst apparent infidelities, and the long series of what have been taken for mistakes proclaims his infallibility.

Talleyrand quotes a saying of Machiavelli, of whom he was as much a disciple as of St. Thomas: "All mutations furnish the material out of which others can be fashioned". All the revolutions with which he had been associated furnished him the material out of which he fashioned a restoration; and all his mutations, having, according to him, the same object, were so many proofs of his invariability. However, when he professes to show in the "intermediate régimes" the phases which he skilfully manipulated in the chrysalis stage of the Restoration, malicious people are inclined to see in his own metamorphoses, not a system of political evolution, but a phenomenon of political mimicry, protecting him by imparting the hues of the day, analogous to the power possessed by certain animals of assuming the colours of surrounding nature and thus protecting themselves. Talleyrand was not one of those who give themselves so entirely to a cause that, when it fails, there remains nothing more for them to do than to wrap themselves in their cloaks and die. He preferred to turn his coat and wait.

To serve every régime without subjection to any; to be prepared to oppose them when disapproving of them; and thus remain doubly true to himself, to his ideas and interests. From 1789 to the end of his career, all his variations were on the same theme: peace at home through liberal institutions; peace abroad through equilibrium of power. Régimes rival each other in their infidelity to their origins and their promises. The Revolution declared peace to the world and flung it into a war which lasted twenty-two years; at home it was to have been the golden age, and it proved to be terrorism and bankruptcy; it was also to have been the reign of virtue and it ended in the putrefaction of the Directory. Napoleon, exalted on high to defend the civil and territorial conquests of the Revolution by restoring its pristine purity, spread his principles abroad in Europe, whence they were soon to be turned against France, but he fertilized them abroad whilst transgressing them at home; he practised liberty by turning the land into a barracks, fraternity by means of slaughter, and equality by pouring out streams of blood to the greater glory of a single man.

Talleyrand's calculated versatility derived its unity from the contradictions of régimes. Seeking the same ends it would have been nothing more than a prudent opportunism as to choice of methods, if among these there had not been the foreign alliance, which, it was said, made it a crime against the country.

Is this conclusion too absolute as regards historical relativity? It requires us, in order to appraise Talleyrand's conduct, to remember that it was certainly of the "period" —to borrow a term from antiquarians. Indeed it was an antiquity that Europe of the old régime, so difficult to picture since the Revolution and the Empire ushered in the era of fierce nationalisms, and substituted, even in the time of peace, the separation of nations for the habit they had of co-operation even during war. Then was the time for the flowering of cosmopolitanism, the ultimate form of humanism, whose capital was Versailles—cosmopolitanism, the flower of internationalism for the use of the élite. At that time, war, the war of kings, was merely a lawsuit as to a matter of succession, or boundaries. It was not, like the war of the nations, a "totalitarian" war, a question of life or death for them. At that time the adversary was less of an enemy than to-day. Even if he were guilty, the hand held out to him across a hardly perceptible frontier was not a parricidal hand. Those who had seen our kings recruit their guards in Switzerland, beat the Germans with Germans, and make one of them a Marshal of France (never had the Franco-German reconciliation been so complete) were not indignant with their compatriots who entered foreign service.

Who was there to throw the first stone at Talleyrand? On the right there were the *émigrés*, who identified king and country and believed they were serving France by taking service with the enemies of the Revolution. On the left were the revolutionaries under the influence of the foreigner and in his pay. A report from La Luzerne, Ambassador in London, refers to Danton as in the pay of the British Government. An agent of the King of

Prussia, in Paris, whose mission was to bring about by any means the rupture of the Franco-Austrian alliance, wrote to Berlin in 1791 that the Jacobin club was solid in the interest of Prussia. So much was that the case that the Assembly offered the command of the French army to the Duke of Brunswick. Moreau, who, under the Empire, dreamed of a "republican Quiberon", and met his death at Dresden was glorified as a martyr to his faith. Patriotic treason was not less honoured abroad. General York, whose defection was caused by Prussia being the ally of France, was admired because he had placed enlightened patriotism above blind military orders. The great Prussian patriot Stein was in the Russian ranks while his own sovereign was the forced ally of Napoleon against Russia.

Under Napoleon charges of intelligence with the enemy were so frequent and in such high places that they remained unpunished. At the close of his reign, when his fall appeared inevitable and desirable, his most reliable servants ceased to be faithful to him. When Talleyrand proposed that he and Caulincourt should work for the restoration of the Bourbons, the latter refused but said nothing and allowed him to intrigue quietly in Paris. At that same period Talleyrand betrayed Napoleon and his own designs to Savary, the Minister of Police, by this remark: "It does not suit everybody to remain in a house on fire". Savary, instructed to have him watched and who was well informed about his intrigues, held his peace. Similarly, the Prefect of Police, Pasquier, hinted to Talleyrand how to remain in Paris—when the Queen Regent, Marie Louise, was fleeing from the Allies—and lay his plans for the return of Louis XVIII. That was one of those periods when "everybody made it a point of honour to be the first to betray". The military were not more chivalrous than the civilians. Old Marshal Jourdan, the victor of Fleurus, who under the Empire was considered a sound republican, was the first to make his troops sport the white cockade. Others did not wait for the passing of the Empire to talk "defeatism" before the foreigner and offer him their services. When, on June 26, 1813, at Dresden, before his celebrated interview with Napoleon at the Marcolini palace, Metternich was passing along the gallery where the marshals were assembled, Berthier, Prince of Neufchatel and Major-General, one of the most devoted of the Emperor's collaborators, encouraged him with the words: "Do not forget that Europe needs peace, France particularly. France wants nothing else but peace."

It was at that interview that Napoleon, throwing his hat across the room, shouted: "I care little about the life of a million men". That was a more immoral remark than any of Talleyrand's and is a plea in defence of his defection. As early as 1808, Joseph de Maistre was writing: "Talleyrand, Berthier, and Lannes told the Grand Marshal at the Court, Comte Tolstoi, that they were tolerably tired of their dear master, and if it should ever suit them to make a half turn to the right, they would be very flattered to be under the sceptre of Alexander". Satiated with honours and grants, grand dignitaries and marshals longed only to enjoy them in peace. The "dear master", who cared even less for their repose than for the lives of a million men, was, in the eyes of this well-fed pack of hounds, a raving madman. Like Queen Louise of Prussia, they saw in him "the monster, the evil principle, the world-scourge, an infernal being, the devil. . . . Doctor Faust and his attendant", said Queen Louise. But the attendant, Talleyrand, bent over his retorts to blow up Faust.

It is in this connection and also because it preceded

other defections that Talleyrand's was different. Was it not more honourable? It signified more risks for him and greater advantages for France than the abjuration of the last, or the rallyings of the first hour. Was it his greatest mistake to have been right first, and to have acted in consequence, while others awaited the accomplished facts to make their obeisance and profit by it? As Talleyrand replied to Alexander, who accused the King of Saxony of having betrayed Europe by his fidelity to Napoleon, himself forgetting the effusions of Erfurt and Tilsit: "Sire, that is a matter of dates". Is not priority here a cause for commendation rather than opprobrium? "I have betrayed Napoleon", he said, "but not France." He even considered that, in his position and with his knowledge, if he had not betrayed a policy fatal to the country and the dynasty, he would have been betraying France and the cause of Napoleon. "Happy treason which only meant the sacrifice of his passions for the benefit of his interests!" —thus does Thiers, often the panegyrist as well as the historian of the Empire, appreciate Talleyrand's "treason" at Erfurt. Stendhal, a great admirer of Napoleon, felt that the "Empire had eclipsed the fatherland". Napoleon turned that fact into a principle when he observed to the son of Louis, the King of Holland: "Your primary duty is towards me and your second is to France". Talleyrand's treason in the rôle he played on the 18th of Brumaire was far less serious than that of Napoleon's brothers and brother-in-law, Murat, who owed him everything, for Talleyrand was by reason of that part rather the creditor than the debtor of the Emperor. His treasons were useless except to himself. For some men, service means obedience, for others it means command: for Talleyrand, then, it meant betrayal. It was even service for Napoleon if the pathway of moderation had not been forbidden him by the blindness of his pride or the implacable logic of the revolutionary heritage.

But for a man like Talleyrand, does not treachery especially mean wealth? Is it necessary to seek for the main-spring of his policy as he exhibits it, any explanation other than his venality? True, he cannot be accused of sacri-ficing the spiritual to the temporal. To judge by certain appearances, the only custom that this ex-Bishop retained of the ecclesiastical calling was that of collecting fees, and the sole receptacle possessing sanctity in his eyes was that which denoted a gratuity. Like Napoleon, who had his collectors of revenue, so he had his collectors of "re-freshers". Here, again, historical relativity is his defender. It has not judged him venal, but has condemned him for avarice, which if it had no limits was not without scruples.

Talleyrand was a man of the eighteenth century. Now, under the old régime, the canons of honesty in the re-lations between authority and money were hardly any better established than the rules of orthography. Perhaps they were not worse observed than the rules of syntax, and particularly those of taste in the matter of style. Virtue would have gained nothing under the Revolution by being codified in laws which claimed to be its grammar and were exalted in speeches that were unquestionably merely rhetoric. Before that time the gratuity was an official institution. Mazarin wrote to Colbert to remind him that in a certain affair a gratuity was stipulated for. Accord-ing to Choisy's memoirs, the King himself "touched" money, only what he received with one hand he gave with the other. "The King, when renewing the lease for the salt-tax, was presented with six hundred thousand francs for commission which he dispensed in liberalities." This was a custom which, had it been kept within certain limits, was no more a source of corruption of the Government than a plaintiff's corruption of a judge by presenting him with a couple of capons, or a ham. The welfare of the State and the cause of justice were matters too sacred to be so cheaply profaned.

In our days, it demands a large dose of pharisaism or ingenuousness to feel indignation at this custom. Talleyrand, musing over his "treasons", observed to Lamartine: "For statesmen there are many ways of being upright". For politicians there are still more ways of being dishonest. A writer who was well acquainted with them and certainly criticized them without malice, Robert de Jouvenel, notes in his book *République des camarades*: "There are grave ministers who consider themselves upright because they have never misappropriated a penny piece for themselves, but have pillaged the budget for the benefit of their families and their acquaintances". The system having reached perfection, pillage is now carried on for the benefit of the electors, in other words, of the member who thus ensures his own election and all the material advantages associated with it. Robert de Jouvenel deplores this: "for the needs of politicians, after all, have some limits, and we know families in Gascony who have none". He therefore proposes to legislate against breach of trust instead of nepotism, and to reserve the crown of civic virtue for "upright ministers who have only despoiled the state for their own advantage."

Let us give to Talleyrand a triple crown: he possessed no electoral family; his principle "refreshers" cost France nothing, for they were procured from other States—they were even of service to public affairs by the use to which he put them. Money, which makes an excellent servant but a bad master, was an excellent servant to him. He spent it freely and considered it rather as a means of power than of enjoyment. His pomp was an element of his success.

He took care frequently to improve his establishment and his expenditure was justified in the use he made of it. It was very largely a propaganda budget. His negotiations were facilitated and his independence was not limited by it. With more truth than Mirabeau he could say: "I see that I am paid, but I do not sell myself".

Concerning this, the testimony of contemporaries who had no love for him is decisive. He was caught in the act of being honest. Having been unable to restore Poland in 1807 as he desired, he spontaneously refunded to the Polish magnates four millions of florins which he had received from them for that service. When he did not refund money, he neither rendered any service if those which were asked from him did not square with his policy. In his relations with the sovereigns who had put him under obligation, his cynicism, which above all was the outcome of his pride, was a source of power for it ensured his independence. The Tsar Alexander supposed he had bound him to himself by his generosity, but he felt no more constraint in having received his liberalities than if he had received a snuff-box.

A snuff-box which a snobbish and ingenuous diplomat receives from a princely donor is far more dangerous to the State than the millions lavished on Talleyrand, who accepted the gifts of sovereigns as their homage and forbade their transformation into a mortgage. When it is a question of "bounty" or "gratuity", where does corruption begin? It is not a matter of figures, like treason—according to Talleyrand—is a matter of dates. Everything resides in the "direction of the intention". A casuist would find it easier to accord Talleyrand absolution, who incorporated into the national fortune the wealth of foreign sovereigns without sacrificing anything to them, than to a Victor Cousin, professor of Philosophy, in enjoyment of State favours, who bestowed a pension on his "muse" Louise Colet, at the cost of the budget and to the prejudice of more worthy associates. Talleyrand appears to advantage, not only as regards the importance of "refreshers", but as regards their origin, use, and especially their counterpart in services rendered to the French State. The case of Cousin is, on the contrary, one of pure corruption.

"Talleyrand is worth more than his reputation, believe me, and there are many apparently honest men who are in the contrary situation." This eulogium comes from Laffitte, a matter-of-fact man, and who, as a banker, took money seriously. On the score of his "venality", as well as his "treasons", Talleyrand merits at least the amnesty of a comparison.

When he had his first interview with Louis XVIII in 1814, Talleyrand, according to his memoirs, received a singularly flattering welcome. The King had said to him: "Our families date from the same period. My ancestors were the ablest. If yours had been cleverer than mine, you would be saying to me to-day: 'Take a seat, come nearer, and let us talk business'. To-day it is for me to say, 'Sit down and let us have a chat'." This language of Louis XVIII requires the hypothesis that if the rôles had been interchanged he would have been asked to "sit down" by a crowned Talleyrand.

The anecdote ill agrees with the haughty irony which, in other circumstances and in the presence of witnesses, he inflicted on Talleyrand. But often it happens that psychologically anecdotes are the more true as literally they are the less so. To those who invent them, to invest themselves with an important rôle, the remark may be addressed: "Tell me what you invent and I will tell you who you are". Such dialogues betray their secrets. They are untrue as to the facts, and only disclose their feelings the better for it.

The only thing deserving attention in the anecdote is that, in his own inner consciousness, Talleyrand acknowledged no master whatsoever, not even his legitimate king. He remained faithful to his motto, "Naught save God". And that loyalty explains, if it does not excuse, what is popularly called his "treason".

This overweening pride was displayed in his private life, to judge by the way it infected the Princesse de Bénévent, the ex-Madame Grant. When a niece of the prince married a member of the Noailles family, the princess exclaimed: "This alliance is not an honourable one for us, for what is the Noailles family in comparison with the house of Périgord?" Although she was a good woman, as she had been a good girl,[1] she insisted on her lady-companion, a countess of the old régime, following her at a respectful distance, and when the countess came within that distance the princess used to turn round, saying, "Countess, you forget your station". Frequently she signed, *"Princesse, souveraine* de Talleyrand, and even, *"Princesse régnante"*.

Mme Grant was a foolish woman and an upstart. Nevertheless, she was only the exaggerated reflection of the prince. When his friends addressed him as "Your Highness", he begged them to call him "Monsieur de Talleyrand"—adding, "I am less, and perhaps *I am more*". He was "less", for he had failed to comply with the formalities necessary for the regularization of the title, but the revenues of which he was content to receive. He was "more"—possibly the most ancient dynast in Europe. M. de Saint-Allais, an authority on heraldry, conscientious

[1] "She was a good woman at bottom, *la belle et la bête*, at one and the same time" (*Recollections of Baron de Frénilly*).—Translators' note.

but courteous, published in 1836, during the prince's life, and probably by his orders, a *Précis historique sur les Comtes de Périgord*. In this genealogy, in which the most important notice was devoted to him, the elder branch is referred to as the *"branche régnante"*, the reigning branch.

To gauge the pride of Talleyrand it is necessary to imagine the pride of the Périgordians, on which his own pride was superimposed, since he was the most distinguished son of the ancient Counts-sovereign of Périgord.

True Périgordians rightly claim to be the greatest lords in the world, if nobility consists in antiquity of civilization and services rendered to humanity. All the aborigines of the region, including especially the most humble among the peasantry, have a right to claim that pre-eminence, for in them the race is purest. Their title-deeds, of which formerly they were but dimly aware, have been vindicated by the most recent and most certain discoveries of science. Glozel is not in Périgord. But, on the banks of the Dordogne and the Vezère, in caves contemporaneous with the early ages of the world, have been discovered the vestiges of an art so many milleniums old that the art of the Pharaohs is but modern in comparison. Good judges have compared it with that of a Rodin for its dramatic and synthetic strength. To-day prehistoric research confirms the local legend which has it that in this region man for the first time took his companion in his arms—no longer the fore-limbs of a beast—and stood upright to look the sun in the face. Inheritors of such a history, the Périgordians discover therein, with the record of pride, that also of scepticism. They doubt everything; or rather, they are dupes of nothing, because during their innumerable previous and cultivated existences they have seen all, studied all, learned or anticipated the hidden reasons of things. They consider themselves superior to everybody, since their ancestors were civilized beings many a century before other races had ceased to be barbarians.

If such is the pride of the humble, what will be the pride of the great? Perigordian gentlemen have the good taste to jest at themselves, but, like Cyrano, dislike that the things they say of themselves be said to them. They attribute their large numbers and their poverty to a gesture of the Eternal. God, having created the nobility on the seventh day, the day of rest, for it cost Him no effort, scattered the seed unequally throughout the world, and then emptied the bottom of the sack over Périgord. Hence that dust of country gentility with which it has been sprinkled.

This residuum of nobility is the pick of it, for all that. In the fields of creation, or the vineyards of the Lord, when the angelic harvesters and fruit-pickers passed that way, they were doubtless provided with baskets, which forthwith they discharged into their Master's sack, so that the top of the basket became the bottom of the sack.

Whatever this postscript to Genesis may be worth, the legend, like pre-history, explains pre-history itself. Each has it that the gentlemen of Périgord are the proudest in the world. They yield to none; neither do they yield to each other. There were four titulars of the four baronies of Beynac, Biron, Bourdeille, and Mareuil, each claiming sole right to the title of premier baron of Périgord. This question of precedence had to be settled in the following manner: in the provincial assemblies the four barons signed their names around a circle drawn upon the minutes of the assembly proceedings.

The pride of these barons gives us a feeble idea of that of their suzerains, the Counts-sovereign of Périgord, and of their most illustrious descendant, who increased their pride by an incalculable personal coefficient. His memoirs show him as profoundly impressed by the traditions of his province and family during the years of childhood passed at Chalais, in the shadow of that tower, which—like its master—decapitated by Richelieu, reminded him of the prerogatives of his ancestors. As a Périgordian he allowed no one to impose on him and was impressed by nothing. Being the leading Périgordian gentleman, he considered himself above all the great ones of this world and quite exonerated from all moral obligations towards them. The consciousness of his talents added to that of his birth increased this feeling of independence. This was a feeling which developed without restraint in revolutionary times. It was then that the institutions and customs which restrained the independence of this last of our great feudal nobles collapsed. The vacation of the monarchy for him was a vacation of legality in general. One single rule existed in that anarchy: the permanent interest of France, of which he considered himself the custodian by a dual right of birth and intelligence. To his accusers, who threw his "treasons" in his face, Talleyrand replied, like Bazaine before the Council of War: "There was nothing". But he added, like the president of the Council of War, the Duc d'Aumale: "There was France". He added further, but in petto: "I was myself the permanence of France, and in ways appropriate to the circumstances, I did my best to fill the interval between her legitimate sovereigns".

Such was his thesis. It would have been stronger had his abnegation been equal to his pride, and if the permanent interests of France, as he conceived them, had not always marvellously coincided with the ephemeral interests of his own fortunes. This coincidence, none the less, exists. When he intrigued with the Tsar and the Emperor of Austria, he imitated the great vassals who ally themselves with foreign princes, but at the same time he considered, and rightly, that the true interests of France were in better accord with general European interests than with the exaggerated dreams of Napoleon. In his eyes, his "dear master" was only a parvenu, who, having been crowned by victory, was deposed by defeat. His right, possessing no foundation other than success, collapsed with him. Talleyrand banished him to "Limoges",[1] just as the King of France would have dismissed his Grand Constable after defeat. He discounted the Emperor's fall and hastened it, but he was not its cause. Before his "treasons" Napoleon had found his Nemesis in himself and in the fatality of his situation. From the historical and psychological aspect, these "treasons" were the "acts of a prince" in the service of a kingdom of which Talleyrand was the trustee in virtue of the secret investiture he had conferred on himself. In 1814 he entrusted France to Louis XVIII, and served him faithfully. He did not betray his legitimate sovereigns. With them he only went into opposition, when they were out of power, which had not been the case under the Emperor. He did not betray Louis XVIII, but he bound him by a constitution. In doing this the last of the great feudal nobles became the first of the great liberals. It was merely a change of labels. Whether for the advantage of the great or of parliaments, both sought as their object the dismemberment and limitation of the royal power.

Merimée said of Talleyrand: "Wherever he goes he forms a court and lays down the law". Foreign sovereigns treated him as one of themselves, when they were not his courtiers. Chateaubriand used to say "Napoleon and I".

---

[1] During the late war, French generals who were considered failures or incompetent were retired and sent to Limoges.—Translators' note.

Talleyrand, even in the livery of Grand Chamberlain, used to think: "I and Napoleon". Expecting, like kings, to die in public, like them also he observed in public the most private ritual of his toilet, including the washing and swathing of his ungainly clubfoot. Judged from this elevated position, the "refreshers" which he accepted were not a salary, but a tribute from other sovereigns. They were portions of the civil list which he assigned to himself in his capacity as European arbiter. He was indeed a native of Gascony, the country where, even in our days, the people criticize while asking for posts, and every transaction is negotiated by the "tuner", that diplomatist of fairs, who even in the sale of a couple of bulls pockets his commission from each party, as a guarantee of his impartiality. Talleyrand introduced this custom into the market for kingdoms when he pocketed his fee from both Murat and the Bourbons of Naples. But, raising himself above the level of the "tuner" of his own province both in principles and the sums at stake, he was more careful of legitimacy than of impartiality.

Let us follow the advice of another Périgordian, Montaigne: "Let us not scrutinize great men in small things". Talleyrand had accomplished great things. In 1814 he had probably saved France from anarchy and dismemberment. She owed him, along with the Restoration, peace at home and abroad. By means of the treaties of Vienna, and the equilibrium obtained from them, he gave peace to Europe as well as to France. In 1870 and 1914 war broke out because a part of his work, the independence of the German states, had been destroyed. But the other part of his work, the Anglo-French alliance and the independence of Belgium, was that which saved, once again, France and Europe.

The events of recent years must not be taken to

diminish his glory and our gratitude. He has especially been reproached for installing Prussia in the Rhineland instead of leaving that province to Saxony. In this question, which is only part of a more important one, France could not invoke the principle of legitimacy to escape her own dismemberment unless she respected it in Saxony. Nevertheless, Talleyrand made no sacrifice to that principle: the same solution was forced upon him by another one from which the old régime never departed, and which enabled him to place France beyond the reach of invasion; namely, the primordial necessity of maintaining the independence of the secondary German states as our clients. Talleyrand perceived in this a safer guarantee than in the temporary displacement of a Prussia which, had she possessed the licence to absorb these states, would have been to us a more formidable neighbour still. It has been said that Talleyrand made a bet on German particularism and that he lost it. He made no bet when he applied an invariable maxim of our old diplomacy. It was rather a bet on French wisdom. He could not foresee that the madness of the Revolution and the Empire would be repeated under Napoleon III, to end in the consummation of German unity which it had prepared. If, in the land of shadows, he has read Stresemann's memoirs, whose author admits that he trembled for the unity of the Reich during the occupation of the Ruhr, he must have concluded that this unity was not necessarily fated to exist. Especially must he laugh in noting what this unity has become under Hitler. In face of this spectacle of frantic neo-paganism, the apostate bishop no doubt flatters himself that he saved Christian civilization in obtaining for it the means to repel the recent aggression of Germanic barbarism.

If Talleyrand's work is worth more than his life, which

itself is worth more than his education, the reason is that this rake had his system of morality. The reason is that, as his compatriot Montaigne has observed, he was not a true sceptic. Neither of these men shared the belief of the world in general, but each believed in things useful to the world in general. At the time of the Wars of Religion, Montaigne believed that no certitude existed which was worthy of being enforced under the pain of death. Talleyrand believed that no conquest was worth the blood it cost. Assuming that legitimacy is a myth, that it has been made a principle out of expediency, or an ideal out of necessity, it none the less is an improvement when compared with the law of conquest; that is, the law of the jungle; the sole law that Napoleon and his opponents recognized. Similarly, he made use of a moral force when he founded French security, less upon a physical fact—such as the tracing of a frontier—than upon the feelings of the people on the other side of it; for instance, when he preferred the maintenance of Germanic liberties to aggrandizement on the Rhine, or the independence of Belgium to its annexation. Whilst not neglecting material power—for during the Congress he advised Louis XVIII to reorganize the army—he still left a great rôle to moral forces in his concept of French greatness. He saw the identity between our interests and public law in a community of civilized nations, of whom, because of her territorial disinterestedness, France would be arbiter, as was the case at the Congress of Vienna, and even the secular arm, as she would prove to be at the outbreak of the Belgian revolution. From 1792 until his death, this doctrine was the unifying force of his political life. It was through this, as much as through the pride which was the focal point of his character, that under all disguises and through all metamorphoses this political Inaudi or Fregoli—for he found solutions as easily as he changed his dress—remained at heart an unchangeable Proteus. It was also through his moderation—the fruit of wisdom, not of weakness—that this man, whose life was an example of licence and excess, was in his thought a model of sobriety. He would have liked to be able to tell Napoleon what Cicero told Caesar: "You seem to have vanquished victory itself, since you do not exact from the vanquished all the profit of your victory". He sought for peace, not in the passing triumph of force, but in the reconciliation of nations, the organization of Europe, and the sense of its solidarity.

Talleyrand teaches us other lessons whose value is enhanced by present errors, just as contemporary events mark his actions with the sign of "plus". His example first of all reminds us that bad institutions corrupt politicians and good ones exalt and sustain them. Mischievous during the Revolution, useless under the Empire, he ensured the salvation of France and Europe under the monarchy. Whilst romanticism was triumphant in the realm of literature he presents us with a model of classic diplomacy, an antidote which is not without its use in a period when romanticism is triumphant in politics. The rôle of reason in the latter diminishes in proportion as blind and collective forces predominate. Will-power also abdicates before these forces, when it does not fade away into the fetishism of the physical sciences, where there reigns a fatalism invoked in politics, though often enough it is only an excuse for cowardice. Talleyrand knew that if there are some events stronger than men, there are some men stronger than events. He knew that if from the Christian point of view statesmen are the actors in a drama whose poet is elsewhere, the actors collaborate more or less with the author. If a classical work is one which has been thought out and willed by the author, then

Talleyrand's work has certainly the classical character. In 1815 and 1830 he intended that which he wrought. If a classical work is one which contains more than appears, and fulfils more than it promises, such also is the character of his art, especially of his masterpiece, Belgian independence, whose significance in 1914 singularly surpassed its initial import.

The bankruptcy of public diplomacy vindicates Talleyrand's: a diplomacy of the cabinet—secret, and therefore all the more fruitful. It saved the nations, unknown to themselves and in spite of themselves, from the calamities they would have provoked had they been left alone. The bankruptcy of signatures does not lessen regret for the good faith of treaties, the foundation of international order, just as respect for contracts is the foundation of the social order. To the faith in treaties—which this renegade professed—are to-day opposed the romantic rights of life, rights invoked in Germany particularly, in order to suppress the rights of other nations and in whose name she has already destroyed some millions of men.

Talleyrand, whose life was full of the romantic, possessed a completely classical mind. It is this which led him to bring more of the moral factor into his politics than into his conduct.

Morality, notwithstanding, was not banished from his conduct or his soul. The latter, like his work, is worth more than his life. During the Revolution and the Empire nothing escaped question; the anomalous was the normal; the frontiers of good and evil were as uncertain as those of States. "In the time of tempest", he said, "all roads are lost". But it was not he who brought the tempest. This classical mind loved neither tempests nor ruins. He preferred harbours. "After the shipwreck, pilots are wanted to pick up the victims. I keep my presence of mind and I steer them to any port; it matters little what port it is, provided that it be a shelter."

When, on the approach of death, he deplored "the errors into which he had been driven by the temptations of the time and human frailty", he rightly put "temptations" in the first place. To judge him fairly we must deduct the tare from the weight of his defects; to calculate the net weight we must deduct that of the "container"; that "time" so charged with errors and with crimes. After this operation the satanical quality of "this devil with an angel's face" seems by no means grave. This is particularly the case when comparison is made with other protagonists in the same drama who, in spite of, or because of a greater perversity, have numbered more friends. From the aspect of his popularity his chief mistake was in being nearly always right; calm in a storm; sober in the midst of excess; human in an inhuman age; in never converting his errors into systems and, above all, into passions. When posterity makes its choice the moderates are caught between the fire of extremists on both sides, as happens in elections. In modern France, where politics are reduced to a struggle of parties, Talleyrand, who never belonged to a party, save in the sense that Brutus played the fool, has been unanimously condemned by partisan tribunals. He has been punished after his death for his virtues as he was rewarded during his life for his vices.

Before the court of the nation he presents a better case, for no one has done more for religious peace and for peace at home and abroad. The nation would have been more grateful to him and he would have won more renown if he had gained less advantage. In his own epic drama with its wonderful good sense, it is not he, but opportunism which is the hero. In the cases where his action seems disinterested, one is left with the impression that he was less moved by patriotism than by dilettantism, or, as he has confessed, by his desire to astonish the world. Then—before the days of Bismarck, of whom it has been said with less truth—he was the only man able to juggle with five balls, two of which were always in the air. If he turned to another task, it was to juggle with difficulties or governments, aided by a conscience as accommodating as the conjurer's hat with its holes. Or, better still, he was the clown who himself placed the obstacles on the track; as, for instance, when in 1814 he forced upon the Allies, with the Bourbons, the solution least convenient for their interests. But it was then that he utilized obstacles to ascend to the highest trapeze and vault from there. Should he fall, it was always without injury. "Thrown from the summit of the Tarpeian rock, he would have found a way to remain in mid-air and to ascend ever higher." When he was no longer at the Capitol he felt homesick for it. In disgrace during the Restoration, already a septuagenarian and in retirement at Valençay, at every ministerial crisis he became restless; just as wine, even when matured, ferments in the cellar when the vine puts forth its buds. This hunger for power alone affected him because it was not ennobled by zeal for public welfare and had been satiated. A nation demands passionate attachment and suffering for its sake.

Talleyrand did not aim high enough to touch the heart of France. The light of his intelligence was too cold to fire humanity. It lighted the path without imparting the power to follow it to the end. He was not "Altissime" like Richelieu, because he was not a man of pure reason. He did not possess that sublime blend of reason and exaltation which creates great statesmen and the great mystic founders of orders. He felt no temptation to renounce himself, to rise above himself. His patriotism took second place. Through an activity analogous to that of Barrès, falling in with

national feeling while interrogating his inner consciousness, he deepened his personal interest down to the point
where it rested on that of the nation.

The most sacred duties of Talleyrand were those he
owed to himself. He knew of others, but those he fulfilled
more willingly when they chimed in with his feelings.
With infinite precautions, to avoid causing the old man
too much emotion, Mme de Dino broke the news to him
of the death of the Princesse de Bénévent. As a funeral
oration he was only able to say: "This greatly simplifies
my position". If, in love, the rôle of the heart only begins
when one loves no longer, with Talleyrand this rôle
showed the height of discretion. He considered that he
owed nothing to that adventuress, that he had given her
far more than he had received by a marriage which, he
said, "was a proof that the half was worth more than the
whole". Nevertheless he had too much in him of the
eighteenth century not to be tender-hearted. He lavished
the tenderest and most delicate affection on his niece,
Mme de Dino, and her daughter, Pauline, the darling of
his old age. He cherished them all the more because he
loved himself in them. Yielding to friendship a fidelity
that politics did not monopolize, he was sincerely
lamented by those who had known him best. His relatives
and servants worshipped him. Assembled around his
deathbed, their grief and tears interceded for him,
mingled with the prayers of the priest.

Like his work, the death of Talleyrand is better than his
life. We may accept for this the word of the eminent priest
who, having given him absolution, administered extreme
unction, not, as in the case of the simple believer, in the
palm of the hand, but outside it. Priests, having received
the unction in the palm of the hand at the moment of
ordination, receive it outside the palm at the moment of

death. It was the dying man himself who, offering his hands for the holy oil, turned them round, and thus reminded the Abbé Dupanloup, who had intended to anoint the palms as in the case of the laity. "You forget", murmured Talleyrand, "that I am a bishop." This was a reply in advance to those who asserted that he was no longer in possession of his faculties when he recovered his soul. We can trust his spiritual adviser, who assures us that Talleyrand's conversion was sincere, and who implored God, "unto whom the secrets of all hearts are known", to give to those who doubted it the grace to die like him. Let us not be duped by the fear of being duped into believing his detractors, who are relentless in discrediting the last peace which he made—the peace with Heaven. Whether he died like a man of good breeding, as Mme de Girardin put it; whether, like a great actor, he sought to make a good exit; whether this illustrious diplomat anticipated supreme promotion in treating with God, and whether this great peacemaker was loth to quit the scene of this world without an intimate concordat with the Eternal; whether he went to God, after evasions and backslidings, as the pilgrims go to St-Jacques de Compostella, taking two paces backward and three forward; whether he adopted that mode of progression, not for superior merit, but for renunciation of the world only on quitting it; whether such a death, in which the human element is not less apparent than the divine, was worthy of such a life. All this is left undetermined. Nevertheless that death is not on that account to be considered as a final imposture, seeing that even in his life, with all its intricacies, room is left for sincerity also. He has, at all events, the right to summon those who condemn him before a tribunal other than theirs. If, in this world, the actions of great men must not be weighed in ordinary scales, the same doubtless is even more true elsewhere. It requires the inhuman pride of a Chateaubriand to presume to dictate to the Sovereign Judge a sentence against Talleyrand without appeal, seeing that if we are not sure we understand the law of God, we are quite sure that we do not understand His jurisprudence.

The more human pride of Talleyrand is more easily conciliated with the idea of the divine. That pride had always bowed down before the mystery of the Beyond. Heir of the Comte de Périgord who asked Hugues Capet: "Who made thee king?" he thought in Napoleon's presence: "Who made thee Emperor?" When, as priest and bishop, he prostrated himself at the foot of the altar, and called down on earth the One who reigns on high, he never felt the temptation to ask, while the consecration was taking place through his ministry: "Who made Thee God?" His motto *Ré qué Diou* flattered him both by its religious and political significance, for God was the unique Being before whom to bow was to be exalted, since it implied entering into relations with the infinite. Talleyrand had never broken those relations. Just as he paid honour to virtues which, he said, he had not practised, but had not blasphemed, so he honoured the God whom he served not, but did not deny. He added: "Religion: I have ceased to be her minister, but I have never ceased to be her child". According to the expression of one of his biographers, he was a man emancipated, not a man in revolt. He asserted that there was no feeling less aristocratic than unbelief, not because the privileged ones of this world, if they have no need of God themselves have need of those who believe in God, but because belief in God raises the greatest above themselves. It was also because he considered himself the equal of the greatest sovereigns that he needed a monarch superior to them all.

God, who brought back this lamb, misled by one of his failings, could not deal harshly with him as regards his other defects. He had not to go far to seek him. At Valençay, Talleyrand piously attended Mass and was never so happy as when he presided at the dinners of the local clergy. This was not only to set a good example to his servants. When he sold his library during the Revolution, he kept only one book as a relic, the *Imitation of Christ*, and he frequently meditated over it.[1] One day he confessed to Mme de Dino: "My favourite prayer is the 'Salve Regina'", and he recited it to her with ardent piety. When he was ambassador in London he dispensed with his carriage, and missed an important appointment so that his grand-niece Pauline might be driven in it to the Catechism.

In these contradictions there is nothing surprising if the human creature is composed of mire and an inspiration of the divine. In Talleyrand there is no mystery other than the human mystery, deeper in his case than with ordinary mortals, because his example illustrates Carlyle's reflection that he had never known a really great man who was not able to be any kind of man.

---

[1] *Talleyrand's Library.*—Although Talleyrand's fine library was dispersed during the Revolution, it is interesting to know that an important section of it still exists in its entirety. This section, formerly part of the library of Georges Pallain, consists of 105 volumes in a uniform ancient binding, and with the ex-libris "Ré qué Diou" in almost all of them; a magnificent collection, which it would be almost impossible to form to-day, since it contains no fewer than 2292 exceedingly rare documents relating to the period of the Revolution. The importance of these works, brought together through the care of one of the chief actors in the historical dramas of the Revolution and the Directory, may be judged from the fact that there has been added to the collection a manuscript catalogue of nearly a hundred pages. This incomparable Bibliothèque Talleyrand is now in the possession of the well-known Parisian bibliophile, M. C. Gaillandre.—Translators' note.

From the human point of view much must be pardoned him, for his services were greater than his vices and they were more his own, his vices being the common lot of his contemporaries. It might even be said that his vices were sometimes necessary to his usefulness. If men of principle are not necessarily bound to succeed, as Thiers has observed, men who succeed under all régimes are not free to betray them. This enabled Talleyrand to serve his own interests simultaneously with those of his country, humanity, and religion.

This last service was not his principal claim to divine mercy. In the cell of another celebrated Sulpician, Renan, there may be read the following passage, taken from the gospel of St. Matthew, xii, verse 32: *Quis dixerit contra filium hominis, ei remittetur, contra spiritum sanctum non remittetur.* The sin against the spirit alone is unforgiven. Talleyrand had never committed this sin. If he was not athirst for the supernatural he cherished a feeling and consciousness of it; he comprehended the incomprehensible as such; he was aware that science and logic are incommensurable with religion, which belongs to another order of things. There was something of value in this attitude in an age which flattered itself that it had abolished the supernatural. He had too much reason to be a rationalist; his mind, which had undergone the triple distillation of the centuries, the seminary, and the world of men, was too subtle to find satisfaction in the crude materialism of the Encyclopaedists.

In his declining years, when his hands were too feeble to retain the worldly goods they had grasped with such eagerness, a sense of his poverty was already the lure for conversion. When he was still a young man, Mme de Staël wrote him: "Are you happy? With so acute a mind do you not at times sink to the bottom of all things—that

is to say, suffering?" He reached now the desolate depths
of his inner consciousness. Having suffered from the discord between his life and his dreams, when his earthly
dreams had become realities, he suffered from the discord
between them and his soul. He spoke of it in the tone of
Ecclesiastes with a *tedium vitae* which aspired after another
life. Gloomy reflections led him to serious thought.

Pauline de Périgord, who in London did not miss her
Catechism, thanks to her good uncle's carriage, repaid him
that kindness by working for his salvation. Her sincerity
restored in him the perfume of the empty vase. Being
one of the converts of Abbé Dupanloup, she introduced
him to the house in the Rue St-Florentin, saying, "My
uncle, not being one of my sins, I never mention him to
my confessor". Another of his grandnieces, Marie de
Talleyrand, took her first communion on the very day of
his death. She came to see him in her white dress, knelt
beside the bed, and asked for his blessing. An eyewitness
has described him sitting on the edge of the bed—a painful
operation which he had just undergone, without chloroform and with admirable stoicism, not permitting him to
lie down. His head swayed at moments from right to left,
and then would suddenly fall on his breast, as though at
that closing debate he alternately replied "yes" and "no"
to the challenge of Death. At the close of his agony he
raised his head, threw back the long curls which covered
his eyes, then opened them, as though—before closing
them for ever—he gazed at something beyond fortune, beyond earthly glory, beyond this world. In the light of the
Beyond, whence divine grace, personified by that maiden
communicant, caused a celestial beam to shine, his own
dazzling life became but darkness.

Weighed most scrupulously, the death of Talleyrand
perhaps deserves Jules Lemaître's sally: "God never has

more than our remains, but our relics are precisely the best portion of us". Weighed in the scales of history, what remains of his work—the integrity of our frontiers, Anglo-French friendship, and Belgian independence—are the best possessions of France and Europe, provided that they learn in his school the art of harmonizing them. They would then recover a lost cause: Equilibrium and Peace.

# INDEX

# INDEX

THE END

*Printed in Great Britain by* R. & R. CLARK, LIMITED, *Edinburgh*